The Third Ohio
Volunteer Infantry
in the Civil War

The Third Ohio Volunteer Infantry in the Civil War

"Obstinate Devils" from Middle Fork Bridge to Cedar Bluff

DAVID D. PERRY

McFarland & Company, Inc., Publishers
Jefferson, North Carolina

LIBRARY OF CONGRESS CATALOGING-IN-PUBLICATION DATA

Names: Perry, David D., 1945– author.
Title: The Third Ohio Volunteer Infantry in the Civil War.
Description: Jefferson, North Carolina : McFarland & Company, Inc., Publishers, 2024 | Includes bibliographical references and index.
Identifiers: LCCN 2024041467 | ISBN 9781476695112 (paperback : acid free paper) | ISBN 9781476653778 (ebook) ∞
Subjects: LCSH: United States. Army. Ohio Infantry Regiment, 3rd (1861-1864) | United States—History—Civil War, 1861-1865—Regimental histories. | Ohio—History—Civil War, 1861-1865—Regimental histories. | Skirmish at Middle Fork Bridge, 1861. | Streight's Raid, 1863. | United States—History—Civil War, 1861-1865—Campaigns.
Classification: LCC E525.5 3rd .P47 2024 | DDC 973.7/471—dc23/eng/20240905
LC record available at https://lccn.loc.gov/2024041467

BRITISH LIBRARY CATALOGUING DATA ARE AVAILABLE

ISBN (print) 978-1-4766-9511-2
ISBN (ebook) 978-1-4766-5377-8

© 2024 David D. Perry. All rights reserved

No part of this book may be reproduced or transmitted in any form or by any means, electronic or mechanical, including photocopying or recording, or by any information storage and retrieval system, without permission in writing from the publisher.

Front cover images: *inset* Lt. Col. John Beatty (National Archives and Records Administration). Lithograph, color titled "All hail to the flag of freedom" Ferd. Mayer & Co., Brooklyn published by Skaats & Knaebel, circa 1861.

*McFarland & Company, Inc., Publishers
Box 611, Jefferson, North Carolina 28640
www.mcfarlandpub.com*

To Richard Francis McGann
Friend, Historian, Politico

O! Lord, when will this war end?
These days of marchings, nights of lonely guard?
This terrible expenditure of health and life?
Where is the glory? Where is the reward,
For sacrifice of comfort, quiet, peace?
For sacrifice of children, wife, and friends?
For sacrifice of firesides—genial homes?
What hour, what gift, will ever make amends
For broken health, for bruised flesh and bones,
For lives cut short by bullet, blade, disease?
Where balm to heal the widow's heart, or what
Shall soothe a mother's grief for woes like these?
Hold, murmurer, hold! Is country naught to thee?
Is freedom nothing? Naught an honored name?
What though the days be cold, or the nights dark,
The brave heart kindles for itself a flame
That warms and lightens up the world!
Home! What's home, if in craven shame
We seek its hearthstone? Bitterest of cold.
Better creep thither bruised, and torn, and lame,
Than seek it in health when justice needs our aid.
Where is the glory? Where is the reward?
Think of the generations that will come
To praise and bless the hero. Think of God,
Who in due time will call His soldiers home.
How comfort mother for the loss of son?
What balm to which her heaviest grief must yield?
Ah! the plain, simple, ever-glorious words:
"Your son died nobly on the battle-field!"
What balm to soothe a widow's aching heart?
The grand assurance that in the battle shock
Foremost her husband stood, defying all,
For freedom and truth, unyielding as the rock.
Then, courage, all, and when the strife is past,
And grief for lost ones takes a milder hue,
This thought shall crown the living and the dead:
"He lived, he died, to God and duty true."

—Colonel John Beatty,
Third Ohio Infantry Volunteers, 1861

Acknowledgments

The "job" of researching and writing historical nonfiction is one that requires patience, peace and quiet. When my last book on the Civil War was published (*Bluff, Bluster, Lies and Spies: The Lincoln Foreign Policy, 1861–1865*), my wife Carmen said, "Finally, I am no longer a widow." She made that statement before becoming aware that I had already started work on *The Third Ohio Volunteer Infantry in the Civil War*. Nevertheless, I must give her credit for her careful copyediting of the manuscript. She pointed out spelling errors as well as factual passages that "didn't make any sense."

In addition to the creative side of historical nonfiction research and writing, there is a technical side of manuscript preparation that can be vexing at best. My thanks go to tech support specialists Sandy Selders and Kayleigh Elbaum whose unique skills unraveled some of the daunting mysteries of Word. I must also thank Lynn Bennett from the Melbourne Florida Public Library for facilitating the interlibrary loan process with the Library of Congress. She was the only one willing to tackle that.

The Prologue of the book began with the first land battle of the Civil War, Philippi. To better understand the movement of troops in the town and its surrounding countryside, I needed the help of a local historian. Fortunately, Philippi resident Ed Larry was helpful in sending me copies of local maps that clarified many of my questions. I was also fortunate to find the complete record of the reunions of the Third Ohio from 1876 to 1929. The minutes of the meetings, roll book, roster book, and the many local newspaper articles included in their scrapbooks provided a degree of detail that was not available in any other source. The reunion documents are housed in the archives of the Ohio History Museum in Columbus, Ohio. Access is limited and by appointment only. As a result, I am grateful to my brother Mark Perry for taking the time to go to the museum and examine the files in advance. This enabled me to read and photograph 61 pages of Third Ohio meeting minutes for the detail provided in the Epilogue. Thanks also to Ms. Abbie Meek, Senior Lincoln Librarian at the

Allen County Public Library (Fort Wayne, Indiana), for assistance with relevant copyright permissions.

For the last chapter of *The Third Ohio Volunteer Infantry in the Civil War*, it was important to obtain as much information as possible about Streight's Raid. The official reports filed by Colonel Abel Streight, Nathan Bedford Forrest, Grenville Dodge and Phillip Roddey provided critical information about the raid. However, many of the more interesting details came from the recollections of Company A sergeant Henry Breidenthal. He kept a small pocket diary, which I discovered at the Huntington Library, San Marino, California. The diary, however, covered only one month, from October to November 1861. It did not cover the period for Streight's Raid and contained no combat detail. It was only when I read Robert Willett's *The Lightning Mule Brigade: Abel Streight's 1863 Raid into Alabama* that I realized that there was another "diary" that Breidenthal kept with excellent, personal details of the raid. I went online to locate the author so I could determine the location of this other diary. Knowing nothing about Robert Willett, I looked him up on the internet and found that he was 97 years young and living in a town next to mine. In addition to the blurb he provided for *The Third Ohio Volunteer Infantry in the Civil War*, Bob also confirmed that there was another Breidenthal diary but believed it was in a library in North Carolina that had burned down many years ago. However, more research uncovered the fact that Breidenthal didn't keep another diary but first published his recollections in *The Rebellion Record: A Diary of American Events with Documents, Narratives, Illustrative Incidents, Poetry, etc.*, by Frank Moore in 1864. Many years later, his narrative on Streight's Raid was published again in the *National Tribune* in 1907.

There are some special people who were also "key players" in providing encouragement, critical advice and new data on a subject on which much has already been written. First among this group is Dr. Wayne C. Temple, chief deputy director of the Illinois State Archives. Dr. Temple's advice and encouragement in my previous book were critical in convincing me that my research was solid and worthy of publication. My three prior journal publications on Abraham Lincoln, John George Nicolay and William Henry Seward were important in that the editors of these publications were also noteworthy in providing helpful criticism as well as significant editing advice. These editors include Dr. Thomas Turner, editor of *The Lincoln Herald*, William Pederson of the *International Lincoln Association Newsletter* and Laurie Verge of *The Surratt Courier*.

My knowledge of the impact of the ironclads during the Civil War came from Howard Fuller, senior lecturer of war studies at the University of Wolverhampton, UK. Howard is the author of several books on maritime history. His knowledge of the Palmerston era and the British navy during the nineteenth century was essential in recognizing the unique limitations with which the British were dealing at this time. Howard's detailed emails and conversations were invaluable. My naval history was also enhanced by Dr. John Coski, Confederate Civil War historian and author of *Capital Navy: The Men, Ships and Operations of the James River Squadron*. Having read John's book, I was curious as to his thoughts on British and Confederate naval strength during the Civil War. I looked up his number on the internet, called him and had an informative discussion of commerce raiders like the *Alabama* as well as the unfortunate Confederate habit of scuttling more of their own ironclads than Farragut could sink. National Park Service historians John Heiser (Gettysburg) and Greg Mertz (Chancellorsville) made contributions to my understanding of the complexities and limitations of mid-nineteenth-century infantry tactics. John's responses to my obviously basic questions were timely and helpful. Greg recommended a book by Earl Hess titled *Civil War Infantry Tactics: Training, Combat and Small-Unit Effectiveness*. It was a good primer on the subject. Alicia Clarke, former curator of the Sanford Museum, was also helpful. This "museum" is unusual in that it contains over 2,000 letters and dispatches from William Henry Seward and his ring of spies and secret agents in Europe to Henry Sanford, U.S. minister to Belgium. Some of Sanford's detectives provide a detailed and intimate look into the world of bribery and surveillance of Confederate activities in England and France during the Civil War. Alicia Clarke was helpful and asked what I had uncovered in my research at the end of a long day. Current curator at the Sanford Museum Brigitte Stephenson was also helpful in making sure that I had workspace and access to the Sanford documents.

Finally, I owe many thanks to a man I never met but have always admired: Carl Sandburg. When I first read his *Abraham Lincoln: The Prairie Years and the War Years*, I was rapt with awe and reverence at the poetic prose of someone with a magical gift. His words and style continue to inspire me. Thank you all.

Table of Contents

Acknowledgments	vii
Preface	1
Introduction: Bushwhackers and Bridge Burners	7
1. Old Rosy and the Paradoxical Cavalier	25
2. Muddle and Confusion	40
3. The Quickness of a Tiger	54
4. Bushwhackers and Scorched Earth	72
5. Men of Iron	85
6. Christmas Crept In	99
7. Make the Sign of the Cross and Go In	111
8. A Bluff Beats a Straight	126
Epilogue	141
Appendix A. Chronology (Annotated): Third Ohio Volunteer Infantry Regiment	153
Appendix B. Roster: Third Ohio Volunteer Infantry	157
Appendix C. Ohio Generals During the Civil War	170
Appendix D. Third Ohio Volunteer Infantry Regiment: Commands, 1861–1864	172
Appendix E. Major General Alexander McCook's Corps: Perryville	173

Appendix F. 14th Army Corps (Army of the Cumberland)   174
Chapter Notes   175
Bibliography   187
Index   199

Preface

American Civil War military history often focuses on the best-known armies, battles and generals. Many are familiar with the Army of the Potomac and the Army of Northern Virginia. Most have heard of Ulysses Grant, Robert E. Lee, George McClellan and Stonewall Jackson. Less known but no less important are the names and deeds of the state regiments, their engagements and their commanders. *The Third Ohio Volunteer Infantry in the Civil War: "Obstinate Devils" from Middle Fork Bridge to Cedar Bluff* is the regimental history of the Third Ohio and their experiences during three years of the Civil War. Ohio sent 260 regiments to fight in the Civil War, including infantry, cavalry and artillery units. Some did not serve with Ohio regiments, however. For example, the Third Independent Company Ohio Volunteer Sharpshooters served throughout the war as Company K of the 66th Illinois Volunteer Infantry Regiment. Although *The Third Ohio Volunteer Infantry in the Civil War* focuses exclusively on this regiment, the Third Ohio also supported the Third Independent Company of Ohio Volunteer Sharpshooters, the Third Independent Battery of Ohio Artillery (three-month and three-year units), the Third Ohio Independent Cavalry Company, and the Third Regiment Ohio Volunteer Cavalry.

In addition to the regiments supplied by the state of Ohio, it also sent some of the most memorable volunteer and general officers to serve in the Civil War. Appendix B lists the names of all serving with the rank of general, three of whom later served as president. Some of the most recognizable names are Don Carlos Buell, George Armstrong Custer, James Garfield, Ulysses Grant, Benjamin Harrison, Rutherford B. Hayes, Joseph Hooker, George McClellan, the "Fighting McCooks" (the McCook family sent six sons to fight as Union generals in the war), Irvin McDowell, John Pope, and William Rosecrans.

The Third Ohio Volunteer Infantry Regiment was first formed as a three-month regiment on April 27, 1861. Regimental officers were Colonel Issac H. Morrow, Lieutenant Colonel John Beatty and Major Joseph

Warren Keifer. This regiment drilled at Camp Dennison, near Cincinnati, Ohio. However, they remained in Ohio and saw no action during the war. It was reorganized as a three-year regiment on June 12, 1861. The three-month volunteers who did not continue with the newly-reorganized regiment were mustered out on August 22, 1861. New, three-year regimental officers were Colonel Issac H. Morrow,[1] Colonel John Beatty, Colonel Orris A. Lawson,[2] Lieutenant Colonel J. Warren Keifer and Major James Vananda.

The new, three-year regiment camped and drilled at Camp Dennison prior to deployment in "western" Virginia on June 22, 1861.[3] The rank and file were paid $8.50 per month. The first recruit was John W. Tignor, Company E. Their battles, engagements and skirmishes included the following:

Middle Fork Bridge	July 6, 1861	"western" Virginia
Rich Mountain	July 11, 1861	"western" Virginia
Elk Water	September 11, 1861	"western" Virginia
Cheat Mountain	September 12–15, 1861	"western" Virginia
Paint Rock	April 28, 1862	Alabama
Bridgeport	April 29, 1862	Alabama
Perryville	October 8, 1862	Kentucky
Stones River, aka Murfreesboro	December 1862–January 63	Tennessee
Streight's Raid, aka Day's Gap	April 21, 1863	Alabama (Raid began)
Hog Mountain	April 30, 1863	Alabama
Blountsville	May 1, 1863	Alabama
Black Creek	May 2, 1863	Alabama
Blount's Plantation	May 2, 1863	Alabama
Cedar Bluff	May 3, 1863	Alabama

The Introduction to *The Third Ohio Volunteer Infantry in the Civil War* concerns a battle and an independent chunk of Virginia that serves as a preview of what would happen in 1861–1865. During the early months of 1861, the first land battle of the Civil War, Philippi, "western" Virginia, took place on June 3, 1861. That fight happened in an independent, mountainous part of Virginia that wanted no part of secession. Philippi is important to the Third Ohio for many reasons. First, the Union victory at Philippi exposed the first crack in an already "divided" Confederacy. This battle created the momentum that took the Third to Rich Mountain and the promotion of George McClellan to full command of all Union forces. Offensively, McClellan would prove to be a failure. Defensively, however, he would show great skill in keeping Washington safe from rebel invasion and seizure. The Third Ohio was also an important factor in denying the Confederacy access to and use of western Virginia, Kentucky, and Tennessee. The fight to deny Jefferson Davis access to the rail lines and good roads that ran over the mountains and through western Virginia was an accurate preview of what would soon happen in Kentucky and Tennessee.

Tennessee wanted things both ways. East Tennessee was pro–Union, but Central and West Tennessee were Confederate-leaning. A good example of Tennessee's ambivalence is found in the pages of the *Nashville Daily Union*. Although Tennessee declared for the Confederacy on June 8, 1861, much of the population was undecided. The poll results taken before the 8th show a preference for the Confederacy but just barely. The *Daily Union* made its position clear on December 4, 1862, when the front page declared,

> The Nashville Union was commenced a few weeks since for opposing the southern Confederacy, and of the restoration of federal authority, without any abatement, over all the states which have attempted to secede. It holds as friends all who support, and as foes all who oppose the Union of the States. It has no Watchword but Freedom and Nationality. With rebels and traitors, there is no compromise to make.... To the people of Tennessee, ever renown for their devotion to liberty and Union, until they were betrayed to the rebel despotism at Richmond by a perfidious Governor and corrupt Legislature.

Page two of the same newspaper, on the same date, praised Confederate general Sterling Price. Three months prior, Price seized an important supply depot in Iuka, Mississippi. He fought against Union general William Rosecrans for control of Iuka and the depot. Yet, the *Nashville Daily Union* declared on December 4, "it appears that Jeff Davis is endeavoring to bring General Price into disgrace. He better not. Price is the most necessary officer in the rebel army."[4] Tennessee had trouble making up its mind. Which side was it on? Kentucky, however, worked hard to maintain some semblance of neutrality. Regardless of allegiance, both states were critical to the success of the war for the Union.

Some historians consider the Battle of Stones River (Murfreesboro), Tennessee, to be the turning point for the Confederacy. It might be considered more significant than Gettysburg. If so, one of the more colorful figures in late 1862 Tennessee is Colonel John Pegram. He was a central figure at Philippi as well as Stones River. Along with rebel cavalry officers John Hunt Morgan (the Wizard of the Saddle), "Fighting Joe" Wheeler and Nathan Bedford Forrest ("Devil" Forrest), John Pegram (the "Paradoxical Cavalier") also conducted some of the cavalry raids that disrupted the supply lines and slowed the advance of William Rosecrans' Army of the Cumberland. John Hunt Morgan, John Pegram and "Fighting Joe" Wheeler were a constant threat to the Third Ohio and Lovell Rousseau's Division during the winter of 1862–1863. In addition to the guerrilla warfare which greatly impacted Union armies in the west, another Philippi alumnus was partly responsible for the disastrous opening shots of the Stones River battle. One of General Ebenezer Dumont's brigades forgot most of their basic training at Hartsville on December 7, 1862.[5] The result allowed John Morgan to walk away with almost 2,000 Yankee prisoners and tons of supplies and ammunition. With the Confederacy outmanned and outgunned at this point in the war, the rebel army decided that the best way to defeat the Yankees was to disrupt their supply lines and destroy their outposts. Deny them the ammunition and food necessary to supply their army, and they would eventually be defeated. Guerrilla strategy and tactics were central to the critical fight in Tennessee. Brigadier General John Pegram, the "Paradoxical Cavalier," played a central role in both Philippi and the disruptive months preceding Stones River.

Five of the Third Ohio engagements were modest in terms of scale and casualties but major relative to their impact on the early stage of the war. The skirmish at Middle Fork Bridge, for example, ensured that McClellan's back was protected and his line of retreat secured as he engaged Confederate forces at Rich Mountain. Compared to casualties at Gettysburg, Rich Mountain was a minor battle. In contrast, however, Rich Mountain was singularly and uniquely significant because it was a critical factor in prematurely elevating George McClellan to command of all Union forces. Later, Perryville, Stones River and all of the engagements linked with Streight's Raid were larger battles in the critical fight to keep the border states from joining the Confederacy.[6] Finally, on May 3, 1863, near Cedar Bluff, Alabama, the Third Ohio was captured by Confederate general Nathan Bedford Forrest. The enlisted men were released in a prisoner exchange on May 15, 1863. The officers were imprisoned at Belle Island in Richmond, Virginia. From August 1863 to June 1864, the Third Ohio Volunteer Infantry Regiment guarded bridges and garrisons throughout Tennessee. Some of the men from the Third, however, were combined with the 88th Ohio in July 1863 to successfully capture John Hunt Morgan. The men of the integral Third Ohio Regiment were mustered out at the end of their enlistment term on June 23, 1864.

Although the Third Ohio saw most of their service as a regiment per se under Colonel John Beatty, the regiment was initially commanded by Issac Morrow. However, Morrow was unpopular with the men in the ranks, and he resigned on February 6, 1862. William Lytle assumed command until he was wounded at Perryville. Lytle was succeeded by John Beatty, who quickly found that he had his hands full. The men of the regiment drank hard and fought harder. Beatty dealt with drunkenness, desertion, insubordination and mutiny. At one point, he tied a drunken mutineer to a tree with the reins from the drunk's horse until the man sobered up. He didn't shoot the man because Beatty needed everyone for service. In frustration, when Division Commander General Ormsby Mitchell was not saluted by some in the rank and file, he angrily referred to the Third as "Obstinate Devils." As a result, the Third Ohio Volunteer Infantry Regiment experienced "combat" on the battlefield as well as on the campgrounds of Virginia, Alabama, Kentucky and Tennessee.

The Third Ohio Volunteer Infantry Regiment was initially part of George McClellan's Department of the Ohio. At Perryville in October 1862, the regiment became part of the 17th Brigade commanded by Colonel William Haines Lytle, which was then part of Lovell Rousseau's Third Division and McCook's Corps. Logistics, tactics and combat attrition forced the Third Ohio to change commands many times. By Stones River, the Third Ohio was part of a division that formed the reserve of Major General George Thomas' center wing of the Army of the Cumberland.

With Lytle wounded at Perryville, Colonel John Beatty now commanded the Second Brigade, Third Ohio under Lovell Rousseau. Nevertheless, it was McClellan who determined the strategy and developed the tactics that brought the Ohio regiment to the first, important land battle of the war, Rich Mountain. Before the Third deployed for service, however, the political landscape in "western" Virginia underwent great change. The hardscrabble men and women from the mountains of this part of Virginia were against secession. The rebel government in Richmond was concerned about a lack of support and possible defection of this mountain region to the Union. By May 1861, Richmond was worried more about a meeting that was taking place in Wheeling, "western" Virginia.

The First Wheeling Convention, and much of the rest of the country North and South, was looking for a leader. The *Wheeling Intelligencer* noted on May 13, 1861, the opening day of the convention, "Now is there a man from all the northwest who has the nerve and the genius to lead this great movement? Is there one who can concentrate the scattered elements and bring their chaotic fragments into form? Such a one is wanted and wanted just now. The man who can do it will be a hero—a hero in the cause of humanity and liberty, and fame is waiting even now to write down his name and imperishable deeds." Western Virginia mirrored the hopes and dreams of the rest of the broken country. Everyone waited for leaders to step forward and fix the complex problems that had been festering for two generations. The men who wrote the Constitution and Bill of Rights didn't solve all of the issues. There were some that they deliberately put off for another day. Nobody knew what to do with slavery. In 1861, a man considered least likely to become that leader believed that he had the answer to the slavery issue. He claimed he knew how to handle a problem that eluded Jefferson, Adams and many others. On March 4, 1861, Abraham Lincoln told his listeners,

> Apprehension seems to exist among the people of the Southern States that by the accession of a Republican administration their property and their peace and personal security are to be endangered. There has never been any

reasonable cause for such apprehension. Indeed, the most ample evidence to the contrary has all the while existed and been open to their inspection. It is found in nearly all the published speeches of him who now addresses you. I do but quote from one of those speeches when I declare that I have no purpose, directly or indirectly, to interfere with the institution of slavery in the States where it exists. I believe I have no lawful right to do so, and I have no inclination to do so.[7]

Lincoln believed that slavery, if left alone in the South, would eventually die by itself—without war. As long as it was not permitted to extend into the new territories that were quickly being formed, then slavery could rest easy and enjoy its liberty. Unfortunately, just how the death of slavery was to happen was never made clear. Nevertheless, Lincoln was an ambitious man whose wife believed that he would become president one day. On election day 1860, when it was clear that Lincoln had won, he went home and told his wife, "We are elected." Hundreds of miles away, however, another man was pulling weeds and watering the roses in his garden when a telegram arrived from Montgomery, Alabama. A group of men from six states that had broken away from the Union had decided that Jefferson Davis would make a great leader for their cause. Unlike Mary Lincoln who eagerly sought the presidency for her husband, Davis' wife, Varina, remembered, "Reading that telegram, he [Davis] looked so grieved that I feared some evil had befallen our family. After a few moments, he told me like a man might speak of a sentence of death."[8] Two leaders with different mandates were about to fight head-to-head.

What about that independent part of Virginia referred to as "western" Virginia? Who was its leader?

Introduction

Bushwhackers and Bridge Burners

O, may those who would plunge us into the horrors of civil discord be overreached by the omnipotent arm of Almighty God. —Reverend Peter T. Laesterley, First Wheeling Convention, May 14, 1861

Great tension hovered low in a small room. Anger was almighty.[1] Rumors were circulating that Stonewall Jackson would attack at any moment.

The first two significant land battles of the American Civil War were fought in "western" Virginia. Prior to June 20, 1863, the western part of the state was referred to as "western" Virginia, even in the *Official Records of the War of the Rebellion*. This part of Virginia is physically different from the eastern part of the state. Mountains, deep valleys and thick forests typify the geography of this part of Virginia. This factor per se helped to produce the independent mindset of the inhabitants and frustrated the tactics and logistics of the large army divisions who attempted to operate there. It is important to know some of the historical background of "western" Virginia to better understand how and why the military history of the Third Ohio and the Civil War rightfully begins here.

On May 16, 1861, the *Cincinnati Enquirer* revealed what many in the mountains of western Virginia were already thinking. Page three shouted, "*Threatened Attack on Wheeling. Apprehension is felt of an attack on Wheeling from Harper's Ferry Tomorrow.*" The threat came from Virginia troops who were thought to be mobilizing for a march on the city of Wheeling. They were planning to shut down a meeting of local leaders who were debating the resolution by the state of Virginia to withdraw from the Union. The tough, weathered men from the mountains never felt any bond with the more decorative politicians from Richmond. The men from the mountains didn't own slaves and felt more connection with the Union from the North. They liked the fact that an "ugly" rail-splitter was president. The biographical "memoirs" of Lincoln's secretary John George Nicolay are relevant here.[2] He and John Milton Hay were like sons to Lincoln.[3] Their biography of the president contains language that often reflected the thoughts of Lincoln himself. According to Nicolay, western Virginia was a "diversified, picturesque, healthful region, a country of pure air, clean springs, magnificent forests and lovely valleys, it gradually gathered a population of hunters and explorers, of lumberman and miners, of herdsmen and small farmers."[4] This contrasted with the population of Richmond who were seen by those around Lincoln as "local magnates who … laid and expended taxes as though the Blue Ridge were the true western boundary of the 'old Dominion' and the great mountain region beyond only a tributary province."[5] The scene was thus set for a clash.

Between May 16 and June 12, 1861, the smoke from the Confederate bombardment of Fort Sumter had cleared. The eight-inch columbiads and 42-pounders that had protected the harbor at Charleston were silent.[6] The dust from defeated casemates finally settled into a soft stratum underfoot. The fort was quiet. In South Carolina, those promoting the "civil discord" mourned by the Reverend Laesterly were full of foolish bluster; but the

Columbiads were big-caliber, smooth-bore guns that were used for seacoast defense. The large 10-inch Columbiad fired a shell weighing 120 lb. almost one mile (Library of Congress).

"fire-eaters" from the Palmetto State were still dangerous. The men and women from the remote western part of Virginia wanted no part of the fight. However, they needed to be better organized. So, at 10:00 a.m. on June 12, 1861, in the city of Wheeling, Virginia, the Reverend Wesley Smith finished a brief prayer to a small group of 30 men from all over the rugged mountain counties of the western part of Virginia. The *Wheeling Intelligencer* called this the Second Wheeling Convention.[7] Conspicuously clean shaven and looking much younger than his 44 years,[8] Senator John S. Carlisle escorted the newly elected committee chair, Arthur I. Boreman, to the podium at the front of the room.[9]

The new chairman spoke about the Ordinance of Secession adopted by the Virginia Legislature in Richmond on April 17, 1861. The men from the peaks as well as the valleys objected to the ordinance. Boreman made it plain that

> we of Western Virginia are asked to concur in this action. We are placed in a peculiar position. We here in Western Virginia have determined that by the help of Him who rules on high we will resist the action of that Richmond Convention, which has practiced upon us a monstrous usurpation of power, violated the Constitution of the country and violated every rule of right. We have determined I say, to resist it, and under this determination we are found here to-day to take definite action. If you gentlemen will go with me, we will take definite, determined and unqualified action as to the course we will pursue. We will take such action as will result in Western Virginia, if not the whole of Virginia, remaining in the Union of our fathers. I am satisfied that the members of this Convention concur with me almost unanimously.... Then, in this Convention we have no ordinary political gathering. We have no ordinary task before us. We come here to carry out and execute, and it may be, to

Arthur I. Boreman. His leadership enabled West Virginia to break from Virginia and become a state in 1863. He was elected the first governor of West Virginia in 1863 (Library of Congress).

institute a government for ourselves. We are determined to live under a State Government in the United States of America and under the Constitution of the United States. It requires stout hearts to execute this purpose; it requires men of courage—of unfaltering determination; and I believe, in the gentlemen who compose this Convention, we have the stout hearts and the men who are determined in this purpose.[10]

Many of those present felt reassured by the dark, penetrating eyes of a man who broadcast the obvious truth. Boreman sat down, and Dr. Dennis B. Dorsey of Monongahela County made the following statement:

Resolved, That it shall be in part the business of this Convention, to make the requisite preparatory arrangements for the separation from Virginia, and the formation into a new State, of such counties as are represented in this body, by delegates or otherwise, and are desirous of entering into the new State organization.[11]

When Virginia seceded from the Union, and western Virginia decided it wanted no part of the fight, the Ohio River was all that separated the nervous state of Ohio from a contest it also wanted to avoid. Lincoln secretary John George Nicolay confirmed this in his Lincoln biography: "With Virginia in secession, and Kentucky setting up the pretense of armed neutrality, the Ohio line became at once a quasi-military frontier."[12] Who was the governor of Ohio, and was he prepared for the challenge? "The officer upon whom the full pressure of this sudden avalanche fell had filled one-half of his term as Governor of the State. [William Dennison] was a man of excellent social connections, of suave, elegant manners, a master of deportment, and a favorite in polite circles. His experience in public affairs had been limited to a single term in the State Senate, and of military matters he was, like most other officials, profoundly ignorant." Although Dennison was proactive in safeguarding Ohio, the rest of the state was concerned about other provlems. Ohio was potentially vulnerable to Confederate attack, but the newspapers of the time do not reflect that alarm. The *Cincinnati Enquirer* headlined the death of Senator Stephen A. Douglas and the health of General Winfield Scott.[13] It also discussed possible recognition of the Confederacy by Europe.

At this time, France was more of a concern to U.S. safety than England. Napoleon III of France was a slippery and aggressive dictator who desperately needed Southern cotton to keep his textile mills operating.[14] The Union blockade was preventing his access to high-grade Southern cotton. However, the emperor was also savvy enough to realize that any such action must only be taken in conjunction with Great Britain. He didn't dare break the Union blockade on his own. British and French cooperation was important at this stage. British minister to the United States at this time was Lord Richard Lyons.[15] "He was the type of what the modern

English diplomatist must be—without initiative or views of his own.... The qualities of caution, discretion, good temper, good sense and steadiness were displayed by Lyons to an uncommon degree during the tense and difficult years of his tenure in Washington."[16] He wrote to the British foreign secretary, Lord John Russell, in Dispatch No. 183 on May 6, 1861, "M. Mercier told me that if England and France acted in strict concert, he did not suppose the announcement [of Confederate recognition] would produce any other inconvenience than a boastful violent note from Mr. Seward; but that the most perfect understanding between the two powers was essential, otherwise it was not unlikely that this government might seek an opportunity to use one or the other as the scapegoat."[17] Soon, Queen Victoria's government declared neutrality. Under accepted international law at the time, neutrality was designed to allow a country to trade with others at war as long as that trade did not include implements of war.

After the Crimean War, the 1856 Treaty of Paris clarified the rights of belligerent parties during wartime. On April 16, 1856, over 40 major powers in Europe signed an agreement that declared (1) the abolishment of privateering; (2) the neutral flag covers enemy's goods with the exception of contraband of war; (3) neutral goods, with the exception of contraband of war, are not liable to capture under an enemy's flag; and (4) blockades, in order to be binding, must

Governor William Dennison considered the defense of Ohio of the greatest importance in 1861. Only the Ohio River separated the state from raiders like Stonewall Jackson. Although he served only one term, his foresight and preparedness helped keep Ohio safe. The Third Ohio regiment trained and departed from Camp Dennison (Library of Congress).

be effective. The queen also wisely declined to challenge the blockade. It was clearly "ineffective" to the extent that Confederate privateers easily breached the blockade and continued to trade with Europe. Nevertheless, Queen Victoria believed that challenging the blockade was too much of a risk. More than the blockade, the issue that more directly impacted the men of the Third Ohio was "shoddy" equipment.[18] The *Cincinnati Enquirer* on May 31, 1861, complained, "Army Supplies-Contractors' Plunder: So much complaint, with charges so serious, has been made against the conduct of army contractors, agents, commissaries, etc. in the manner of which they have been and are plundering the government that we wonder that some prompt and proper action has not been taken by the proper departments to put a stop to it." James Gordon Bennett of the *New York Herald* added his grousing but influential voice to the outrage: "Bennett was especially upset with stories of war profiteering and shoddy uniforms for Union soldiers. Complaining that the troops were 'half naked' with uniforms that disintegrated in bad weather, Bennett further complained that 'it is by such contracts as these that the life-blood is being sucked out of the nation by the vampires.'"[19]

George McClellan gave Arthur Boreman and western Virginia hope with a proclamation he issued from his desk in Cincinnati on May 26, 1861:

Proclamation to the People of Western Virginia

Headquarters Department of the Ohio,
Cincinnati, May 26, 1861

To the Union Men of Western Virginia:

Virginians: The general government has long enough endured the machinations of a few factious rebels in your midst. Armed traitors have in vain endeavored to deter you from expressing your loyalty at the polls. Having failed in this infamous attempt to deprive you of the exercise of your dearest rights, they now seek to inaugurate a reign of terror, and thus force you to yield to their schemes, and submit to the yoke of the traitorous conspiracy dignified by the name of Southern Confederacy.

Geo. B. McClellan,
Major-General, Commanding[20]

Western Virginia was still part of the state of Virginia. Would Robert E. Lee and Governor Lechter allow a vital part of their state to be chopped off without a fight? Colonel George A. Porterfield, Virginia Volunteers, was stationed in Philippi, western Virginia. On May 29, he informed Colonel Robert S. Garnett of the true situation in his area. Porterfield refers to the city of Bellaire, Ohio, which was a staging area for the Third Ohio after leaving Camp Dennison and crossing the Ohio River into western Virginia.

> Colonel: On the 27th instant, I received reliable information of a contemplated movement among those hostile to us, by which a large body of men were intended to be precipitated on me in the rear, by the railroad, without notice, and in a few hours' time. I was also assured that about fifteen hundred Federal troops had collected at Marietta, some at Bellaire.... I also sent an expedition to destroy a bridge of the Northwestern Virginia Railroad.... I caused a small bridge of the same road ... to be destroyed, but I learn that it has been repaired.[21]

Anticipating that bridges would be burned and railroad track torn up, McClellan began to attach engineer brigades to the regiments operating in this theater of war. As a result, the bridges being burned by George Porterfield were quickly repaired by Union engineers. Throughout the South, the Civil War was a multifront campaign. Men fought on land as well as the rivers, gulfs and lakes that ran through the Confederacy. In addition, there was a constant battle to maintain the railroad bridges and tunnels that kept the trains functioning. Those rails quickly transported men and supplies from one theater of war to another. Without the trains, bad roads would slow down and help defeat an army, Union or rebel. Porterfield continued his wire to Garnett and set the stage for the first land battle of the Civil War: Philippi. Although the Third Ohio was not yet deployed, the actors on both sides at Philippi will return later in the war to impact the Third. It is important to get to know them now. On the 29th, Porterfield continued,

> Considering our very inadequate supply of ammunition, particularly caps, and that our number of infantry was small (not more than about five hundred and fifty) and the want of any sort of training or military discipline among our men, and being informed that other bodies of men besides those first spoken of, had passed the burned bridges by means of temporary repairs of them.... I concluded to remove the State of arms and stores to Philippi.[22]

As a result of Porterfield's establishing his supply depot at Philippi, that small town became the scene of the first land battle of the Civil War.

Before the Third Ohio crossed the Ohio River into western Virginia, the growth and power of North versus South was evident to many. Maybe the *Intelligencer* was right: this will be a short war. During this time, North and South were growing dangerously apart. In 1857, New York senator William Henry Seward purchased a copy of a new book that was making a sensation all over the country. A North Carolinian, Hinton Rowan Helper, published *The Impending Crisis of the South: How to Meet It*. The book became very controversial. Helper was raised in a slave-owning family

Philippi was the first land battle of the Civil War. It is distinguished from Fort Sumter in that Sumter was a siege rather than a land battle between two opposing infantry regiments. Shown here are Union troops turning right on Main Street and attempting to capture rebel forces escaping to the South (Library of Congress).

but grew to hate slavery. He used statistics to show the relative strength of North versus South. The contrasts were compelling.[23]

1855	North	South
Import Tonnage	236	24
Export Tonnage	167	107
Value Mfg. Products	$842,000,000	$165,000,000
Railroads (miles)	17,855	6,859
Bank Capital	$230,000,000	$102,000,000

Helper's statistics are especially significant when railroad numbers are considered. Armies moved by foot and rail. However, when Lincoln's strategy of fighting the Confederacy on multiple fronts simultaneously was put into practice, Jefferson Davis and Robert E. Lee could not move troops fast enough to meet the threat. They did not have the railroad infrastructure to do this. Their limited scope of track in multiple gauges greatly compromised their mobility.[24] There are many accounts of Stonewall Jackson's forced marches on foot to reinforce one overwhelmed general after another. To force the army to move faster still, Lee issued General Order No. 102 which stated, "All cannoneers are positively prohibited from riding on the ammunition chests or guns." According to Alan Nevins, "The point of perhaps the greatest and most rapidly growing disparity between Northern and Southern strength, however, lay elsewhere: in the railroads."[25] The Third Ohio was initially sent to western Virginia to protect the railroad bridges and tunnels that rebel guerrilla forces were burning as fast as they could.

On June 22, 1861, men from the Third Ohio Volunteers crossed the Ohio River and became the first Ohio regiment to enter Virginia. The *Cincinnati Enquirer* noted the event: "Camp Dennison: The attendance of visitors at Camp Dennison yesterday was larger than on any day this previous week, but the intense heat prevented many from perambulating the camp ground. The preparation and departure of the Third Regiment, Colonel Marrow (sic), and Fourth Regiment, Colonel Andrews, was the special feature of the day. The troops were furnished with improved muskets, and the flank companies of each regiment received an Enfield rifle. Their equipment was complete, and as the train moved off, the air was rent with their huzzas and cheers for the Union and the Stars and Stripes.... The regiments number 1,000 men each and go to Bell Air via Columbus. They were provided with two days rations.... The Third, Fourth and Tenth regiments have been assigned to General Schleich's command as a brigade."[26] It was hotter than usual at that time of the year, and the men were forced to live in leaky tents with poor uniforms. General Henry Carrington complained as well, "The militia of Ohio had been thus hurried off, and none too soon; but the inferior clothing that had been sent from Philadelphia, of the same kind as that first furnished the Pennsylvania troops, was almost worthless, and there had not been time for the State authorities to buy material and manufacture simply transferred to the field, there to be useless for want of common necessaries in the way of outfit."[27]

Late in June, security improved when the Third Ohio Volunteer Infantry Regiment was converted from three months to three years of service in the U.S. Army. Some of the three-month volunteer enlistments left for home, but most signed on in the "regular army." Negative feelings ran high against those electing to go home. Ohio adjutant general Catharinus Buckingham did his best to manage a sensitive issue:

> When the three-years' recruits began to come in, it was found that the presence of the three-months' men, who had declined to reenlist, was the cause of much inconvenience, and greatly tended to demoralize the entire force. The quarters were crowded, jealousies sprang up, doubts arose as to the rights of the different classes of troops, ill-feeling was engendered, and general insubordination, in most regiments, was the result. It became absolutely necessary to separate the three-months' men from the others. Instead of mustering them out of the service, however, as would seem to have been the proper method, no directions were received from the War Department as to the disposition to be made of them, though sought by the Governor and officers often and earnestly. At length the colonels of the regiments took the responsibility of sending their three-months' men home, on furlough, till further orders.[28]

Later that summer, Lieutenant Colonel Rutherford B. Hayes of the 23rd Ohio Volunteer Infantry Regiment arrived at Clarksburg, Virginia, on July 27, 1861. He commented in his diary on the joy shown by the residents when they saw the three-month enlistments go home: "All the way, one hundred and thirty miles, in Virginia, greeted by shouts and demonstrations of joy. The people had seen many three-months men going, leaving western Virginia for home. This, with the defeat at Washington perhaps, led the people to fear that the Union men were left to the Rebels of the eastern part of the State. Our coming relieved them and was hailed with every demonstration of joy."[29] Nevertheless, the Ohio River was still a critical barrier. Governor William Dennison proclaimed, "We can let no theory prevent the defense of Ohio. I will defend Ohio where it costs least and accomplished most. Above all, I will defend Ohio beyond rather than on her border."[30]

Long before the Third Ohio arrived in western Virginia, the area was in turmoil. On May 29, 1861, Confederate colonel George Porterfield reported from his camp in Philippi, "I ordered some of the bridges of the Baltimore and Ohio railroad northwest of Fairmont to be destroyed, which order was carried into effect by the destruction of two between Farmington and Mannington, about thirty-five miles northwest of Grafton."[31] That rail was a vital part of communication and military logistics from Washington to the Ohio River. Initiated by merchants and investors from Baltimore, Maryland, the line first ran from Washington to Baltimore and then on through Harpers Ferry, Virginia, Cumberland, Piedmont, Grafton and Parkersburg in western Virginia, finally reaching Cincinnati, Ohio.

All of the new technology began to play an important role in warfare—on land and sea. On land, the railroad, telegraph, rifled guns and the minié ball began to have an impact on strategy, tactics and logistics. At sea, ironclad warships and Monitor-class harbor vessels ultimately convinced Great Britain that challenging the Union blockade of Southern ports was not worth the risk.[32] The railroad was, however, so vital that both North and South considered it worth fighting for. On April 29, 1861, Lee ordered Major General Alonzo Loring to "muster into the service of the State such volunteer companies as offer themselves in compliance with the call of the Governor, take command of them and direct the military operations for the protection of the terminus of the Baltimore & Ohio Railroad and also of the road."[33] The CEO of the Baltimore and Ohio Railroad (B&O), John W. Garrett, didn't want to see his business destroyed. He tried to play both sides and declared, "Our road is regarded, both in Maryland and Virginia, as a monument of the common enterprise of their people, and as the means of a common prosperity."[34] The Union advantage in railroads was decisive, however. The B&O had 1,231 more cars available for supply and troop transport than all of Virginia rails combined. The Pennsylvania

Railroad had 1,479 more cars.[35] Although burning B&O bridges became critical in protecting the life of the young Confederacy, those bridges were also needed to ensure the independence of western Virginia.

In addition to the logistical importance of the railroad, the telegraph quickly assumed vital significance as well. At this time, the men laying the wooden ties and driving spikes to secure the rails also erected the poles that held the telegraph wires. "By the eve of the Civil War, telegraph mileage exceeded railroad mileage, with some fifty thousand miles of line in successful operation throughout north America, over fourteen hundred stations, and a telegraph force of nearly ten thousand operators and clerks."[36] The railroad was a critical factor in quickly moving large numbers of troops into position within hours or days rather than the weeks it would otherwise have taken by foot over difficult terrain. First-person accounts of forced marches over long distances often talk about starvation and dehydration. Many marched barefoot or with shoes completely worn out. In western Virginia, however, the rivers and valleys through which the railroad must pass were forded by the wooden bridges that George Porterfield was intent on burning. Quickly securing these passages before Porterfield applied his torch could only be done with the help of a telegraph that ordered men to move before the damage was done. Before Middle Fork Bridge and Rich Mountain, George McClellan informed Winfield Scott, "I was engaged in maturing plans to carry out the General's telegraphic instructions, when I learned by telegram that two bridges on the Baltimore and Ohio Railroad, near Farmington Station, had been burned on Saturday night…. Col. Kelley, of the First Virginia Volunteers, with his own regiment and four companies of the Second, are ordered by telegraph to move without delay from Wheeling towards Fairmont, guarding the bridges as they proceeded."[37] Later in the war, Edwin Stanton would comment, "The military telegraph has been of inestimable value to the service, and no corps has surpassed, few have equaled, the telegraph operators in diligence and devotion to their duties."[38] The North had the financial resources to buy the wire, insulators and battery acid necessary to build the United States Military Telegraph. This system allowed generals in the field to talk in real time with central command in Washington.

When George McClellan eventually crossed the Ohio River with men from the Third Ohio, his troops were equipped with rifled muskets and 12-pound cannon. Most Confederate infantry at this time were still armed with smooth-bore muskets. They loaded from the muzzle and fired a round .58 caliber ball that wobbled and quivered as it forced its way through currents of air to find the target. The enemy had to be close because that ball was accurate at less than 100 yards. When it hit its target, however, that oscillating round ball tore a large, jagged hole in a man's body. This helped contribute to the amputations that disabled so many war veterans. In contrast, Yankee minié balls were merciful. They were rifled and cut a smaller hole when they struck: at a greater and more accurate distance of 250 yards. In addition, the Union army had already begun to use the 12-pound gun versus the six-pounder used by the Confederacy.

May 26, 1861 Soldiers: You are ordered to cross the frontier and enter upon the soil of Virginia. Your mission is to restore peace and confidence, to protect the majesty of the law, and to rescue our brethren from the grasp of armed traitors.

Geo. B. McClellan,
Major-General, U.S. Army,
Commanding Department[39]

By May 1861, Abraham Lincoln had called for 75,000 volunteers. This was in response to the bombardment of Fort Sumter in the harbor at Charleston, South Carolina. Lincoln's focus was not on western Virginia, however. The president had never heard of Philippi. He was more interested in the railroad that ran from Alexandria to Manassas, Virginia. From there, he could send troops straight to Richmond and end the rebellion before it started. The man in charge of the Confederate armed forces in Virginia was Robert E. Lee. He didn't want to lose control of the B&O railroad that ran through Harpers Ferry and one-third of the state of Virginia, but Manassas and Richmond were more immediately important. As a result, Lee had only a few regiments under Colonel George Porterfield available to contest the Ohio and Indiana regiments now crossing the Ohio River into the Kanawha Valley.

In western Virginia, both the B&O and the Northwestern Virginia rail systems were critical. Railroads could move fighting men faster through terrain that was mountainous and heavily forested than could be achieved on foot. In addition, six- and twelve-pound artillery pieces were easier to move by rail or macadamized road. Horses needed forage, water and rest to haul a heavy load. A steam engine needed only water. "Pro-Southern historian Douglas Southall Freeman wrote 'from the very hour of secession, the Federals realized that the Baltimore and Ohio Railroad between Washington and Parkersburg [Virginia] was at once the most important and the most exposed link in the iron chain that bound together the East and the Midwest. Not only must the railroad be held but also it must be free to operate without the threat of raids.'"[40] Ultimately, an act of Congress gave Abraham Lincoln the authority to take federal control of all railroads if necessary for the defense of the Union.[41] This was timely because Secretary of War Simon Cameron had a conflict of interest with a competing railroad, the Northern Central, in which he held a substantial interest. This led to lax protection for the B&O. John Hunt Morgan and his raiders initially found the rail an easy target. Succeeding war secretary Edwin Stanton had no competing interest, and the B&O became more secure.

Porterfield's command consisted of 600 infantry and 175 mounted cavalry. He was based in Philippi, which allowed him to secure supplies from Beverly and march north to burn bridges in Grafton. However, George McClellan had just ordered a force three times that of Porterfield to advance on Philippi and capture or chase them all into the mountains. To make matters worse, Porterfield was also out of ammunition and out of support from the local citizenry who wanted him gone.

After burning the railroad bridge at Grafton, Porterfield and his men retreated south to Farmington and then to Philippi. Union brigadier general Thomas A. Morris came to Grafton and replaced the burned ties on the damaged bridge.[42] He immediately detailed Colonel Benjamin F. Kelley to chase the bridge burners who were still in Farmington, three miles to the south.[43] The *Wheeling Intelligencer* told its readers, "It was rather exciting to see the scouts or 'snake hunters' as they styled themselves on a trail.... In the evening the companies returned from Farmington, bringing with them several prisoners, and reporting that their scouts had killed one secessionist and wounded another."[44] Attempting to capture Porterfield himself might be a problem, however, because Morris heard a rumor that spies from Pruntytown were watching and reporting his movements. So Morris met with Colonel Kelley and devised a scheme to fool the Confederate partisans. The following morning, June 2, at 9:00 a.m., Kelley and the regiments of James Irvine and Robert Milroy would board the B&O east toward Harpers Ferry. Hopefully, Porterfield would believe that Harpers Ferry was the target. Kelley's force would disembark from the train, six miles out in Thornton, and march 25 miles south to Philippi. Due to the poor roads on this route, Kelley needed the extra time. To continue the ruse, Colonel Ebenezer Dumont would leave at 8:30 p.m. on June 3. He would take the B&O heading west. Four miles later, in Webster, he would meet up with the regiments of Thomas Crittenden and Frederick Lander who were waiting for him just outside of town. It was particularly important to avoid Fetterman because the telegraph operator there was a known Confederate sympathizer. The basic plan was to squeeze Porterfield between their forces positioned east and west of Philippi. What happened next? Dumont would take the Beverly-Fairmont Pike to Philippi. The pike was better maintained and would allow Dumont to leave later than Kelley but hopefully arrive in Philippi at the same time.

The use of untrained, volunteer troops was a gamble. As a result, Kelley's men left Grafton without provisions. As the men starved on the long march, they begged for food at farmhouses along the way. Without water in their canteens, they drank the muddy water that filled the potholes during a torrential rain at night. Finally able to procure some flour to bake bread, they were frustrated when the rain extinguished their fires. By the time they reached Tracy, some of the men declared that they would prefer death to continuing the march. Fifteen hundred exhausted men were now stretched out in a line almost two miles long. How could they be expected to fight when they reached their destination? Dumont and his men marched on better road conditions but soon realized that they would not be able to arrive at 4:00 a.m. In an attempt to quicken the pace, many of the companies in the Dumont regiment threw away everything except their musket. They covered the last five miles in one hour. Were they able to surprise Porterfield's pickets and squeeze the rebels tight?

> Daylight came. Porterfield's pickets, taken by surprise, had given to warning of enemy approach. The first intimation was received when shots from the Federal battery on the hill began falling into the Confederate camp and the village street. Porterfield's untrained men, already overwrought by a night of nervous tension, believing they were trapped, became completely demoralized. In spite of Porterfield's personal coolness and his efforts to rally them into a semblance of disciplined order, they fled in the utmost confusion. Discarding their equipment, and even their guns, they ran through the muddy streets in uncontrollable panic—many on foot, some on horses—all made haste to escape down the pike toward the south. Fortunately for them, through some failure still unexplained, the southern road which was to have been blocked remained ahead of them open and unobstructed, while Kelley mistakenly approached the northern end of the town.[45]

Newspaper accounts of the skirmish at Philippi referred to the Confederate defeat as the "Philippi Races." George McClellan was still in Ohio but filed the first report of the action on June 3, 1861.

> Headquarters Department of the Ohio,
>
> Cincinnati, June 3, 1861
>
> I have just received a telegram, dated today, from General T.A. Morris, Indiana Volunteers, commanding United States troops at Grafton, Va. In which he says: We surprised the rebels, about two thousand strong, at Philippi this morning. Captured a large amount of arms, horses, ammunition, provisions and camp equipage. The attack was made after a march during the entire night in a drenching rain. The surprise was complete. Fifteen rebels killed. The gallant Colonel Kelley, of the First Virginia Volunteers, I fear, is mortally wounded. No other important casualties on our side.
>
> Geo. B. McClellan,
> *Major-General, Commanding*
> Col. E.D. Townsend, *Assistant Adjutant-General*[46]

Introduction   21

What really happened at Philippi? "The investigations of the commission had developed that a main and picket guard as strong as was consistent with the effective infantry force present was regularly detailed and posted at distances sufficiently far out to accomplish the object in view, provided they knew and did their duty, which the latter is strongly to be suspected from the fact that although in advance they failed to give any intimation of the enemy's approach, a conclusion that is strengthened by the official report of the mounted officers out with the scouting parties on the night of June 2 that they had neither seen an infantry picket nor been challenged by its sentinels going from or returning to the town that night."[47]

The night of June 2 was pouring rain, and all troops were intended to arrive at their destination by 4:00 a.m. Twenty-five miles from Webster to Philippi was a great distance to cover in a short time. Dumont was fortunate, however, in being able to take advantage of the Beverly-Fairmont Turnpike. Nevertheless, some of the men in his regiment fainted from exhaustion, while others threw away their gear to be able to keep up the required pace. Dumont covered the last five miles in one hour. The plan was to arrive at a point 400 yards outside of Philippi. Kelley, Irvine, Milroy and Crittenden were to attack from the east and Dumont from the west.

Attacking from the west, however, involved crossing a narrow bridge over the Tygart River. This forced Union regiments to cross tightly packed and company by company. If Porterfield's men were better trained and stood their ground, they could have fired into the bridge and forced the troops back. In the panic to escape, this did not happen. As a result, the Seventh Indiana, 14th Ohio and Sixth Indiana charged over the bridge, fully exposed and vulnerable. Porterfield and some of his men fled south to Beverly. With Dumont and Kelley covering all escape routes, north and south, Porterfield still managed to escape. How did this happen?

The problem lay with Kelley's troops marching in from the east. Just south of Nestorville, the road from Grafton divides in two. The approach from Tracy ran straight into the center of Philippi. The road coming in from the northwest was part of the Beverly-Fairmont Turnpike. The supply depot for Confederate forces in northwestern Virginia was in Beverly. The fastest route to Beverly was over the turnpike. Kelley was supposed to be blocking the turnpike route. However, when he arrived with his men on the morning of June 3, he took the shorter route which took him away from the pike. Ultimately, Porterfield took an alternate route and emerged south of Kelley on the turnpike to Beverly.

At this point, the report filed by Dumont and those reported in the *Wheeling Intelligencer* by the men in the field begin to disagree. Dumont stated that his six-pounders opened up on the center of Philippi when pickets first opened up on him. With the pickets still sheltering from the rain, Dumont's credibility is in question. In addition, Colonel Dumont supports this with a statement that he drew picket fire first because his men were poised on the opposite side of the Tygart Valley River due to the confusion as to which of the two roads leading into town was the correct route. Allegedly, this left his men exposed and awaiting orders, thus allowing Porterfield pickets time to get their range and open fire. In fact, the two approaches to the narrow bridge over the river are too far back to allow for effective musket fire. The immediate approach to the bridge was accessed by one road, not two. With a substantial head start, it is more likely that Kelley was the first to arrive in Philippi. His men entered the town to the north and unintentionally allowed Porterfield to escape. However, when Dumont arrived and his guns began to fire, Porterfield and his men were trapped and they fled in panic. Rather than take their provisions and ammunition with them, some cut the horses loose from the wagons and fled on horseback. Others threw down their muskets and ran. Apparently, one of Porterfield's men was too overweight to keep up. In desperation, he turned and fired his pistol at his mounted pursuer and shot. The bullet pierced Colonel Benjamin F. Kelley in the chest.[48]

What was the reaction of Robert E. Lee? The general in charge of the Virginia militia sent his quartermaster, Major Michael G. Harman, to get more information and send supplies and ammunition if needed. Harman wrote to Lee on June 6, 1861, "From all the information I have received, I am pained to have to express my conviction that Colonel Porterfield is entirely unequal to the position which he occupies. The affair at Philippi was a disgraceful surprise, occurring about daylight, there being no picket guard or guard of any kind on duty."[49] At this point, Lee decided to replace Porterfield with his adjutant, Colonel Robert Garnett. Nevertheless, Lee wanted to let Porterfield down easily. He wrote on June 13, "Colonel: Your letter of the 9th has been received. I regret much the unfortunate circumstances with which you have been beset, and appreciate the difficulties you have had to encounter."[50]

The buildup of rebel forces in western Virginia and the transfer of General Robert Garnett to the Rich Mountain area would require McClellan to leave his comfortable headquarters in Cincinnati and cross the Ohio. McClellan's habit of delaying offensive action was finally starting to concern Ohio governor Dennison. This was the first of many delays that would come to characterize his command style. On May 10, 1861, Dennison contacted McClellan and urged him to cross the river and fight in Virginia, not on Ohio soil. McClellan responded, "I have carefully considered your letter of the 10th.... I advise delay for the present. I fear nothing from Western Virginia."[51] With railroad bridges being burned and the vital passes at Rich Mountain and Laurel Hill now occupied by rebel troops, McClellan should have mobilized faster. Nevertheless, on June 22, 1861, the Third Ohio Volunteer Infantry Regiment crossed the Ohio River at Bellaire and reached Grafton, western Virginia, by 1:00 p.m. on the 23rd.

1

Old Rosy and the Paradoxical Cavalier

>	Headquarters, Department of the Ohio
>	Grafton, Va. June 23, 1861
>
> *Colonel: Having completed as far as possible the necessary arrangements for Company I, Fourth Artillery, and the Company of Chicago Rifles. I reached here about 2 a.m. having left the Ninth Regiment at Webster. The Eighth and Tenth Indiana, Loomis' Michigan Battery, and Captain Barker's company of Illinois cavalry reached Clarksburg today. The Third and Fourth Ohio also reached Fetterman today.*
>
>	Very Respectfully Your Obedient Servant
>	Geo. B. McClellan
>	*Major General*
>	Lieutenant Col. E.D. Townsend
>	*Assistant Adjutant General*[1]

    The telegraph operator at Fetterman, western Virginia, was a Confederate spy. "Bushwhackers" had been burning railroad bridges near Fetterman and Grafton, western Virginia, for weeks.

    Throughout their entire service in the Civil War, the Third Ohio traded shots with "bushwhackers" and "partisan rangers" in "western" Virginia, Alabama, Tennessee and Kentucky. John Hunt Morgan, Nathan Bedford Forrest, John Pegram and "Fighting Joe" Wheeler were responsible for many of the burned bridges that the Third Ohio was directed to protect. One of the stops on the B&O railroad line was Cincinnati, Ohio. If Stonewall Jackson got control of the rail line, Ohio was vulnerable. The Ohio River might not stop him. Major General George McClellan, commander of the Department of the Ohio and "western" Virginia, was sent to stop the "bushwhackers" and protect the rail line. The bridges and tunnels servicing those lines were vulnerable. Unfortunately, when McClellan arrived with the Third Ohio, those Confederate "guerrillas" had become an army. They were commanded by Confederate general Robert S. Garnett.[2]

The immediate danger to the B&O, however, was Stonewall Jackson. Colonel Thomas Jackson and his troops occupied the B&O railroad crossing at Harpers Ferry, Virginia. To go from Baltimore to Wheeling, all trains passed over the Potomac River at Harpers Ferry. At this early stage in the war, Harpers Ferry was critical. Every day, Jackson and his men watched as B&O trains came east loaded with coal. Wheezing smoke, yellow spark and pounding their way to northern factories, Jackson was concerned that the coal would fire the furnaces that made good Yankee guns. But how to put a stop to it? Impulsively, he rationalized that the noise was keeping his men up at night. They were getting no sleep. He came up with the idea that the railroad run only during daylight hours. Although the railroad agreed, the coal kept coming. Jackson exercised patience in part because Virginia was still a member of the Union. The legislature had already decided to secede, but the people hadn't voted yet. That would happen on May 23. By the 21st, however, Harpers Ferry suddenly got busy. Commanding Virginia troops in the area was Brigadier General Robert S. Garnett. On the 21st, Inspector General George Dees told him about the forces ready at Harpers Ferry. If the vote should go for secession, then the B&O railroad bridge should be held, and no Yankee trains should be allowed to pass. Dees told Garnett, "The force assembled at this place and its outposts consists of the First, Second, Third, Fourth and Fifth Virginia Regiments; the Fourth Regiment from Alabama; two Regiments from Mississippi; five Companies of

George Brinton McClellan, major general, Department of the Ohio and Western Virginia. Although he graduated second in his class from West Point, McClellan's curriculum focused more on engineering than the infantry tactics needed in the Civil War (Library of Congress).

Virginia Artillery; eight companies of Virginia cavalry; four companies of Kentucky infantry."[3] Jackson was ready. Nevertheless, the coal trains still came. So Jackson came up with another idea. He requested that the trains run east for only two hours per day. His argument was that two hours would not interfere with the transport of Virginia troops. When Virginia voted to secede on the 23rd, Jackson lost patience and seized the railroad between Point of Rocks, Maryland, and Martinsburg, Virginia. Fifty-six locomotives and 300 freight cars were captured. The B&O was shut down. However, research has shown that the seizure of the B&O backfired because it further hardened the pro-Union attitude of western Virginia and even some in Virginia. Their economy depended on that railroad. Seizure of the B&O threatened their livelihood.

Thomas "Stonewall" Jackson earned the nickname after other regiments at First Manassas saw him standing like a "stonewall: against Union infantry charges." He died on May 10, 1863, after being accidentally shot by one of his own pickets at Chancellorsville (Library of Congress).

After the successful vote on the 23rd, however, the presence of the Third and other troops on Virginia soil sparked strong reaction. Colonel Christopher Q. Tompkins, Company K, Second Virginia Infantry Regiment declared,

> Charleston, Kanawha County, Virginia
> May 30, 1861
>
> *Men of Virginia! Men of Kanawha! To Arms!*
>
> The enemy has invaded your soil and has threatened to overrun your country under the pretext of protection. You cannot serve two masters. You have not

the right to repudiate allegiance to your own state. Be not seduced by his sophistry or intimidated by his threats. Rise and strike for your firesides and alters. Repel the aggressors and preserve your honor and your rights. Rally in every neighborhood with or without arms. Organize and unite with the sons of the soil to defend it. Report yourselves without delay to those nearest you in military position. Come to the aid of your fathers, brothers, and comrades at arms at this place, who are here for the protection of your mothers, wives and sisters. Let every man who would uphold his rights turn out with such arms as he may get and drive the invader back.[4]

C.Q. Tompkins
Colonel, Virginia Volunteers, Commanding[5]

By June 28, Colonel John Beatty and the men of the Third Ohio were on the move. Beatty noted in his diary,

At twelve o'clock to-day our battalion left Clarksburg, followed a stream called Elk Creek for eight miles, and then encamped for the night. This is the first march on foot we have made. The country through which we passed is extremely hilly and broken, but apparently fertile. If the people of Western Virginia were united against us, it would be almost impossible for our army to advance. In many places the creek on one side, and the perpendicular banks on the other, leave a strip barely wide enough for a wagon road. Buckhannon, twenty miles in advance of us, is said to be in the hands of the secession troops. To-morrow, or the day after, if they do not leave, a battle will take place. Our men appear eager for the fray, and I pray they may be as successful in the fight as they are anxious for one.[6]

Lieutenant Colonel John Beatty served as a private at the Battle of Rich Mountain. By 1863, he was promoted to brigadier general. His 1879 book, *Citizen Soldier, or, Memoirs of a Volunteer*, provides colorful detail of the action seen by the Third Ohio Volunteer Infantry Regiment (National Archives and Records Administration).

Although Beatty didn't know it then, his regiment would soon be surrounded and in a fight for their lives. The first engagement for the Third Ohio in the Civil War happened at Middle Fork Bridge. Confederate general in command William Garnett knew the bridge was critical. His forces were guarding the passes on Rich and Laurel Mountains. With George McClellan marching in his direction from the west, that bridge was the only natural obstacle between him and the Yankees. Two weeks before the skirmish at Middle Fork Bridge, the *Richmond Dispatch* was already reporting activity at the bridge. Lieutenant Colonel Jonathan M. Heck, 25th Virginia Infantry, told the paper that an incident happened after he left Camp Garnett on June 26.

> I left this camp for Buckhannon on the 26th instant with a force amounting in all to three hundred men, and made a march of eighteen miles, encamping for the night five miles east of Buckhannon. Scouts were sent out on all the roads leading from our camps or from Buckhannon in the direction of Philippi or Clarksburg. About one o'clock, the scouts on the road leading to Buckhannon, 10 in number, having advanced within one mile of the town to guard a mill, were fired upon by a party of Union men. On the 27th, our forces marched into the town of Buckhannon and purchased sufficient quantity of corn, oats, quartermaster and ordinary stores.... Our scouts, left to guard the bridge over the Middle Fork River, were fired at this morning, one shot taking effect in the hip of one of the scout's horses.[7]

The Confederate forces of General Garnett were relying on being able to purchase food for their men in Buckhannon. They had to cross the Middle Fork River to get there. When they returned to camp, they were fired on by advance skirmishers of George McClellan's brigade. Realizing that control of the bridge was critical to their positions on Rich Mountain, Heck and his company were left to ensure that Union troops didn't take the bridge and put Camp Garnett at risk.[8]

General Garnett posted his forces at the gap on Laurel Mountain and the regiments of Confederate colonel John Pegram at Middle Fork Bridge and Rich Mountain.[9] He knew that holding these passes would not be easy. In addition to a lack of troops and percussion caps for his muskets, he also lacked the support of western Virginia itself. However, if the Confederate forces trying to hold on to western Virginia were struggling to mount effective resistance, the Yankee troops under George McClellan were laboring with shortages as well. Colonel Beatty of the Third went begging for his breakfast to a local farmer on June 29. He remembered, "Provisions outside of camp are very scarce. I took breakfast with a farmer this morning, and can say truly that I have eaten much better meals in my life. We had coffee without sugar, short-cake without butter, and a little salt pork, exceedingly fat. I asked him what the charge was, and he said 'Ninepence,' which means one shilling. I rejoiced his old soul by giving him two

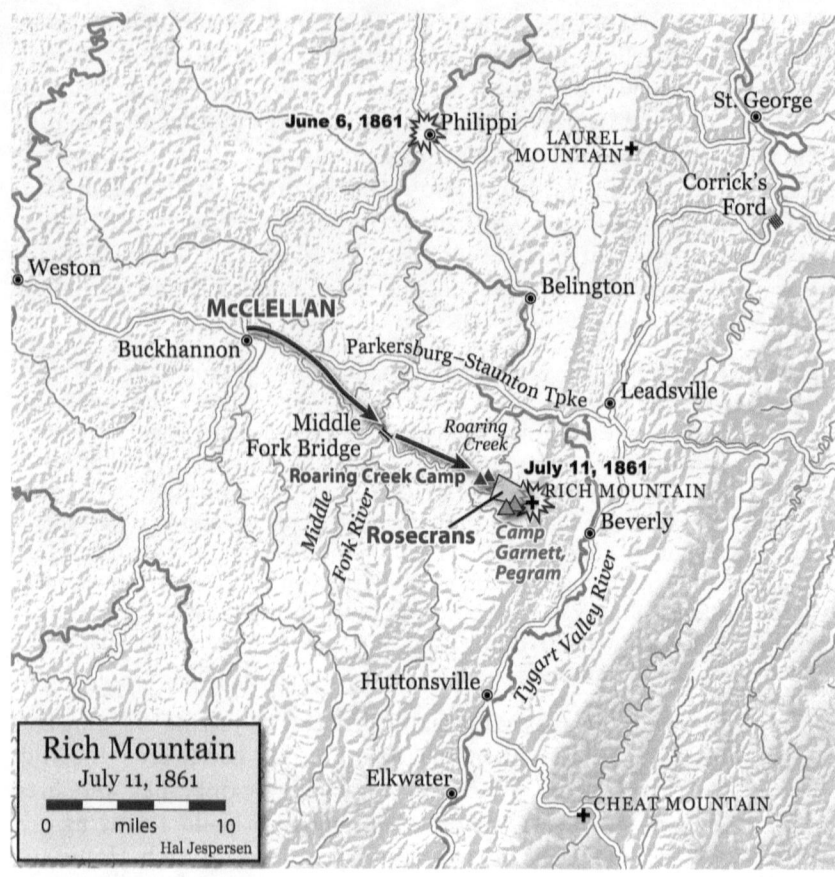

The Middle Fork Bridge and Rich Mountain engagements are shown here. McClellan's job was to protect the pass over Rich Mountain accessed via the Parkersburg-Staunton Turnpike. Securing Middle Fork Bridge cut off Confederate supplies from Buckhannon and protected McClellan's back as he camped at Roaring Creek and prepared to assault Rich Mountain (map by Hal Jespersen, www.cwmaps.com).

shillings."[10] The "old soul" was typical of many in western Virginia at the time. They were independent and favored the Union.

"Western" Virginia was beautiful, rugged, mountainous and separated from the eastern part of Virginia by men who were independent, hated slavery and found it easy to relate to another tough individual, President Abraham Lincoln. The governor and citizenry of "eastern" Virginia felt threatened by this independent streak and were prepared to remedy the situation. What was McClellan's plan? In his communication to Townsend, the general continued, "As soon as I can get my command well in hand and obtain more reliable information ... I propose moving with all my available forces from Clarksburg on Buckhannon, then on Beverly, to turn entirely the detachment at Laurel Mountain."[11]

Why was Rich Mountain so strategically significant that George McClellan was willing to divert troops and attention away from the heart of western Virginia and focus on a mountain covered with thick brush, rattlesnakes and a small log tavern at the top? Writing to Adjutant General Edward Townsend on July 5, 1861, McClellan mentions Rich Mountain for the first time. He stated that his position in Buckhannon was important because of its location on the Parkersburg-Staunton Turnpike. From here, he had access to wide, smooth roads going over Rich Mountain and connecting to Beverly, Clarksburg, Grafton and Philippi. He could quickly move troops by rail and march them to anywhere in the northern part of western Virginia. He told Townsend, "I expect to find the enemy in position on Rich Mountain, just this side of Beverly. I shall, if possible, turn the position to the south, and thus occupy the Beverly road in his rear."[12]

Colonel John Pegram, the "Paradoxical Cavalier," was not well liked by his men. To make matters worse, they were all poorly trained and short of ammunition as well as artillery. Most available resources were concentrated at Manassas. He was killed on February 6, 1865, at the Battle of Hatcher's Run, Virginia (Library of Congress).

Rich Mountain was more of a clash than a battle. All of the action took just three hours, and most of the heavy fighting consumed only 20 minutes. The Union lost 46 soldiers and the Confederacy 300. This is in sharp contrast to Antietam (22,000 casualties), Chancellorsville (30,000 casualties) and Gettysburg (50,000 casualties). In other ways, however, Rich Mountain, Laurel Hill and Cheat Mountain might be considered more significant than some of the better-known engagements later in the war. George McClellan viewed Rich Mountain as a great victory, which happened just in time for the Union to save face after the unexpected defeat at Bull Run. All of the newspapers in early July 1861 were talking about the conventions at Wheeling and Richmond. Yet, by the middle of the month, those newspapers now concerned themselves with the Battle at Manassas (Bull Run). Nevertheless, Jefferson Davis was deeply concerned that part of Virginia might defect and join the Union. While Davis considered his options, the Third Ohio was enjoying camp life. By July 5, 1861, they were camped just outside the town of Buckhannon. This put them within a few miles of their objective: the strategic pass over Rich Mountain. According to John Beatty, "Reached Buckhannon at 5 P.M., and encamped beside the Fourth Ohio, in a meadow, one mile from town. The country through which we marched is exceedingly hilly; or, perhaps, I might say mountainous. The scenery is delightful. The road for miles is cut around great hills, and is just wide enough for a wagon. A step to the left would send one tumbling a hundred or two hundred feet below, and to the right the hills rise hundreds of feet above. The hills, half way to their summits, are covered with corn, wheat, or grass, while further up the forest is as dense as it could well have been a hundred years ago."[13]

The beautiful view was quickly interrupted by General McClellan who came to review his troops. According to Beatty, "At ten o'clock the Third and Fourth Regiments were reviewed by General McClellan. The day was excessively warm, and the men, buttoned up in their dress-coats, were much wearied when the parade was over."[14] McClellan's objective was to secure the passes on Rich and Laurel Mountains. This would help ensure safe and easy passage of Union troops through "western" Virginia. Failure to control these mountain gaps would enable Confederate forces to control all of Virginia, the B&O railroad and the river separating Ohio from Virginia. The first objective was Rich Mountain. Unfortunately, the Middle Fork Bridge was the only bridge that crossed the Middle Fork River in this area, and it stood in McClellan's way. Guarding the bridge and blocking access to the mountain pass were the pickets of troops commanded by Colonel John Pegram.[15] The *Wheeling Intelligencer* on July 1, 1861, detailed some of the damage already done to the B&O by Pegram and his men: "Actual Loss of the Baltimore and Ohio Railroad over $2,000,000:

1. Old Rosy and the Paradoxical Cavalier 33

In addition to the locomotives destroyed at Martinsburg, there were three hundred and sixty freight cars and five passenger cars (destroyed). The engines prove to be so sprung, from the intense heat of the fire built around them, that they are now worthless. Such wanton destruction of property is as villainous as the crime of murder.... Northern men found the means and the brains to build their roads and canals, and now the traitors cut and slash away with the consciousness that the loss is not theirs."

At this time, McClellan's small Department of the Ohio consisted of three brigades. There were no divisions under his command in Virginia. They were all headed for Manassas. Brigade commanders included William Rosecrans, Newton Schleich and Robert McCook. Unfortunately, Union forces dispatched to Middle Fork Bridge were under the command of Brigadier General Newton Schleich. Considered one of the most incompetent political generals in the war, Lieutenant Colonel John Beatty, Third Ohio, had bitter words for his commander. Writing after the war, Beatty complained, "[Schleich] is a three-months' brigadier, and a rampant demagogue.... He is what might be called a tremendous little man, swears terrible, and imagines that he thereby shows his snap. Snap, in his opinion, is indispensable to a military man. If snap is the only thing a soldier needs, and profanity is snap, Schleich is a second Napoleon. The General Snap will go home at the expiration of his three-months' term, unregretted by officers and men."[16]

McClellan knew he had to secure the bridge over the Middle Fork River. To attack the force on Rich Mountain, he needed to have the bridge intact and at his back. This would be his only effective line of retreat. Writing to Adjutant General Townsend, McClellan reports, "Buckhannon, July 6, 1861 ... My advance guard goes at 4 in the morning to occupy the Middle Fork Bridge. By the 8th or 9th at the latest, I expect to occupy Beverly."[17] Schleich sent out that advance guard under Captain Orris Lawson.[18] Lawson was ordered to gather intelligence and clear the bridge if possible. However, hearing that Lawson and the Third might have been surrounded at the bridge, John Beatty of the Third Ohio took the lead in the attempt to rescue Lawson and his men.

> On the 5th instant a scouting party, under Captain Lawson (Third Ohio), started for Middle Fork Bridge, a point eighteen miles from camp. At eight o'clock last night, when I brought the battalion from the drill-ground, I found that a messenger had arrived with intelligence that Lawson had been surrounded by a force of probably four hundred, and that, in the engagement, one of his men had been killed and three wounded. The camp was alive with excitement. Each company of the Third had contributed five men to Captain Lawson's detachment, and each company, therefore, felt a special interest in it. The messenger stated that Captain Lawson was in great need of help, and General

McClellan at once ordered four companies of infantry and twenty mounted men to move to his assistance.[19]

What was happening with Lawson and the Third Ohio at the bridge? A correspondent for the *Cincinnati Commercial* told his readers,

A gallant band of fifty Buckeyes, Third Ohio Regiment, under Captain O.A. Lawson of Columbus, made a good record yesterday afternoon at Middle Fork Bridge.... The expedition proceeded by bridle paths across the hills to a point on Beverly Pike, five miles this side of Middle Fork Bridge, and encamped for the night. About midnight, Union men appealed to them for protection against marauding rebels, who had forced their women and children to flee to the woods for safety, and had pillaged their houses. Lawson scaled a rough mountain and crossed Middle Fork in the morning, two and a half miles above the bridge. He followed the stream with great difficulty through unbroken thickets, until he reached a good ambush within musket range of the bridge, which was crowded with rebels. The enemy discovered his party, and an advance guard of five cautiously approached him from the bridge, all ready with their muskets. His men stood up and both parties fired simultaneously. Three of the rebels fled at the first round, and the other two dropped immediately afterwards. The enemy now opened upon his little band from three sides ... the effect was awful imprecations and screams of "murder." After firing four rounds into the bridge, he ordered a retreat.... An Irishmen in the party said it was "hot as hell."[20]

The first of the Third Ohio to die was Samuel W. Johns of Hamilton, Ohio. He was shot in the chest. Corporal Joseph High of Columbus was shot in the ankle and hoped that the surgeon wouldn't cut his foot off. Before fainting from the wound, he stood on one foot and fired two more rounds into the rebels at the bridge. Nicholas Black from Cincinnati was shot in the forehead with buckshot pellets. William Denning from Hamilton had the skin on his right ear cut off. When the smoke cleared, Samuel Johns lay dead and six more were wounded.

Believing that Lawson and the Third Ohio were surrounded by rebels, John Beatty set out to help. He remembered, "I had command of the detachment, and left camp about nine o'clock P.M., accompanied by a guide. The night was dark. My command moved on silently and rapidly. After proceeding about three miles, we left the turnpike and turned onto a narrow, broken, bad road, leading through the woods, which we followed about eight miles, when we met Captain Lawson's detachment on its way back. Here we removed the wounded from the farm wagon in which they had been conveyed thus far, to an ambulance brought with us for the purpose, countermarched, and reached our quarters about three o'clock this morning."[21]

Company A of the Third Ohio was responsible for pushing back the Confederate pickets that had surrounded Lawson. On July 9, 1861, the

Wheeling Intelligencer gave a short note of praise for the work of the Third Ohio at Middle Fork Bridge:

> Fight near Buckhannon—Onward Movement—General Engagement Expected. A dispatch was sent from Buckhannon, Va. On Sunday night (which for some unaccountable reason we did not get) announcing that forty-five men, belonging to the Third Ohio Regiment, under Captain Lawson, while on a scouting expedition, on Sunday night, fell into an ambuscade of several hundred rebels at Middle Fork Bridge, twelve miles east, and were surrounded. After a desperate fight, they cut their way through, losing one killed and five wounded. The enemy lost some twenty killed. Five dead bodies were found on Sunday. Col. McCook with the 4th and 9th Ohio regiments, the 10th Indiana under Colonel Morrow, with the Loomis Battery, and Burdsall's company of cavalry, moved on and took possession of the bridge early Sunday morning—General Morris advanced from Philippi to within a mile and a half of Laurel Hill—Ex Congressman Garnett is in charge of the rebel forces there. Gen. McClellan with a large force intended to move toward Beverly yesterday morning. A battle is anticipated within forty-eight hours.

When the Middle Fork Bridge was finally secured, McClellan established his base at Roaring Creek, two miles from the trail leading up Rich Mountain. The brigade of General William Rosecrans was selected to lead the attack. William Rosecrans, "Old Rosy," was a West Point graduate but was trained as an engineer, not a tactical infantry commander. Nevertheless, after the war, Confederate general Daniel H. Hill commented that Rosecrans "has a fine practical sense, and is of a tough, tenacious fiber."[22] By contrast, "Pegram was Lee's paradoxical cavalier. While the very model of courage and comportment, style and spirituality, Pegram was a poor leader of volunteers and a mediocre tactical commander."[23] More important, McClellan's forces were well armed and well fed. By comparison, Pegram's pickets slept in the rain without tents, his men got diarrhea from poor food, they suffered a lack of the correct-size percussion caps with which to fire their muskets, and used six-pound artillery whose shot consistently landed 300 yards short of Rosecrans' front lines. To make matters worse, logistics was a nightmare. Virginia governor Lechter sent additional cannon, but they were useless because they arrived without their caissons.[24] As early as June 1861, Confederate major Michael G. Harman complained to Robert E. Lee, "We are sadly in want of ammunition, our whole supply being exhausted by this expedition. I hope you will have sufficient supply forwarded as soon as possible to this point."[25] By the middle of July, Harman desperately wrote directly to President Jefferson Davis that more ammunition needed to be sent from Richmond because local suppliers either refused to sell or hid their ammunition from anxious Confederate forces.

Although it looked like McClellan couldn't lose, the general commanding faced geographic obstacles that might still have resulted in defeat. "Country like this part of West Virginia is indeed no place for large armies for manifest reasons, but when forces are limited to the nature of the region, it can readily be seen that the larger has great advantages. It is by division of forces that results can be obtained. Holding, with a number equal to the work, the smaller enemy, there are fine opportunities for flanking with the rest, when fogs and rains and night and adjacent hills, streams, and mountains offer cover for the movement."[26] To his credit for good tactical planning, McClellan took advantage of western Virginia's natural resources and harsh terrain. His initial plan, however, was not Rich Mountain. He wanted to secure an important part of the region: the Kanawha Valley. The Kanawha River flowed through the area and provided troop and supply transport to whomever controlled it. George McClellan was sufficiently interested to wire Assistant Adjutant General Lieutenant Colonel Edward Townsend on May 30, 1861, "I am now organizing a movement on the valley of the Great Kanawha; I will go there in person and endeavor to capture the occupants of the secession camp at Buffalo, then occupy the Gauley Bridge."[27]

However, believing that securing the roads over Rich Mountain and Laurel Hill would give him better strategic opportunities, McClellan sent General Jacob Cox to face Confederate general Henry Wise in the Kanawha. Cox had his hands full because Wise was known as "an animated buzz-saw with

General William S. Rosecrans, "Old Rosy," graduated from West Point and worked as a mining engineer in western Virginia in 1855. He surveyed the territory in which he later led troops to victory at Rich Mountain. Rosecrans was known for leading his troops from the front, not the rear. He had a sharp temper and gave Third Ohio colonel John Beatty a "tongue lashing" that Beatty remembered years later (Library of Congress).

sound and fury and any number of dangerous teeth."[28] The "Paradoxical Cavalier" on Rich Mountain seemed like an easier target. Before Pegram had a chance to fire a shot, the Third Ohio heard from the son of the older "buzz saw." On July 8, Obidiah Jennings Wise made his presence known. According to Beatty, "As we were leaving camp this morning, an officer of an Ohio regiment rode at break-neck speed along the line, inquiring for General McClellan, and yelling, as he passed, that four companies of the regiment to which he belongs had been surrounded at Glendale, by twelve hundred secessionists, under O. Jennings Wise…. Our men, misapprehending the statement, thought Buckhannon had been attacked, and were in a great state of excitement."[29]

After Middle Fork Bridge was secured, the Third Ohio, along with McClellan's three brigades, marched to the river. According to Beatty,

> This morning, at seven o'clock, our tents were struck, and, with General McClellan and staff in advance, we moved to Middle Fork Bridge. It was here that Captain Lawson's skirmish on Saturday had occurred. The man killed had been buried by the Fourth Ohio before our arrival. Almost every house along the road is deserted by the men, the women sometimes remaining. The few Union men of this section have, for weeks past, been hiding away in the hills. Now the secessionists have taken to the woods. The Dutch regiment (McCook's), when it took possession of the bridge, had a slight skirmish with the enemy, and, I learn, killed two men. On the day after to-morrow I apprehend the first great battle will be fought in Western Virginia.[30]

The *Intelligencer* also told its readers that another battle was expected. At midnight on July 10, 1861, Third Ohio colonel Isaac Morrow told his men to turn out. Morrow was a married man of 40 and just as nervous as his men. Nevertheless, he hid his emotions and addressed the Third Ohio. They were half-asleep. According to John Beatty, "It was the hour when graveyards are supposed to yawn, and the sheeted dead to walk abroad."[31] Morrow's speech didn't sit well with Beatty or the rest of the men. Standing stiff with arms at his side, Morrow told his men,

> Soldiers of the Third: The assault on the enemy's works will be made in the early morning. The Third will lead the column. The secessionists have ten thousand men and forty rifled cannon. They are strongly fortified. They have more men and more cannon than we have. They will cut us to pieces. Marching to attack such an enemy, so intrenched and so armed, is marching to a butchershop rather than to a battle. There is bloody work ahead. Many of you, boys, will go out who will never come back again.[32]

Major Joseph Warren Keifer of the Third Ohio took a dim view of Morrow and a positive opinion of Beatty. He later recalled,

> The Colonel of my regiment (Morrow) so magnified a Mexican war experience as to make the unsophisticated citizen-soldier look upon him with awe,

yet he never afterwards witnessed a real battle. John Beatty, who became later a Colonel, then Brigadier-General, was my Lieutenant-Colonel; he did not, I think, even possess the equivalent of my poor pretense of military training. He was, however, a typical volunteer Union soldier; brainy, brave, terribly in earnest, always truthful, and what he did not know he made no pretense of knowing, but set about learning. He had by nature the spirit of a good soldier; as the war progressed the true spirit of the warrior became an inspiration to him; and at Perryville, Stone's River, Chickamauga, and on other fields he won just renown, not alone for personal gallantry but for skill in handling and personally fighting his command."[33]

Major J. Warren Keifer was ordered to push Pegram's skirmishers away from the mountain road entrance, which Rosecrans was expected to take to the top of the mountain. According to Keifer, "I was then Major of the Third Ohio Infantry serving in McClellan's army, and was, the night of July 10, in command of a detachment in charge of the pickets on its front and covering—the turnpike road well up towards the base of the mountain and closely confronting the enemy's pickets."[34]

This is the log tavern owned by Joseph Hart. It was located near the turnpike crossing the top of Rich Mountain. Although badly damaged from cannon fire, the tavern was used as a Union hospital after the battle. Joseph Hart filed a claim for his losses from the battle, which included 15 steers, 5 cows, 20 hogs, and lumber and crops valued at $2,500 (Library of Congress).

Rosecrans' brigade employed a local scout who knew a secret path up the mountain. The path was probably unknown to Pegram's men. The path would connect with the Parkersburg turnpike near the crest of the mountain, near the small, log tavern and farm owned by Joseph Hart. Keifer and the men of the Third Ohio remembered watching Rosecrans and his men as they rode past the pickets and up the secret mountain path:

> My small force took up a position less than one half mile from the enemy's fortified position, driving back his pickets at the dawn of day through the dense timber on each side of the road. About 9 A.M. a mounted orderly from McClellan came galloping from camp carrying a message for Rosecrans, said to be a countermand of former orders, and requiring him to halt until another and better plan of movement could be made. The messenger was, as he stoutly insisted, directed to overtake Rosecrans by pursuing a route to the enemy's right, whereas Rosecrans had gone to our right and the enemy's left. Of this the orderly was not only informed by me, but he was warned of the proximity of the Confederate pickets. He persisted, however, in the error, and presented the authority of the commanding General to pass all Union pickets. This was reluctantly respected, and the ill-fated orderly galloped on in search of a route to his left. In a moment or two the sharp crack of a rifle was heard, and almost immediately the horse of the orderly came dashing into our picket lines, wounded and riderless. The story was told. The dispatch, with its bearer, dead or alive, was in the enemy's hands. The orderly was, however, not killed, but had been seriously hurt by a rifle ball. He and his dispatch for Rosecrans gave Pegram his first knowledge of the movements of the column to the mountain summit.[35]

Ultimately, the skirmish at Middle Fork Bridge was significant because it enabled George McClellan to secure the pass at Rich Mountain. Both of these successful engagements helped strengthen the resolve of those meeting in Wheeling. They wanted no part of secession. By 1863, they successfully joined the Union as the state of West Virginia.

Middle Fork Bridge was a modest but significant engagement. Was the headless body the Third Ohio found at Roaring Creek the next day a sign of the fighting to come?

2

Muddle and Confusion

As the Third Ohio crossed the Middle Fork Bridge and approached Roaring Creek,[1] the sight of a headless torso got Lieutenant Colonel John Beatty's attention.

It became clear that Union sympathizers living in the area were hated by the few still loyal to Virginia and its secession resolution. Although Beatty published his memories of the Third Ohio almost 20 years after the war, he never forgot what he saw as his regiment reached the creek on June 8, 1861: "The few Union men of this section have, for weeks past, been hiding away in the hills. Now the secessionists have taken to the woods. The utmost bitterness of feeling exists between the two. A man was found to-day, within a half mile of this camp, with his lead cut off and entrails ripped out, probably a Union man who had been hounded down and killed."[2]

George McClellan had intelligence that convinced him that securing passage over Rich Mountain through the Parkersburg-Staunton Turnpike would be difficult. He believed that the turnpike route from the west would be heavily defended by Confederate forces. This was never a problem for McClellan because he preferred to maneuver and surround his enemy rather than fight. Writing to Adjutant General Edward Townsend on July 5, he stated, "Assure the General (Scott) that no prospect of a brilliant victory shall induce me to depart from my intention of gaining success by maneuvering rather than by fighting."[3] In this, he remained the faithful student of the leading military theorists of the day—Antoine Jomini, Dennis Hart Mahan and William Hardee.[4] On July 9, McClellan ordered General Thomas A. Morris to Laurel Hill to pin down General Garnett and prevent him from sending reinforcements to Rich Mountain.[5] On July 10, McClellan sent a wire to Adjutant General Edward Townsend: "In sight of the enemy, who is strongly intrenched [sic] and holds firm. A strong armed reconnaissance is now starting out. I think I can turn his position."[6] McClellan believed that he could turn the Confederate position because William Rosecrans convinced him that it could be done.

Earlier on the 10th, 22-year-old David Hart tried to get through Union pickets so he could walk up the turnpike to his father's house on top of Rich Mountain. He was taken to General Rosecrans who listened as Hart told him that there was a little-used path up the mountain to the left of Camp Garnett. Hart had walked that little-known route the month before. Rosecrans took Hart to see McClellan. Both believed that Hart was honest and loyal. They convinced him to show Rosecrans and his men the way. Early the next morning, Rosecrans' men filled their canteens and took one day's rations. It was now 4:00 a.m., and the sight of the men gathering earlier than usual caused the nervous bugler in the 19th Ohio to mistakenly sound "first call." Everyone was anxious. The men knew that real combat was coming. Rosecrans reprimanded the bugler and instructed him to wait and sound assembly later, at the usual hour. This would convince enemy pickets that nothing was imminent in the Union camp. The sky was cloudy, but rain was threatening. To avoid excess noise, Rosecrans' men didn't use their axes as they clawed their way slowly up the mountain. David Hart took the troops up the Confederate left. The objective was to reach the turnpike at the top of the mountain, flank the Confederate forces and attack from the rear. Upon hearing the opening shots, General McClellan was to attack Camp Garnett in a frontal assault. They would catch the enemy between them. The outspoken editor of the *Richmond Examiner*, Edward Alfred Pollard, wrote his version of what happened next: "As [Rosecrans] advanced, our artillery, posted on top of the mountain, opened upon them, but with little effect as their lines were concealed by the trees and brushwood. The earth of the mountain seemed to tremble under the thunder of the cannon. The tops of trees were cut off by our fire which was aimed too high.... An incessant fire of musketry was kept up in the woods, where the sharpshooters, wet to the skin in the rain, kept the advancing lines of the enemy at bay."[7] The reality was significantly different from Pollard's embroidered prose, however.

Rosecrans' first encounter with the small force of Captain Julius DeLagnel at the Hart farm was from those sharpshooters who gave Rosecrans temporary pause. They attempted to force Rosecrans' men out from the cover of dense brush. Their efforts were successful, and the single six-pound cannon roared into action. Only one gun was available because Pegram was keeping the other one for himself as he faced what he believed would be a frontal assault from McClellan. He would send the extra gun to DeLagnel if so requested.[8] Nevertheless, that one six-pounder fired four shots per minute with spherical case on a short fuse.[9] Hundreds of grape the size of a baby's fist poured down on Rosecrans' men. An account later recorded by David Hart reveals that Pegram and his men knew all about McClellan's plan of attack. They just didn't know by which flank, left or right, the enemy was approaching. According to Hart, "We pushed through the bush, and rocks, followed by the whole division in perfect silence. The bushes wetted us thoroughly, and it was very cold. Our circuit was about five miles. About noon, we reached the top of the mountain, near my father's farm. It was not intended that the enemy should know of our movements, but a dragoon with dispatches from General McClellan, who was sent for us, fell into the hands of the enemy, and they found out our movements."[10]

When Rosecrans finally reached the top of the mountain and got to the rear of DeLagnel's men, fierce fighting broke out. With men untested in battle on both sides, confusion was epidemic. For example, the Eighth and 10th Indiana regiments were ordered to form in column and attack the Confederate trenches. The 10th formed by column and charged, but the Eighth mistakenly formed in line. Although not intentional, Rosecrans left this plan intact because the line fired a massive volley across a broad front, which provided some protective cover for the advancing 10th. At this point, Confederate forces began to fall back, and Rosecrans personally led the 13th Ohio into the charge on the enemy works. He almost lost his life, however. When Colonel Jeremiah Sullivan of the 13th filed his battle report with Rosecrans, he remembered that Rosecrans had exposed himself to an extent that a rebel sharpshooter took aim and was about to shoot the Union general. Private Benjamin Smith of Company H took quick action and shot the rebel.

Muddle and confusion continued without restraint when Confederate forces near the Hart farm realized they were in trouble and sent word to Pegram for the other gun. The gun crew began to bring the artillery piece into action faster than anticipated. As they approached the top of the mountain, a captain from the Powhattan Rifles mistook his own gun for that of the enemy. He ordered that the horses pulling the heavy load to be shot so that the gun could not be hauled into firing position. At this point in the battle, McClellan was supposed to initiate a frontal attack on Camp Garnett. Where was he? How come he never joined the battle as planned?

According to McClellan, "during the progress of [Rosecrans'] march, he was to communicate with me every hour. The remainder of the force under my command to be held in readiness to assault in front as soon as Rosecrans' musketry should indicate that he was immediately in their rear."[11] Did McClellan hear the "musketry," and if so, why didn't he commence his planned frontal attack? According to Lieutenant Colonel John Beatty in command of the Third Ohio,

> Between two and three o'clock we heard shots in the rear of the fortifications; then volleys of musketry, and the roar of artillery. Every man sprang to his feet, assured that the moment for making the attack had arrived. General

McClellan and staff came galloping up, and a thousand faces turned to hear the order to advance; but no order was given. The General halted a few paces from our line, and sat on his horse listening to the guns, apparently in doubt as to what to do; and as he sat there with indecision stamped on every line of his countenance, the battle grew fiercer in the enemy's rear. Every volley could be heard distinctly. There would occasionally be a lull for a moment, and then the uproar would break out again with increased violence.[12]

As per Beatty and other participants that day, McClellan heard the "musketry" but went back to camp and didn't attack. What was he thinking? Major Joseph Warren Keifer, Third Ohio, had a clear memory of McClellan's actions at Rich Mountain. Keifer was in charge of the picket forces at the base of Rich Mountain and watched as Rosecrans and his men disappeared into the trees on the mountain. It was sunrise on July 11, 1861. Keifer remembered what happened next:

Major Joseph Warren Keifer wrote *The Battle of Rich Mountain and Some Incidents*. In his memoir, he was critical of McClellan for failing to engage Pegram in the planned frontal assault at Rich Mountain (Library of Congress).

About nine A. M., a mounted orderly from McClellan came on a gallop from his headquarters with a large envelope carried under his belt addressed to General Rosecrans, since known to be an order to him countermanding his order to make the movement then under way and devised. The messenger was directed to overtake Rosecrans by a route to the enemy's right, whereas Rosecrans had gone to our right, the enemy's left. Of this I informed the orderly and offered to put him on Rosecrans' trail. He haughtily spurned my advice and produced a written order from General McClellan signed by his Adjutant General Major Seth Williams of the regular army, commanding all officers in charge of grand guards and pickets to let him pass unmolested. I warned him of the certain danger of proceeding further on the main road, but he persisted in his superior's error, and as he held the supreme authority to go as directed and as I was green in the army and somewhat then in awe of a Commanding General I let him pass my advance pickets in search of the trail to our left, the enemy's right."[13]

McClellan's mixed messages became a problem. In this case, the orderly was captured but could not remember whether Rosecrans was marching up the right or left side of the mountain. The work of the Third Ohio was more routine, however. Colonel John Beatty recorded in his diary, "Arriving on yesterday's battlefield, the regiment was allowed a half hour for rest. The dead had been gathered and placed in a long trench, which was still open. The wounded of both armies were in hospital, receiving the attention of the surgeons. There were a few prisoners, most of them too unwell to accompany their friends in retreat."[14]

The dead from the attack on Rich Mountain were buried at the top of the mountain where they lay. What happened to Confederate general Garnett? The report filed by McClellan on July 14 stated, "I here learned that General Garnett, as soon as he discovered we were approaching his rear and had cut off his retreat in this direction, abandoned his intrenchments [sic] at Laurel Hill, leaving his tents and other property, and had made a hasty retreat in the night over a rough country road leading towards St. George."[15]

Confederate reports on the aftermath of the battle were not so "routine." Lieutenant Colonel John M Heck, 31st regiment Virginia Volunteers, filed a detailed report on July 13, 1861, in which he related, "The enemy, having charged and taken our piece of artillery, were bayonetting our wounded soldiers, who had been shot at their posts."[16] What else was the Third Ohio doing during this time? On the 14th, McClellan filed his report in which he stated that Garnett had been killed at Carrick's Ford: "General Garnett and about twenty others of the enemy were killed, and fifty prisoners and two stands of colors, and one rifle cannon taken, besides the baggage train and a large amount of other property."[17] George McClellan ordered that Garnett's body be packed in ice and sent to Grafton. From there, it would be sent with an honor guard to Baltimore, Maryland, where he would be buried. The *Wheeling Intelligencer* on July 17 reported, "Arrival of General Garnett's remains: The remains of Confederate General Robert Garnett, of the secession forces at Laurel Hill, who was killed at the Cheat River Battle, on Sunday morning, were brought up to the city yesterday evening, having been placed in a metallic coffin sent out from the city to Grafton. All of the general's private effects have been carefully preserved.... The ball which caused the death of General Garnett was from a Minnie musket and the wound produced is said to be a most terrible one.... The ball entered the middle of the back and came out just above the breast, tearing through two coats, a vest and under-clothing." Where was the Third at this time?

On July 16, 1861, the Third Ohio was in camp at the foot of Rich Mountain. The dead from the battle had been buried in long trenches at the top of the mountain. The report filed by General Rosecrans simply stated, "Colonel Beatty (Third Ohio) entered the upper camp at about the same time (6 a.m.) and occupied it, taking charge of the property, among which were two brass 6-pounders and some eighty tents, four caissons and one hundred rounds of ammunition."[18] To an extent, the dead were lucky. The *Washington Evening Star* reported the scene on Rich Mountain after the battle. From July 20, 1861: "It was a sickening sight to see the surgeons amputating the limbs of the wounded. They took off the legs of two soldiers while I was there. Some were shot in the legs, some in the thigh, some in the back and some arms were broken and shattered by grapeshot. One man, who had just had his right arm cut off near the shoulder, seemed to be in the greatest agony. I saw the prisoners at Beverly (Pegram's men) about seven hundred in number.... Col. Beatty took out a detachment and arrested sixty men last night.... One of the artillery men had seven shots in him before he left his gun. He finally fell down, rolled toward a stable, and never got up again." With the fighting over, however, some men from the Third rode into Huttonsville on the 18th. When they arrived, they were surprised to find almost 400 rebel soldiers asking to be taken prisoner. They had fled Laurel Hill after Rosecrans' victory on Rich Mountain but were exhausted, hungry, shoeless and complaining that they had been deceived about the righteous cause of the Confederacy and the fire-breathing dragons from the North. Apparently the dragon was preferable to the "Stars and Bars."

The *Wheeling Daily Intelligencer* was more specific about the flight of the rebel forces at Laurel Hill. On July 17, it reported, "They left their camp on Thursday night, and evidently in a great hurry.... Arms, cooking utensils, shirts, blankets, tents and stores ... were left scattered helter skelter all over the camp—in fact the entire camp presents unmistakable evidence of a sudden and precipitate movement."

The men of western Virginia rejoiced in the defeat of rebel forces at Rich Mountain. The *Wheeling Daily Intelligencer* continued, "Clean Sweep of the Traitors from Northwestern Virginia: From all the information that is before us at this writing, it would seem that the combined columns of Gens. McClellan, Morris and Hill have made and are making a clean sweep of the rebels from out of Northwestern Virginia. They have been driven from their prey like a pack of sheep-stealing dogs. Their commander has been killed, and they themselves surrounded, cut off and captured. They have been ignominiously foiled in every attempt to retrieve their fortunes—completely out-generaled and most disgracefully whipped.... Garnett shot and Wise's head in the gibbet, our troubles in Western Virginia will be ended."[19]

The men of the Third Ohio shared the feelings of their lieutenant colonel, John Beatty. They all felt that the policy of some of the Union generals was too lenient. To an extent, this began with General George McClellan. On May 26, 1861, he told his Ohio troops, "Preserve the strictest discipline. But remember that your only foes are the armed traitors—and show mercy even to them."[20] That policy provided aid and comfort to the enemy. George McClellan told his men not to destroy private property. He also strictly enforced the Fugitive Slave Act and returned runaway slaves to their owners to the extent that this was practical in wartime. By contrast, General Benjamin Butler and others welcomed runaways into their camps. This encouraged others throughout the South to follow. Before long, Lincoln realized that the black man might make a good soldier. Ultimately, 10 percent of all Union forces were black. Thousands served with bravery and distinction during the Civil War. Nevertheless, the lieutenant colonel of the Third Ohio, John Beatty, disagreed with the "rose-water" policy of the Lincoln administration.

The star of the Confederacy appears to be rising, and I doubt not it will continue to ascend until the rose-water policy now pursued by the Northern army is superseded by one

General Benjamin Butler was one of the most controversial generals in the Civil War. He helped liberate Washington in 1861 from the grip of Confederate "bushwhackers" blocking the B&O railroad; labeled runaway slaves as "contraband" of war, thus subject to seizure and not subject to return under the Fugitive Slave Act; and threatened Confederate women of New Orleans for disrespecting the Union soldiers who camped there (Library of Congress).

more determined and vigorous. We should look more to the interests of the North, and less to those of the South. We should visit on the aiders, abettors, and supporters of the Southern army somewhat of the severity which hitherto has been aimed at that army only. Who are most deserving of our leniency, those who take arms and go to the field, or those who remain at home, raising corn, oats, and bacon to subsist them? Plain people, who know little of constitutional hair-splitting, could decide this question only one way; but it seems those who have charge of our armies cannot decide it in any sensible way. They say: "You would not disturb peaceable citizens by levying contributions from them?" Why not? If the husbands, brothers, and fathers of these people, their natural leaders and guardians, do not care for them, why should we? If they disregard and trample upon that law which gave all protection, and plunge the country into war, why should we be perpetually hindered and thwarted in our efforts to secure peace by our care for those whom they have abandoned? If we make the country through which we pass furnish supplies to our army, the inhabitants will have less to furnish our enemies. The surplus products of the country should be gathered into the Federal granaries, so that they could not, by possibility, go to feed the rebels. The loyal and innocent might occasionally and for the present suffer, but peace when once established would afford ample opportunity to investigate and repay these sufferers. Shall we continue to protect the property of our enemies, and lose the lives of our friends? It is said that it is hard to deprive men of their horses, cattle, grain, simply because they differ from us in opinion; but is it not harder still to deprive men of their lives for the same reason? The opinions from which we differ in this instance are treasonable. The man who, of his own free will, supplies the wood is no whit better than he who kindles the fire; and the man who supplies the ammunition neither better nor worse than he who does the killing. The severest punishment should be inflicted upon the soldier who appropriates either private or public property to his own use; but the Government should lay its mailed hand upon treasonable communities, and teach them that war is no holiday pastime.[21]

Soon, the exploits of guerrilla bands like that of John Hunt Morgan and others inspired revenge by Northern officers.

Before the policy of the administration changed, however, General Ivan Turchin finally got sick and tired of the constant guerrilla raids that took advantage of his rear guard. Turchin was part of Ormsby Mitchell's Third Division, Army of the Ohio. Near Athens, Alabama, Turchin had had enough. He told his men that he would close his eyes for two hours, and they could do as they wished with the population and property of the town.

> Turchin's brigade has stolen a hundred thousand dollars' worth of watches, plate, and jewelry, in Northern Alabama. Turchin has gone to one extreme, for war cannot justify the gutting of private houses and the robbery of peaceable citizens, for the benefit of individual officers or soldiers; but there is another extreme, more amiable and pleasant to look upon, but not less fatal to

the cause. Buell is likely to go to that. He is inaugurating the dancing-master policy: "By your leave, my dear sir, we will have a fight; that is, if you are sufficiently fortified; no hurry; take your own time." To the bushwhacker: "Am sorry you gentlemen fire at our trains from behind stumps, logs, and ditches. Had you not better cease this sort of warfare? Now do, my good fellows, stop, I beg of you." To the citizen rebel: "You are a chivalrous people; you have been aggravated by the abolitionists into subscribing cotton to the Southern Confederacy; you had, of course, a right to dispose of your own property to suit yourselves, but we prefer that you would, in future, make no more subscriptions of that kind, and in the meantime we propose to protect your property and guard your negroes." Turchin's policy is bad enough; it may indeed be the policy of the devil; but Buell's policy is that of the amiable idiot. There is a better policy than either. It will neither steal nor maraud; it will do nothing for the sake of individual gain, and, on the other hand, it will not crouch to rebels; it will not fear to hurt the feelings of traitors; it will not fritter away the army and the revenue of the Government in the insane effort to protect men who have forfeited all right to protection. The policy we need is one that will march boldly, defiantly, through the rebel States, indifferent as to whether this traitor's cotton is safe, or that traitor's negroes run away; calling things by their right names; crushing those who have aided and abetted treason, whether in the army or out. In short, we want an iron policy that will not tolerate treason; that will demand immediate and unconditional obedience as the price of protection.[22]

Ivan Turchin was court-martialed for his policy. Colonel John Beatty of the Third Ohio served on the board that oversaw the process. In the end, Lincoln stepped in and saved his favorite Russian general. Turchin became a hero and represented the fact that winning this war would take every effort by the Lincoln government, whether hard or soft, chivalrous or not.

Before leaving Rich Mountain, however, the men from the Third heard some exciting news. Rumors quickly began to fly that the rebel defeat at Rich Mountain would bring Robert E. Lee himself to the battlefield. Now there would be some real fighting. The scene in "western" Virginia was changing rapidly. Union forces had been defeated near a creek named Bull Run, close to a town called Manassas. Right after that, all of the fancy troop reviews with bands, gold buttons and expensive horses stopped. George McClellan had been called to Washington to take charge of all Union forces. Some of the officers had their doubts about McClellan, but their opinion didn't matter. Abraham Lincoln had made up his mind.[23]

"Western" Virginia was still threatened by rebels, however. The Staunton turnpike, which ran all the way from the B&O railroad line near Clarksburg to Beverly, Huttonsville and farther south, was still at risk. Charged with its protection was Major General Joseph Reynolds. During the summer of 1861, he built a fortified camp south of Huttonsville. He

2. Muddle and Confusion

called it Camp Elkwater. In addition, he fortified the top of Cheat Mountain with a small earthwork fort called Fort Milroy. Ordered to keep the vital Confederate railroad lines in the area open and free of interference was Brigadier General William Loring. He was responsible for ridding Cheat Mountain of Yankee invaders. Confederate president Jefferson Davis, however, believed that Loring needed help. General Robert E. Lee was sent to provide that assistance. It is ironic that when still an officer in the U.S. Army, Lee was offered the position of commander of all U.S. forces at the start of the Civil War. Abraham Lincoln often referred to him as "Bobby Lee" and hoped that Lee would take the position. Instead, Lee chose to resign his commission and return to his native Virginia. He was placed in charge of all Virginia state troops. His loss was immediately felt by Lincoln and General-in-Chief Winfield Scott. Scott commented, "Even God had to spit on his hands when he made Bob Lee."

Union troops on Cheat Mountain threatened the security of the Staunton-Parkersburg Turnpike. As early as August 6, 1861, Winfield Scott knew that Cheat Mountain was vulnerable and warned Rosecrans.

> Brig. Gen. Rosecrans USA
> *Commanding, Clarksburg, Va.*
>
> It is said that Lee intends attacking Cheat Mountain Pass. It is advisable for you to push forward rapidly the fortifications ordered by General McClellan on that mountain and near Huttonsville. No intelligence of any move on Red House via Romney.
>
> Winfield Scott[24]

Although the strategic pass over Rich Mountain was now secure, rebel forces were still in the area. What eventually happened to Julius DeLagnel who stood alone on top of Rich Mountain as Rosecrans moved in? For the next four weeks, Confederate captain Julius DeLagnel hid in bushes near the Hart cabin and watched as Union soldiers began to bring their wounded into the cabin. The farm was now being used as a field hospital. Again, Major Keifer of the Third Ohio recalled,

> On August 14, 1861, while Captain Henry E. Cunard, of the 3d Ohio, with part of his company, was on advanced picket on the Brady's Gate road, privates Vincent and Watson, under Corporal Stiner, discovered a man stealthily passing around them through the woods, whom they halted and proceeded to interrogate. He professed to be a farm hand; said his employer had a mountain farm not far away, where he pastured cattle; that a two-year-old steer had strayed away, and he was looking for him. His clothes were fearfully torn by brush and briars. His hands and face were scratched by thorns. He had taken off his boots to relieve his swollen feet, and was carrying them in his hands. Imitating the language and manners of an uneducated West Virginian, he asked the sentinel if he "had seed anything of a red steer." The sentinel had not.

After continuing the conversation for a time he finally said: "Well, I must be a-going, it is a-gettin' late and I'm durned feared I won't get back to the farm afore night. Good-day." "Hold on," said the sentinel; "better go and see the Captain." "O, no, don't want to trouble him, it is not likely he has seed the steer, and it's a-gettin' late." "Come right along," replied the sentinel, bringing down his gun; "the Captain will not mind being troubled; in fact, I am instructed to take such as you to him."

The boots were discovered by the keen instinct of the inquiring Yankee to be too neatly made and elegant for a Western Virginian mountaineer employed at twelve dollars a month in caring for cattle in the hackings. When asked the price paid for the boots, the answer was fifteen dollars. The suspect was a highly educated gentleman, wholly incapable of acting his assumed character. He had touched the higher education and civilization of men of learning, and his tongue could not be attuned to lie and deceive in the guise of one to the manor born. Though at first Captain Cunard hesitated, he told the gentleman he would take him for further examination to camp. Finding the Captain, in his almost timid native modesty, was nevertheless obdurate, the now prisoner, knowing hope of escape was gone, declared himself to be Captain Julius A. De Lagnel, late commander of the Confederates in the battle of Rich Mountain, where he was reported killed. His tell-tale boots were made in Washington. He was severely wounded July 11th, and had succeeded in reaching a friendly secluded house near the battle-field, where he remained and was cared for until his wound healed and he was able to travel. He had been in the mountains five days and four nights, and just as he was passing the last and most advanced Union picket he was taken. His little stock of provisions, consisting of a small sack of biscuits, was about exhausted, and what remained was spoiled. He was taken to camp, wet, shivering, and exhausted from starvation, cold, and exposure.[25]

DeLangel was taken to the headquarters of General Joseph Reynolds. The general was in command of about 4,000 troops on Cheat Mountain, a few miles south of Rich Mountain. The two had known each other from previous service in the U.S. Army. DeLagnel was sent to a prison camp that had been established at Fort McHenry. He was soon released in a prisoner exchange and continued to serve the Confederacy throughout the war.

By September 1861, "Western" Virginia was working hard to break away from the Confederacy and join the Union. Confederate president Jefferson Davis now faced his first potential setback after his success at Bull Run in July. "Western" Virginia needed to be held. Lee's orders for September 9, 1861, were

> Headquarters of the Forces
> *Valley Mountain, W. Va.*, September 9, 1861
>
> The forward movement announced to the Army of the Northwest in Special Orders No. 28, from its headquarters, of this date, gives the general commanding the opportunity of exhorting the troops to keep steadily in view

the great principles for which they contend and to manifest to the world their determination to maintain them. The eyes of the country are upon you. The safety of your homes and the lives of all you hold dear depend on your courage and exertions. Let each man resolve to be victorious, and that the right of self-government, liberty and peace shall in him find a defender. The progress of this army must go forward.

R.E. Lee
General, Commanding[26]

The plan that Lee developed was simple and classic. Essentially, one brigade would create a diversion in front of the forces of Union colonel Nathan Kimball on top of Cheat Mountain. While this was happening, another brigade would carry the main assault while a third brigade would cut off the avenue of retreat to the west of Cheat Mountain. Lee intended that all three brigades would coordinate their actions at the same time. However, Lee's officers were inexperienced and the weather did not cooperate. What happened and what part did the Third Ohio play?

Confederate brigadier general Henry Jackson's diversion began their attack on Cheat Mountain. He traded fire with Union pickets who fell back to their primary post and held firm. Jackson's men were held in place and could not advance farther up the mountain. However, Brigadier General Samuel Anderson's brigade succeeded in fighting their way to the rear of Cheat Mountain. They cut the telegraph connection to Union general Reynolds' headquarters at Elkwater camp. When the frontal assault of Colonel Albert Rust finally got under way, Reynolds became concerned for Kimball and his small force at the top of the mountain. It was essential to reestablish communication. In his report of September 17, Brigadier General Reynolds stated, "Determined to force a communication with Cheat, I ordered the Thirteenth Indiana under Colonel Sullivan, to cut their way, if necessary, by the main road, and the greater part of the Third Ohio and the Second Virginia, under Colonels Morrow and Moss, respectively, to do the same by the path. The two commands started at 3 o'clock a.m.... Early on the 13th, the small force of about 300 from the summit engaged the enemy, and with such effect that he ... retired in great haste and disorder, and our relieving force (Third Ohio and 2nd Virginia) ... marched to the summit securing the provision train and reopening our communication."[27] When Lee initiated the initial attack on the 12th, he also decided to attack Reynolds' headquarters on the Elkwater. According to Third Ohio major Warren Keifer,

> Early on the 12th of September I was sent with a detachment of four companies of the 3d Ohio, as grand-guard at an outpost and for picket duty as well as scouting, to the point of a spur of Rich Mountain near the mouth and to the north of Elk Water, west of the Huntersville pike, and about one mile and

a half in advance of the camp. This position covered the Elk Water road from Brady's Gate, the pike, the narrow valley of the Tygart's, and afforded a good point of observation up the valley towards the enemy. A portion of the time I had under me a section of artillery and other detachments. Here Reynolds determined to first stubbornly resist the approach of the enemy, and consequently I was ordered to construct temporary works. Another detachment was located east of the river with like instructions. On the 12th the enemy pushed back our skirmishers and pickets in the valley and displayed considerable disposition to fight, but as we exchanged some shots and showed our willingness to give battle, no real attack was made.[28]

Lee backed off because Loomis' artillery opened up with a ten-pound Parrott gun. "Bobby" Lee decided it might be better to fight some other day.

Camped on the banks of the Tygart Valley River, the Third Ohio waited for orders. Everything was quiet except for the occasional skirmishing. According to Beatty on September 19, "There was lively skirmishing for a few days, and hot work expected; but, for reasons unknown to us, the enemy retired precipitately."[29] Shortly after the capture of DeLagnel, camp life was disturbed by an incident that Major Keifer recalled many years later. The Third Ohio had established a field hospital on a small island in the middle of the Tygart Valley River. This would keep the doctors and patients safe from animals or unexpected enemy attack. On August 20, however, the water level in the river began to rise. The hospital tents might be swept away by the force of the uprooted trees that were surging down the river out of control. No one knew what to do. Unless action was taken soon, doctors and patients would be swept to their death. According to Keifer,

> Lieutenant-Colonel John Beatty, of the 3d Ohio, with that Scotch-Irish will and heroic determination which characterized him in all things, especially in fighting the enemy, met the emergency. He got into an army wagon and compelled the teamster to drive into the rushing stream above the island so that he could move, in part, with the current. Thus, by swimming the horses, he, with a few others, escaped the floating timbers and reached the imperiled hospital. He found at once that it was impossible to carry back the occupants or even to return with the wagon. He promptly ordered the driver to unhitch the horses and swim them to shore, and to return in like manner with two or three more wagons. Two more wagons reached Beatty, but one team was carried down the stream and drowned. He placed the three wagons on the highest ground, though all the island was soon overflowed, chained and tied them securely together to stakes or trees. On the wagon boxes the hospital tent was rolled, and the sick and wounded were placed thereon with some of the hospital supplies. He, with those accompanying him, decided to remain and share their fate, and he, with some who could not get into the wagon, climbed into the trees. The river at 10 P.M. had reached the hubs of the wagons and threatened to submerge them, but soon after it commenced to recede slowly, though a rain

The Parrott Gun was a muzzle-loading, rifled gun that was made from cast iron. To give it strength from cracking, a band was wrapped around the breach. Shown here is the 20-pound gun, the largest used by the Union army during the war (Library of Congress).

again set in, lasting through the night. Morning found the river fast resuming its normal state, and the Colonel and his rescuing party, with the hospital occupants, were all brought safely to the shore.[30]

The hospital was secure and so was western Virginia. In two years, the latter would become the 35th state. Until then, northern victories at Rich Mountain, Laurel Hill and Cheat Mountain helped ensure that Jefferson Davis and "Bobby" Lee could not take advantage of its mountain passes and turnpikes. The Third Ohio, along with other regiments from bordering states, helped provide hope and confidence through these early victories for a struggling Union.

Shooting at men standing in the distance in front of you was easier than firing at someone who hid behind a tree or sneaked up on your hindmost. Guerrilla tactics weren't fair.

3

The Quickness of a Tiger

> Guerilla warfare was a high risk activity, and [John Hunt] Morgan immediately acquitted a taste for it. Raids relieved the pain of boredom and insidious depression, and the excitement provided short-term pleasure. Totally immersed in the activity, [Morgan] learned that depression was blotted out, and outside reality did not exist. He experienced a sense of power, control and triumph in the face of despair and helplessness.[1]

"William Henry Seward is a vaporing, blustering, ignorant man," shouted British prime minister Lord Palmerston.[2]

Before Secretary of State William Henry Seward had an opportunity to impact the Third Ohio and the Civil War, the Third was spending most of the fall of 1861 and winter of 1862 disrespecting their officers, fighting rebel skirmishers and praying for the rains to stop. On September 27, 1861, John Beatty recalled,

> To-night almost the entire valley is inundated. Many tents are waist high in water, and where others stood this morning the water is ten feet deep. Two men of the Sixth Ohio are reported drowned. The water got around them before they became aware of it, and in endeavoring to escape they were swept down the stream and lost. The river seems to stretch from the base of one mountain to the other, and the whole valley is one wild scene of excitement. Wherever a spot of dry ground can be found, huge log fires are burning, and men by the dozen are grouped around them, anxiously watching the water and discussing the situation. Tents have been hastily pitched on the hills, and camp fires, each with its group of men, are blazing in many places along the side of the mountain. The rain has fallen steadily all day.[3]

When not fighting with the weather, the men had too much free time on their hands. The officers of the Third were embarrassed when the men in the ranks began to make fun of the colonel commanding, Issac Morrow. They recalled his speech just before the fighting on Rich Mountain began. They were looking for real leadership, and that excluded Morrow. Soon,

Beatty and some of the other officers were discussing ways to have Colonel Morrow transferred. He didn't know what he was doing and was dangerous because he was unable to inspire the men of the Third. False alarms were often sounded in the middle of the night. Inexperienced sentries with little training were standing guard. Anyone going beyond the perimeter and reentering later needed to give the password or risk being shot as a spy or the advance guard of an approaching enemy. Shortly after the hospital rescue incident, Private Francis Union, Company A, Third Ohio, was shot by a nervous sentry when the password wasn't uttered fast enough. Incidents like these gave the rank and file cause for concern. They had little faith in the leadership they were counting on to guide them in battle and keep them safe. Morrow had to go before more fighting resumed. With Robert E. Lee on the way, the sooner the better!

By October 8, the Third Ohio was assigned to a new brigade commanded by Brigadier General Ebenezer Dumont. According to Beatty, "he is a small man, with a thin piping voice, but an educated and affable gentleman."[4] By November 1, the Third was in Kentucky. They were headed for Louisville. That would be the supply hub for all activity in the Bluegrass State. That's when Queen Victoria heard from Prime Minister Lord Palmerston about William Henry Seward.

It was November 10, 1861, and Queen Victoria had just learned about the seizure of two Confederate representatives who were on board a British packet ship bound for London. The Confederacy needed cash to buy guns and gunpowder. The blockade was making it harder and harder to ship

Secretary of State William Henry Seward was educated, talented, and impulsive. He served as Lincoln's secretary of state. Initially, he considered himself to be the de facto president. On the wall in his home in Auburn, New York, he had framed pictures of some of the famous people he knew. All of the pictures are numbered. Lincoln is #6 and Seward is #6.5 (Library of Congress).

cotton to their agents at Fraser and Trenholm in Liverpool. Cotton was no longer king, and Jefferson Davis needed to borrow money. In addition, he was also hoping to convince the British and the French to force their way through the blockade so that the hungry mills of Manchester and Leeds could start production again. The basic facts of the *Trent* incident are relatively simple and well known. On November 8, 1861, Captain Charles Wilkes, aboard the *San Jacinto*, intercepted the *Trent* on the high seas off the coast of Cuba. On board were Confederate ministers James Mason and John Slidell, their secretaries and some members of their families. Mason and Slidell had evaded the Union blockade of Charleston by slipping quietly out at 1:00 a.m. on the night of October 12. Blockade runners were often painted a dull gray so that they were harder to detect at night. They burned smokeless anthracite coal to help avoid detection. Many were equipped with powerful engines whose steam-driven paddle wheels could cruise at 26 revolutions per minute. When pursued by federal cruisers, they could sprint at 33 revolutions per minute. They were built for speed.

Before reaching England, brief accounts of the Mason and Slidell mission appeared in the Northern newspapers. It has been suggested that the mission was so well publicized that the publicity itself became an incentive for the captain of the *San Jacinto*, Charles Wilkes, to capture the ship and seize the Confederate envoys. This is unlikely. The *New York Times* on October 31, 1861, reprinted an October 29 article from the *Richmond Examiner*. The article read, in part, "By this time our able representatives abroad, Messrs. MASON and SLIDELL, are pretty well on their way over the briny deep towards the shores of Europe.... The malice of our Yankee enemies will thus be foiled, and the attempt to capture them fail of success." What was Seward's part in this? He was Lincoln's secretary of state and was regarded by politicians in England and France as the de facto president who was really responsible for the war. Although they were wrong, they needed someone to blame, and Seward was always an easy target.

The Third Ohio was impacted because they were part of an army charged with securing Tennessee for the Union. Its rivers and railroads were vital assets. West Tennessee had a rich soil that allowed cotton to flourish. If Tennessee effectively remained Confederate, then cotton might eventually reach the loading docks in Liverpool and enrich the rebel treasury. The Army of the Cumberland and the Third Ohio were there to ensure that the cotton fields remained empty. Jefferson Davis hoped that war with England over the *Trent* incident would ultimately render fighting by the Army of the Cumberland and the Third Ohio moot. British gunboats would smash their way through the blockade and open Confederate ports to cotton and anything else the Confederacy had to sell for ready cash. Although the *Trent* incident was settled without war with Britain,

3. The Quickness of a Tiger

the Third Ohio was fighting a personal war of its own.

By December 13, the Third was reassigned to the 17th Brigade, Third Division of General Ormsby Mitchell.[5] By the end of the month, everyone knew something was up. Major General Don Carlos Buell arrived. By this time, however, life in camp was poor. Regulations and discipline were lax and getting worse. It was at this time that Ormsby referred to the Third Ohio as "Obstinate Devils" because of their general lack of order and respect. The men wanted Morrow out and were even starting to lose faith in the next in command, Colonel John Beatty. According to Beatty,

James Mason (shown here) and John Slidell were charged with trying to obtain loans and possible recognition for the Confederate government from England and France during the war. They were captured on board the HMS *Trent* in November 1861. Their capture caused sufficient outrage in the British Foreign Office that war with Britain might have resulted if not for skillful negotiations by Lincoln and Secretary of State William Henry Seward (Library of Congress).

To-day a soldier about half drunk was arrested for leaving camp without permission and brought to my quarters; he had two canteens of whisky on his person. I remonstrated with him mildly, but he grew saucy, insubordinate, and finally insolent and insulting; he said he did not care a damn for what I thought or did, and was ready to go to the guard-house; in fact wanted to go there. Finally, becoming exasperated, I took the canteens from him, poured out the whisky, and directed Captain Patterson to strap him to a tree until he cooled off somewhat. The Captain failing in his efforts to fasten him securely, I took my saddle girth, backed him up to the tree, buckled him to it, and returned to my quarters. This proved to be the last straw which broke the unfortunate camel's back. It was a high-handed outrage upon the person of a volunteer soldier; the last and worst of the many arbitrary and severe acts of which I had been guilty. The regiment seemed to arise *en masse*, and led on by a few reckless men who had long disliked me, advanced with threats and fearful oaths toward my tent. The bitter hatred which the men entertained for me had now culminated. It being Sunday the whole regiment was off duty, and while some, and perhaps many, of the boys had no desire to resort to violent measures, yet all evidently sympathized with the prisoner, and regarded my action as arbitrary and cruel. The position of the soldier was a humiliating one, but it gave him no bodily pain. Possibly I had no authority for punishing him in this way; and had I taken time for reflection it is more than probable I should have found some other and less objectionable mode; confinement in the guard-house, however, would have been no punishment for such a man; on the contrary it would have afforded him that relief from disagreeable duty which he desired. At any rate the act, whether right or wrong, had been done, and I must either stand by it now or abandon all hope of controlling the regiment hereafter. I watched the mob, unobserved by it, from an opening in my tent door. Saw it gather, consult, advance, and could hear the boisterous and threatening language very plainly. Buckling my pistol belt under my coat where it could not be seen, I stepped out just as the leaders advanced to the

Brigadier General Ormsby Mitchell was the commander referring to the Third Ohio as "Obstinate Devils." He was an amateur astronomer who financed and built one of the most powerful telescopes in America at the time. He was a professor of mathematics at West Point and was often called "The Professor" (Library of Congress).

tree for the purpose of releasing the man. I asked them very quietly what they proposed to do. Then I explained to them how the soldier had violated orders, which I was bound by my oath to enforce; how, when I undertook to remonstrate kindly against such unsoldierly conduct, he had insulted and defied me. Then I continued as calmly as I ever spoke, "I understand you have come here to untie him; let the man who desires to undertake the work begin—if there be a dozen men here who have it in their minds to do this thing-let them step forward—I dare them to do it." They saw before them a quiet, plain man who was ready to die if need be; they could not doubt his honesty of purpose. He gave them time to act and answer, they stood irresolute and silent; with a wave of the hand he bade them go to their quarters, and they went.[6]

Although unwilling to challenge Beatty, Morrow was another matter. Feeling the heat, the other officers of the Third looked to Beatty to settle matters with Morrow. They all wanted him out, and they looked to Beatty to get the job done. On January 28, Beatty met with Morrow and told him of the issues as expressed by the men and other officers. One hour later, Colonel Issac Morrow reluctantly agreed to resign from command of the Third Ohio Volunteer Infantry. On February 8, he finally left camp and boarded a train to take him back to Ohio. His escort to the train returned to camp drunk and happy. Very soon, however, the snow and bitter cold dampened any feelings of relief or joy.

On February 10, 1862, the Third Ohio left Bacon Creek, Kentucky, at noon. Before crossing the Green River later that night, some of the officers were as drunk as the men. According to Beatty, "Many of the officers imbibed freely, and the senior surgeon, an educated gentleman, and very popular with the boys, became gloriously elevated. He kept his eye pealed for secesh, and before reaching Munfordville found a citizen twice as big as himself in possession of a doublebarreled shot-gun. Taking it for granted that he was an enemy, the Doctor drew a revolver and bade him surrender unconditionally. The boys said the Doctor was as tight as a little bull."[7] As the Third Ohio, along with the Army of the Cumberland, chased Braxton Bragg farther south, they suddenly saw smoke on the horizon. They were near Bowling Green on February 14. The Third was sure they were in for a fight. As they got closer to the city, they could hear musket fire and artillery. This was it! However, when the army got closer to Bowling Green, they discovered that the fire and smoke were from burning warehouses and supply wagons. The rebels decided it was better to run than stay and fight. Before leaving, they destroyed anything that might help the Yankees. According to Beatty, "When within ten miles of Bowling Green the guns opened in our front. Leaving the regiment in charge of the Major, I rode ahead rapidly as I could, and reached the river bank opposite Bowling Green in time to see a detachment of rebel cavalry fire the buildings which contained their army stores. The town was ablaze in twenty different places. They had destroyed the bridge over Barren River in the morning, and now, having finished the work of destruction, went galloping over the hills."[8] The fire at Bowling Green was a troubling sign for the Third Ohio. The Bluegrass State was guerrilla territory, and John Hunt Morgan was in the area. On March 1, 1862, the Third Ohio was headed for Murfreesboro where they heard that a rebel cavalry unit was near. According to Colonel Beatty, "Our brigade, in command General Dumont, started for Lavergne, a village eleven miles out on the Murfreesboro road, to look after a regiment of cavalry said to be in occupation of the place. Arrived there a little before sunset, but found the enemy had disappeared. The troops obtained whiskey in the village, and many of the soldiers became noisy and disorderly."[9] The Third was always eager for a fight. When disappointed, they fought with whiskey and anything else they could find. When they arrived in Murfreesboro, Morgan and his cavalry had fled. Bushwhackers and cavalry raiders were always willing to shoot from behind a tree. When faced with combat face-to-face, they preferred to leave and come back another day. Morgan and his men didn't run very far, though. The men of the Third Ohio Volunteer Infantry Regiment did what they did best when there was nobody around to fight: they got drunk. On March 1, General Dumont and the Third heard that there was a guerrilla band in the area around Lavergne, so they set off in pursuit. After searching the town and questioning some of the residents, the Third Ohio emptied the homes and local taverns of any spirits that had not been hastily hidden before their arrival.

The regiment was still "under the weather" when they were ordered to march back to Nashville. Whether or not John Hunt Morgan was in the area, his local reputation personified his spirit all over Tennessee. Newspapers in Kentucky and Tennessee frequently reported him attacking in several different places at the same time and on the same day. Morgan loved the publicity, and so did his imitators. Independent, outlaw bands marketed the Morgan "brand" for their own benefit. Whether real or facsimile, the Third was always looking out for Morgan. On March 8, 1862, their concerns were justified:

> March 8, 1862. This afternoon the camp was greatly excited over a daring feat of a body of cavalry under John Morgan. It succeeded in getting almost inside the camps, and was five miles inside of our outposts. It came into the main road between where Kennett's cavalry regiment is encamped and Nashville; captured a wagon train, took the drivers, Captain Braden , of Indiana, who was in charge of the train, and eighty-three horses, and started on a by-road back for Murfreesboro. General Mitchell immediately dispatched Kennett in pursuit. About fifteen miles out the rebels were overtaken and our men and horses recaptured. Two rebels were killed and two taken; Kennett is still in hot pursuit. Captain Braden says, as the rebels were riding away they were exceedingly jubilant over the success of their adventure, and promised to introduce him to General Hardee in the evening. Without asking the Captain's permission they gave him a very poor horse in exchange for a very good one, put him at the head of the column and guarded him vigilantly; but when Kennett appeared and the running fight occurred he dodged off at full speed, lay down on his horse, and although fired at many times escaped unhurt. Morgan's men know the country so well that all the by-roads and cow-paths are familiar to them; the citizens keep them informed also as to the location of our camps and picket posts, and if need be are ready to serve them either as guides or spies, hence the success which attended the earlier part of their enterprise does not indicate so great a want of vigilance on the part of our troops, as might at first thought be supposed.[10]

Cavalry regiments served many important functions for armies north and south. For both, cavalry served as a mobile intelligence-gathering unit. As the army marched forward, it was important to know where your enemy was and how he was armed. What was the topography of the ground to which you were marching? Was it open ground that could not conceal men and arms, or were there trees sufficient to give pause for what might be concealed behind them? Was there sufficient forage in the area for the horses and mules pulling the heavy artillery caissons? Was there water for man and beast? A marching army corps might stretch for several miles. Cavalry was used to screen the area in front and in the rear. Men like Morgan, Wheeler and Forrest were adept at attacking the rear of the corps as it marched. Although protected by skirmishers, Morgan and other rebel cavalry bands could sometimes destroy a skirmish line and burn as many unguarded supply wagons as possible. In addition, cavalry regiments were expected to burn the railroad bridges that transported men and supplies to the front. They also tore down telegraph lines that were increasingly important for both Washington and Richmond to communicate in real time with their commanders in the field. Rosecrans and Bragg both had cavalry regiments performing all of these functions. However, the Confederate cavalry units were generally more numerous and more aggressive. It has been suggested by some that the smaller and thus more vulnerable Southern male population were quick to volunteer for cavalry duty before they were conscripted for the infantry. Nevertheless, the Army of the Cumberland had an effective cavalry regiment. The Fourth Ohio

General John Hunt Morgan was a legendary figure in newspapers North and South. He was born in Alabama but grew up in Kentucky. His first wife was the sister of General A.P. Hill. After she died, Morgan remarried in 1862. He is best known for his successful raids on Union supply lines. Those raids resulted in the loss of millions of dollars in ammunition and staple supplies (Library of Congress).

cavalry regiment was commanded by Colonel John Kennett. On April 7, 1862, the men of the Third Ohio watched as Kennett's cavalry regiment went out in search of Morgan. Beatty recalled, "Colonel Kennett at the head of three hundred cavalry, made a dash into the country toward the Tennessee River, captured and destroyed a train on a branch of the Nashville and Chattanooga Railroad, and returned to camp to-night with fifteen prisoners."[11]

What was the objective of Morgan, Wheeler, Pegram and the other Confederate guerrilla bands that were a constant thorn in the side of Union armies operating in the South? As far as the Third Ohio was concerned, Morgan was a threat to the supply lines that fed an army that was determined to catch Braxton Bragg. Who was John Hunt Morgan, and why was he a threat to the Third Ohio and the Union war effort in the western theater? John Hunt Morgan was born in Alabama in 1825. Abraham Lincoln was born in the state where John Hunt Morgan later grew up—Kentucky. Ironically, both men opposed secession, but Lincoln fought to resist it, and Morgan battled to sustain it. Both men were ambitious risk-takers, and both dealt with depression. The similarities ended here, however. Lincoln was molded by a culture that generally took a negative view toward slavery. By contrast, Morgan was cast by a society that either tolerated or made a good living from slavery. The newspapers from the Deep South, both Republican and Southern Democrat, covered the exploits of Morgan and his cavalry the way that dime novels expanded their circulation writing about Wild Bill Hickock and Billy the Kid. "In a world of his own; [Morgan] was the master of fate; the sky was the limit; everything was possible.... The state of euphoria was as addictive as alcohol or drugs.... Morgan conducted four or five raids every week; as soon as he was rested from one, he began planning and anticipating the next."[12]

The Third Ohio and all of the men under General William Rosecrans were vulnerable. At Perryville in Kentucky, their supply base was Louisville. At Stones River in Tennessee, the Third relied on supplies of food and ammunition coming from Nashville. Morgan and his men were constantly burning the railroad bridges and supply wagons that sustained the Army of the Cumberland. Battles could not be won without men who were healthy and supplied with enough powder and shot to subdue the enemy. Both George McClellan and Winfield Scott advised Lincoln to take advantage of his superiority in money and troop numbers to create a battle front so long that Jefferson Davis would not be able to effectively challenge every fight. The Union plan was to attack north, south, east and west at the same time. Eventually, the rebels would be forced to give up. The only practical alternative for Jefferson Davis was the guerrilla tactics provided by men like John Hunt Morgan, Nathan Bedford Forrest and "Fighting Joe" Wheeler.

3. The Quickness of a Tiger 63

In addition to constantly watching out for Morgan and "Fighting Joe," the Third was also compromised by the constant flow of runaway slaves coming into Union camps. This was a problem in every theater during the Civil War. Abraham Lincoln's initial position was one of ordering Union generals to honor the Fugitive Slave Act and return slaves that come into their lines to rightful "owners."[13] The president did not want to antagonize the border slave states. The position of the Lincoln administration was that accepting slaves into their lines amounted to an informal form of emancipation. General Benjamin Butler was one of the first to take a controversial public stand on the matter. When slaves came into his camp and asked for protection, Butler considered them war "contraband" and thus subject to lawful seizure. Butler refused to honor the law and return them. He argued that the seceded states were foreign countries. As a result, the Fugitive Slave Act did not apply. On March 18, 1862, the camp of the Third Ohio was forced to deal with this sensitive political issue. While the Third Ohio was outside Nashville, Major Warren Keifer recalled, "At Nashville the 3d Ohio's officers (especially Colonel Beatty) were charged with harboring negro slaves, and Buell gave some slave-hunters permission to search the regiment's camp for their escaped '*property*.'[14] The Colonel ordered all the colored men to be assembled for inspection, but it so happened that not one could be found. One of the slave-hunters proposed to search a tent for a certain runaway slave, and he was earnestly told by Colonel Beatty that he might do so, but that if he were successful in his search it would cost him his life. No further search was made."[15] Beatty agreed with Butler. Ultimately, Lincoln backed down. Runaway slaves were welcomed into Union lines.

The day after John Beatty took a stand against the Fugitive Slave Act, John Hunt Morgan struck again. The Third was on the march to Murfreesboro. They had to take an extended detour because of bridges constantly burned. However, two days later, brigade commander Ebenezer Dumont was reassigned. The brigade to which the Third was attached was now commanded by Brigadier General William Haines Lytle.[16] Who was in overall command? Who was constantly watching their columns from the rear and the flank? The new Army of the Cumberland was commanded by General William S. Rosecrans.[17] However, the Third Ohio was part of the corps commanded by a Virginian, General George H. Thomas. Some military historians consider Thomas to have been the greatest commander in the Civil War. He died relatively young in 1870. This allowed Ulysses Grant and William Sherman the opportunity to rewrite history and promote their own story. A prolific observer and writer of the Civil War was Major Donn Piatt, 13th Ohio Volunteer Infantry.[18] To him, "Grant felt uneasy and ashamed in the presence of Thomas, and both Grant and Sherman were troubled with the thought that truth and justice would award to their subordinate in office the higher position on the honor roll."[19] Thomas was born into a slave-owning family in Virginia. One of his earliest memories was of he and his family running from home and hiding in a swamp as Nat Turner and his small band of runaway slaves murdered white families in southern Virginia. The Turner rebellion remained clearly in the minds of men and women throughout the South. Slave owners conveniently justified their position by convincing themselves that their slaves were happy and would never revolt and harm them. On the other hand, those same men were constantly afraid that their slaves would do to them what Nat Turner did to many they personally knew. They slept with a pistol under their pillow.[20]

George Thomas was a quiet man, a West Point graduate, an amateur botanist and a tenacious fighter. Wherever his corps was directed to stand, the Third Ohio knew there would be

William Haines Lytle was born in Cincinnati and graduated from Cincinnati College. He was wounded at Carnifex Ferry, Virginia, in 1861, and later at Perryville in 1862. Lytle was taken prisoner during Perryville but was soon exchanged. He died at Chickamauga on September 20, 1863. Lytle is also known for his poetry. After he died, Confederate soldiers came to honor his remains at a place now known as Lytle Hill (Library of Congress).

action. Although Thomas commanded the corps, the Third were closer to their division commander, Lovell Rousseau. "He was no West Pointer, which made his rise to Major General all the more impressive. Rousseau advanced by virtue of his native intelligence, his talent for learning from experience, and his very visible courage. Rousseau did not try to lead from behind; he was a cheerful warrior on horseback who seemed to be inspired by danger—and inspired his men in turn. In this way, too, Rousseau reminds one of [Andrew] Jackson and [Sam] Houston. They were all born to command."[21] With George Thomas and Lovell Rousseau always ready for action, the Third Ohio realized they would be busy in this war.

The Third Ohio knew Major General Ormsby Mitchell the best. Mitchell was born in Kentucky but was raised in Ohio. His father died when he was very young, and Mitchell grew up poor. By the age of 15, he was the primary wage earner for the family. He was fortunate to gain entrance to West Point where he interacted with Robert E. Lee and Joseph Johnston. His roommate at the academy was Jefferson Davis. Ormsby Mitchell graduated 15th in his class and Davis 23rd.

Major General George Thomas, later the "Rock of Chickamauga," is considered by many military historians to be the best fighter in the Union army. However, he died relatively young in 1870, thus allowing both Ulysses Grant and William Sherman time to revise history in their favor (Library of Congress).

After graduation, Mitchell remained at West Point and became a professor in the math department. As a result, he was later often referred to as "The Professor." Perceptive observer of Civil War battles and leaders Whitelaw Reid characterized Ormsby Mitchell as "beginning as an errand-boy and store-clerk, he had risen to rank among the foremost scientific men in the nation. He was esteemed a skillful railroad engineer and manager. He had been a college professor of high standing. He was reckoned among the most brilliant of scientific lecturers in the country, and among the most effective of popular orators. He was a successful author. His reputation as an astronomer was as high in Europe as in his own country."[22] Ormsby Mitchell's diary entries reveal an articulate man with great curiosity about the world. His inquisitiveness and ceaseless energy is reminiscent of men like Benjamin Franklin and Thomas Jefferson. After touring Europe for the best telescope lenses, Mitchell worked hard to raise the funds to build one of the largest refracting telescopes in the world at that time. When it was dedicated, former president John Quincy Adams spoke at the laying of the cornerstone. As a graduate of West Point, however,

Ormsby Mitchell was a strict disciplinarian. The reference to Obstinate Devils comes from Mitchell. On April 4, 1862, John Beatty recorded the incident that provoked the label.

> At Murfreesboro heavy details were made for bridge building, and one day, while superintending the work, the General addressed the detail from the Third in a very uncomplimentary way: "You lazy scoundrels, go to work! Your regiment is the promptest in the division to report for duty, but you will not work." At another time he gave an order to a soldier which was not obeyed with sufficient alacrity, when he yelled: "What regiment do you belong to?" "The Third." "Well, sir, I thought you were one of the obstinate devils of that regiment." At another time he rode into our camp, and the boys failed to rise at his approach, when he reined in his horse suddenly and shouted: "Get up here, you lazy scoundrels, and treat your superiors with respect!" Riding on a little further, a private passed without touching his cap: "Hold on, here," said the General, "don't you know how to salute a superior?" "Yes," stammered the boy, "but I did not see you." "Hold up your head like a soldier, and you will see me." One night I was making the rounds in the Second Ohio with the General. The guard did not turn out promptly and he became angry; diving into the guard-tent to rout them up, he ran against a big fellow so violently that he was nearly thrown off his legs. This increased his fury, and seizing the soldier by the coat collar he shook him roughly, and said: "You insolent dog, I'll stand insolence from no man. Officer, put this man under arrest immediately."[23]

Major General Lovell Rousseau congratulated the Third Ohio after the Battle of Perryville. He told them that they stood like "men of iron" (Library of Congress).

The Third Ohio wanted to fight, not repair bridges.

News about battles in Tennessee was eagerly sought by the men of the regiment. On April 10, 1862, the Third Ohio was in Fayetteville, Tennessee. Farther west of Fayetteville, the Tennessee River flowed casually through the town of Pittsburg Landing. Near the riverbank was a small, log church with a name that sounded strange to the men of the Third—Shiloh.[24] According to Beatty, "There are various and contradictory rumors afloat respecting the condition of affairs at Shiloh. The rebel sympathizers here are jubilant over what they claim is reliable intelligence, that our army has been surprised and defeated. Another report, coming via Nashville, says that a part of our army was terribly beaten on Sunday; but reinforcements arriving on Monday, the rebels were driven back, and our losses of the first day retrieved."[25]

Shiloh created a storm of finger-pointing by newspapers, politicians and President Lincoln. Ulysses Grant fought against Albert Sidney Johnston. When Johnston was killed, he was replaced by the hero of Bull Run, Pierre Beauregard. The killing was awful, and the public on both sides was sickened. Rumors began to fly. Supposedly, Grant was caught surprised because he was drunk? Union soldiers were bayonetted in their tents? Lincoln came to Grant's support by claiming, "I can't spare this man. He fights." Mary Lincoln called him a butcher and wanted her husband to replace him. Lincoln held firm. The newspapers didn't let up, however. Although the New York papers were especially harsh, the *Cincinnati Daily Enquirer* in April 1862 summed up the debate: "*The Surprise at Pittsburg Landing—Our Mistakes*. Who is responsible for this condition of things? No one but the general in command. Who else is censurable for the great loss of life? No One! A Colonel of an Indiana regiment, who did noble fighting, said to me, 'I have had forty years of experience in military life, and have always been taught to respect my superior officers, but I will say what can be proved if court-marshaled [sic], that if General Grant had been hired to serve our army on a plate and hand it over to the enemy, he could not have done it more handsomely.'"

Why was Shiloh important and how did it impact the Third Ohio? Shiloh (Pittsburg Landing) was important because it sat right on the banks of the Tennessee River. That river provided access to one of the most critical waterways in one of the vital states in the Confederacy. The Third Ohio Volunteer Infantry Regiment played a central role in the Battle of Stones River (Murfreesboro), which helped to secure Tennessee and its river for the Union. Why else was Tennessee so important? Geographically, the state's borders allowed access to much of the Confederacy. Union control of East, Central and West Tennessee would ultimately ensure the probable defeat of the Confederacy. The Tennessee River not only flowed through most of the state, northeast to southwest, but it also coiled and twisted its way through the city of Chattanooga. That city was at the junction of the East Tennessee Railroad, the Nashville and Chattanooga Railroad, the Western and Atlantic Railroad and the Memphis and Charleston Railroad. It also had access to the Virginia and Tennessee Railroad. That was especially important because that railroad allowed access to Richmond, New Orleans, Nashville and Savannah. Chattanooga had a target on its back from the start of the war. Directly or indirectly, the Virginia and Tennessee Railroad provided entry to most of the rebel states. In addition, the loss of Tennessee would represent a crippling loss to the Confederacy. Part of the state, east Tennessee, already sympathized with the Union cause and had no intention of helping the rebels if it could be avoided. Central and West Tennessee were more agricultural and considered the "breadbasket" of the South. Tennessee grew the wheat that Robert E. Lee's army needed to live and fight. Nashville was the jewel, however. Its mills and forges produced small arms, percussion caps and the gunpowder necessary to fight in any theater of war. However, the blockade was already beginning to strangle the South. Its major seaports were guarded by Union gunboats that sailed just far enough offshore to block and supply ships trying to get through. There is a large, credible body of research that shows that fewer and fewer blockade runners were getting through to Europe. Those few that managed to sail or power past Gideon Welles' blockade found that Union purchasing agents were all over Europe outbidding the few Confederate agents who managed to land. Henry Shelton Sanford, unofficial head of Lincoln's secret service, had his agents following rebel arms purchasers all over London, Paris and Germany.[26] Sanford also controlled the banks that directed the cash flow needed to outbid and buy arms and saltpeter. Nashville was a prosperous and cultured city. Edwin Booth and Jenny Lind played and sang in its theaters. Although Lincoln believed that losing Kentucky would ensure loss of the war, he should have said Tennessee was more critical, not Kentucky. To the Third Ohio, it didn't matter if they were in Kentucky or Tennessee because when they weren't fighting, they were drinking.

According to Colonel John Beatty, on April 14, "the Fifteenth Kentucky remains here. The Third and Tenth Ohio moved at three in the afternoon. Roads bad and progress slow. Bivouacked for the night near a distillery. Many of the men drunk; the Tenth Ohio particularly wild."[27] On the 23rd, a rebel guerrilla force attacked the skirmish line protecting the Third in an attempt to take over a bridge near the Third's campsite. An officer of the Third estimated that they were 300 strong. The Union skirmish line drove them off with only one man wounded. By April 27, 1862, the Third and 10th Ohio regiments crossed over to the north side of the Tennessee River at Tuscumbia. Not wishing to be outdone by Morgan and his guerrilla band, Lieutenant Colonel Joseph Walter Burke of the 10th Ohio torched the bridge crossing behind them. According to Beatty, "the flames were hissing among its timbers, and the smoke hung like a cloud above it."[28]

By 5:00 p.m., April 29, the Third Ohio was just outside the town of

Bridgeport, Alabama. The bridge was guarded by Confederate brigadier general Danville Leadbetter.[29] To confront a larger Union force, all Leadbetter had were two, old six-pound guns and 400 infantry. Knowing he could not hold off a larger opposing force, Leadbetter ordered that the east side of the bridge be packed with 200 pounds of powder. His only means of escape would be to blow up the bridge before the Yankees got there. As the Third Ohio and the rest of Ormsby Mitchell's regiments approached, Leadbetter ordered that the fuse be shortened and lit. Unfortunately, the charge was not enough to destroy the bridge. In his report to Major General E. Kirby Smith, Leadbetter stated, "I determined therefore to carry out the spirit of your instructions and burn the East Bridge [and] it was soon in flames and impassable to the enemy."[30] Union engineers, who were embedded in many Union brigades, quickly rebuilt the bridge. Mitchell's infantry crossed on the double-quick. With Colonel John Beatty and the Third on the run, Beatty recalled,

> About five o'clock we formed in line of battle, on high ground in the woods, one-half mile from Bridgeport, the Third having the right of the column, and moved steadily forward until we came in sight of the town and the enemy. The order to double quick was then given, and we dashed into the village on a run. The enemy stood for a moment and then left as fast as legs could carry him; in fact he departed in such haste that but few muskets and one shot from a six pound gun were fired at us; one piece of his artillery was found still loaded. We captured fifty prisoners, a number of horses, two pieces of artillery and many muskets. The bridge over the Tennessee had already been filled with combustible material, and when the rear of the rebel column passed over the match was applied; the fire extended rapidly, and we found it impossible to proceed further. The fright of the enemy was so great that, after getting beyond the river a mile or more, he threw away over a thousand muskets, and abandoned everything that could impede his flight. Unfortunately, however, before a raft could be constructed to convey our troops across the river, the rebels recovered from their panic, backed down a railroad train, and gathered up most of their arms and camp equipage. A little more coolness on the part of our troops would have enabled us to capture twenty-five or thirty cavalrymen, who came riding into Bridgeport, supposing it to be still in the hands of their friends. As they approached, a few scattering shots were fired at them by the excited soldiers, when they wheeled and succeeded in making their escape.[31]

On April 30, the Third marched all night to reach Stevenson. By May 1, however, trouble found the Third Ohio again.

> General Mitchell is well pleased with my action in the Paint Rock matter. The burning of the town has created a sensation, and is spoken of approvingly by the officers and enthusiastically by the men. It is the inauguration of the true policy, and the only one that will preserve us from constant annoyance.
> Col. John Beatty, Third Ohio, May 5, 1862, Paint Rock, Alabama[32]

What happened at Paint Rock? The skirmish at Bridgeport, Alabama, had stretched the Third Ohio thin of ammunition and provisions. By May 2, they were headed for Huntsville to resupply. Before they got there, however, they were attacked by "bushwhackers" who were constantly sniping at the men of the Third.

The snipers suddenly came out from behind the trees, from under the bridges and the caves in the area. Before reaching Huntsville, the Third passed through Paint Rock. The area was a haven for the bushwhackers and bridge burners. Beatty recalled what happened: "At Paint Rock the train was fired upon, and six or eight men wounded. As soon as it could be done, I had the train stopped, and, taking a file of soldiers, returned to the village. The telegraph line had been cut, and the wire was lying in the street."[33] In 1904, T.P. O'Shea of the Third told about the caves in his minutes: "There were caves at Paint Rock where the rebels fired on our train. We stopped that train and chased them to a hole in the ground through which they disappeared, followed by our boys who chased them through the mountains to an opening large enough to contain a number of covered army wagons they had stolen."[34] Beatty and the men of the Third were more than annoyed at the constant threat of rebel sniping from the woods. Beatty decided to let Paint Rock know that there would be serious consequences if the sniping continued.

> Calling the citizens together, I said to them that this bushwhacking must cease. The Federal troops had tolerated it already too long. Hereafter every time the telegraph wire was cut we would burn a house; every time a train was fired upon we should hang a man; and we would continue to do this until every house was burned and every man hanged between Decatur and Bridgeport. If they wanted to fight they should enter the army, meet us like honorable men, and not, assassin-like, fire at us from the woods and run. We proposed to hold the citizens responsible for these cowardly assaults, and if they did not drive these bushwhackers from amongst them, we should make them more uncomfortable than they would be in hell. I then set fire to the town, took three citizens with me, returned to the train, and proceeded to Huntsville.[35]

The Third Ohio quickly became celebrities for their "scorched earth" policy.[36] General Ormsby Mitchell was pleased, and the area around Huntsville, Alabama, temporarily got quiet. Beatty's regiment captured 26 men from the Paint Rock area and took them to Huntsville with them. The newspapers complained that some bushwhackers were true Confederates while others were just roving bands of outlaws taking advantage of the chaos of war. The *Wheeling Intelligencer* on June 2, 1862, reminded its readers of one such bandit: "We have received a Daguerreotype likeness of Wat Cool, the king of Western Virginia Guerillas, who was captured by Captain Moses S. Hall, of the Third Virginia Regiment, half a mile above Addison, on the Elk River, in Webster County. Captain Hall bagged the whole party, consisting of four guerillas, on their way back from a marauding expedition into Randolph County. They had seven stolen horses in their possession, which they had taken from Wm. Hyer on the Friday previous. They robbed the house of sheets, blankets, clothing, and even the finger and ear rings and breastpins of the women." Later, the *Louisville Courier Journal* complained that a train coming from Nashville was full of women and children fleeing fighting. The newspapers reported, "The story related by these unhappy people is most lamentable. They tell of respectable law-abiding men being tied up and whipped until they are streaming with blood; of houses plundered and sacked; of crops destroyed and every species of outrage. Small companies of outlaws belonging to neither side, taking advantage of the anarchy which prevails in the country, roam about for the sole purpose of plunder."[37]

The Third Ohio Volunteer Infantry Regiment fought in what was termed then and now as the western theater of war. Although names like Bull Run and Fredericksburg in the eastern theater generated more headlines in the newspapers, places like Perryville and Stones River were just as critical to the ultimate success of the Civil War. Through places like Vicksburg, Perryville and Murfreesboro—the vital rivers, turnpikes and railroads that held the Confederacy together—were the seeds of defeat initially sown. By the fall of 1862, the Third Ohio was about to play a significant part in the struggle for union.

4

Bushwhackers and Scorched Earth

It was hot and dry. Many of the waterholes were full of dead dogs and lifeless horses.[1]

Although Perryville, Kentucky, was just a place to get water for thirsty men and their mounts, it was also part of a larger battle for those border states that were trying to remain neutral in the war. Maryland, Delaware, Missouri and Kentucky wanted to stay out of the fight. All four were on the border between north and south. Both Abraham Lincoln and Jefferson Davis considered these four states as critical to the prosecution of the war. Kentucky, Maryland, Delaware and Missouri were geographically essential to controlling the rivers and boundaries that would dictate military strategy in that region. Maryland was especially important because the nation's capital was located within its borders. If Maryland seceded, what would happen to Washington? Baltimore "Plug Uglies" had already tried to stop Lincoln from reaching Washington for his inauguration.[2] When Mary Lincoln and her sons took the B&O through Baltimore to the capital, her car was assaulted. There was fear that she might be kidnapped or killed. In addition, the B&O railroad was the lifeline to the capital. It ran from Washington to Baltimore and then to points west. If that rail line was threatened by rebel forces, Washington's only relief came from the vulnerable Potomac River. The B&O branch servicing the capital needed protection.

Brigadier General Benjamin Butler was in charge of the two Massachusetts regiments sent to help protect the capital. Because Baltimore was threatening to block rail passage to Washington, Butler helped to find a way around the city before Washington was cut off from the rest of the country.[3] In the end, most in Maryland were more loyal to the Union than originally anticipated. What about Kentucky? Lincoln was born in Kentucky and claimed, "I hope to have God on my side, but I must have Kentucky."[4] Culture and slavery tied these states to the South, but the railroad bound them to the North. Those four border states would see a stressful tug-of-war for the next four years. With over 100,000 men under arms marching through Tennessee and Kentucky, the general population struggled for their safety and their livelihood. With the logistics necessary to feed, arm and shelter thousands of men, armies were often encouraged to live off the land. As a result, homes were plundered, chickens butchered and crops seized from the soil of small farms that were barely surviving without the war. "Scorched earth" made a difficult situation much worse. Forced marches by the Third resulted in men walking day and night for mile after painful, shoeless mile. Part of the problem was that not only did the men need to eat and drink water, so did the horses and mules that pulled the commissary wagons, bake ovens, artillery and ammunition wagons. Forage and water were constantly on the minds of the men and their officers. Unfortunately, a man from the 86th Illinois complained, "Much of the water we drink is mixed with the filth of the mules, hog and goose."[5] The memoirs of the rank and file as well as the officers who filed the reports available in the *Official Records* all complain about the hot summer of 1862 and the lack of water in Tennessee and Kentucky.

Even General Buell complained in a communication with Henry Halleck: "The whole army had for three days or more suffered from a scarcity of water. The last day particularly the troops and animals suffered exceedingly for the want of it and from hot weather and dusty roads. In the bed of Doctor's Creek, a tributary of the Chaplin River about 2½ miles from Perryville, some pools of water were discovered, which the enemy show a determination to prevent us from gaining possession of."[6] As Don Carlos Buell's massive army slowly lumbered north into Kentucky, Confederate soldiers threw dead animals into the few remaining water holes to make it harder for Union men to find potable water. Clean, drinkable water was so hard to get that summer that Major Warren Keifer of the Third Ohio recalled, "I remember Colonel John Beatty and I, on one occasion near Cave City, stood in a hard rain storm holding the corners of a rubber blanket so as to catch a supply of water to slake our thirst."[7]

Due to logistics and politics, the policy toward the border states, north and south, was one of conciliation and a soft touch. "[Lincoln] thought that the Border States must be conciliated and kept in the Union by pleasant promises. The hyena was fed with sugar plums, and it snapped at the hand which caresses it.... The Border State policy has proved a failure, and those states which it was designed to conserve to the Union, are, possibly more dangerous and more difficultly dealt with for the reason that they are out of the Union while they profess to be in it."[8] With emancipation always on Lincoln's mind, part of his tactical plan was to offer compensated emancipation to the slave owners in the border states. With slaves working on the plantations and in the warehouses, the slave owner was free to grab his gun and fight the Yankees. Although slaves were already running away from the farms and coming into Union lines, this was not enough. If the border states would agree to free their slaves and accept government compensation, then the rebels might desert the battle front and return home. Their families came first. That might help end the war. Compensated emancipation had been successfully accomplished in the British colonies in 1833. Denmark and France followed in 1843 and the Netherlands by 1863. Always concerned with anything that might drive the four border states into the Confederacy, Lincoln ultimately threatened that it would be wiser to take the compensation money now rather than wait for a Union victory that would free the slaves. Then they would get no money. However, where would the funds for compensation come from? Lincoln was shortsighted and naive in this regard. Jay Cooke, Anthony Drexel and hundreds of their agents were all over the states of the Union selling bonds to help support the army and navy to win the war on the military, not the political front.[9]

Nevertheless, in April 1862, Congress passed the Compensated Emancipation Act, which compensated slave owners for freeing their slaves in the nation's capital. In the end, however, the border states rejected compensated emancipation. Lincoln's "sugarplum" policy failed. Force would be necessary. To Lincoln, Kentucky was important personally and strategically.[10] It was now up to Don Carlos Buell and his army. With 55,000 men in the ranks, this should be an easy job for the Army of the Ohio.

Months before the Third Ohio took the lead in the attack against Confederate forces at Perryville, the Union grip was slowly tightening on the Confederacy. Winfield Scott's "Anaconda Plan" for strangling the rebellion was starting to have an impact.[11] With Union warships blockading key Southern ports, the South was slowly starving for guns as well as butter. Blockade runners were having modest success at slipping past the Union ironclads. They were selling small quantities of cotton at high prices through the offices of Fraser and Trenholm in Liverpool, England.[12] Eventually, however, few got through the blockade. Jefferson Davis quickly realized that the men under arms and those at home needed to eat. King Cotton was sacrificed and staple food planting took its place. The *Nashville Daily Union* commented on April 15, 1862, about a resolution to the Confederate Senate in Richmond: "The resolution which was sent to the Senate from the House of Representatives proposed to advice the planters of the Confederacy to abstain from raising cotton and tobacco this year, and to devote themselves exclusively to the production of grain and provisions."

4. Bushwhackers and Scorched Earth 75

Originally, the Confederacy had hoped to use the money from cotton sales to buy guns and gunpowder from their sources in Germany. However, the unofficial head of Lincoln's secret service, Henry Shelton Sanford, was successful in blocking Confederate arms agents. Nevertheless, if the army was starving, more guns weren't the issue. Guns won't fire themselves.

Before the Third Ohio could fix bayonets and charge against Braxton Bragg at Perryville, Kentucky, the regiment had to fight its way north to get there. On April 10, 1862, the Third Ohio was in Fayetteville, Alabama. By April 15, the Third Ohio had marched to Huntsville, Alabama, and was headed for the Tennessee River. Constantly marching long distances caused many hardships. The infantry often outpaced the commissary wagons. When stopping for the night, the men were sometimes on their own for food. On the march through Tennessee, one Ohio recruit remembered catching a frog and grinding it up into small pieces. He ate this with an ear of green corn. On the march north, the 42nd Indiana was camped next to the Third Ohio. In Tennessee, they opened a barrel of flour and dumped in a cup of water to make "sinkers"—rock-hard dough. The men kept marching. By the 27th, the Third had reached the Tennessee River, crossed to the north side, and burned the bridge behind them to protect the rear of their column. By the next day, they reached Stevenson and camped for the night. Regimental colonel John Beatty remembered,

> Ordered to move to Stevenson. Took a freight train and marched until twelve o'clock at night, and then bivouacked on the railroad track. Resumed the march at daylight; one mile beyond Stevenson we found the Ninth Brigade, Colonel Sill, in line of battle; formed the Third in support of Loomis' Battery, and remained in this position until two in the afternoon, when General Mitchell arrived and ordered the Ninth Brigade, Loomis' Battery and my regiment to move forward. At Widow's Creek we met a detachment of the enemy; a few shots from the battery and a volley from our skirmish line drove it back, and we hastened on toward Bridgeport, exchanging shots occasionally with the enemy on the way.[13]

Throughout May 1862, the Third Ohio remained camped in the Huntsville area. Beatty complained that his horse got too fat during this period. With New Orleans falling to Union admiral David Farragut on May 1, 1862, a major lifeline for the Confederacy was now closed. Vicksburg, on the Mississippi River, however, remained vital as a distribution center for Confederate supplies coming in through the port of Matamoros, Mexico.

If Vicksburg could be captured, the Confederacy would eventually starve. After Grant defeated Beauregard at Shiloh, Tennessee, in April, Grant set his sights on Vicksburg. Jefferson Davis was getting desperate and knew he had to act fast. He fired Beauregard and promoted Braxton

Bragg. The new army was called the Army of Tennessee.[14] Bragg's plan to save Vicksburg was to combine forces with Edmund Kirby Smith and march north to invade Kentucky. Hopefully, this would divert Union forces away from the Mississippi. It didn't work. Grant never took his eyes off Vicksburg, and Buell moved to catch up to Bragg and Smith who were sprinting for Louisville, Kentucky. Where was the Third Ohio Volunteer Infantry at this time?

Earlier, on July 19, 1862, the Third was reassigned to Brigadier General Lovell Rousseau's division. The officers of the Third regiment were pleased. According to the colonel commanding, John Beatty, "General Rousseau has been assigned to the command of our division. I am glad to hear that he discards the rose-water policy of General Buell under his nose, and is a great deal more thorough and severe in his treatment of rebels than General Mitchell. He sent the Rev. Mr. Ross to jail to-day for preaching a secession sermon last Sunday. He damns the rebel sympathizers, and says if the negro stands in the way of the Union he must get out. Rousseau is a Kentuckian, and it is very encouraging to learn that he talks as he does."[15]

Tough talk was needed at this time. McClellan had already launched his Peninsula Campaign to capture Richmond and end the war.[16] However, Lincoln and McClellan disagreed on the strategy to accomplish this. If the Union army captured Manassas, the rail line that ran direct from there to Richmond could be utilized to rapidly transport troops and capture the city. McClellan disagreed with the logistics of this approach and believed that it would be faster and easier to go by water to the Yorktown peninsula and march north to Richmond from there. McClellan won the debate but lost the battle. In July 1862, the slow Peninsula Campaign quickly degenerated into the Seven Days Battles around Richmond. The city was surrounded by Robert E. Lee and so many forts that McClellan could not penetrate. At the same time, General John Pope was facing defeat near Manassas during what became known as Second Bull Run. Frustrated with his failure during Peninsula and Seven Days, McClellan declined to come to Pope's rescue. "Little Napoleon" finally skulked his way north toward Pope, but it was too late. Rumors of defeat were all over the camps in Kentucky. By July, the Third Ohio was desperate for credible news of the campaigns. According to Colonel Beatty of the Third,

> We know, or think we know, that a great battle has been fought near Richmond, but the result for some reason is withheld. We speculate, talk, and compare notes, but this makes us only the more eager for definite information.... A lieutenant of the Nineteenth Illinois, who fell into the enemy's hands, has just returned on parole, and claims to have seen a dispatch from the Adjutant-General of the Southern Confederacy, stating that McClellan had been defeated and his army cut to pieces. He believes it.... An Atlanta paper of

the 1st instant says the Confederates have won a decisive victory at Richmond. No Northern papers have been allowed to come into camp.[17]

Where did all of this leave the Third Ohio volunteers?

All remained quiet until August when the "bushwhackers" and snipers sneaked back. This time, they shot Union brigadier general Robert McCook on August 6, 1862.[18] According to Beatty, "As General Ammen and I were returning to camp this evening, we were joined by Colonel Fry, of General Buell's staff, who informed us that General Robert McCook was murdered, near Winchester, yesterday, by a small band of guerrillas. McCook was unwell, riding in an ambulance some distance in advance of the column; while stopping in front of a farm-house to make some enquiry, the guerrillas made a sudden dash, the escort fled, and McCook was killed while lying in the ambulance defenseless."[19] McCook was part of the famous "Fighting McCooks." Fifteen members of the family fought for the Union in the Civil War. Six of them became generals.[20]

Perryville, Kentucky, became a clash between Don Carlos Buell's Army of the Ohio against Braxton Bragg's Army of Mississippi. The Third Ohio Infantry Regiment was literally caught in the middle of the two armies. The battle for control of Kentucky was significant, in part because the objective was no longer a fight for control of a capital city, river or railroad. By 1862, Kentucky became a fight to capture or kill an army. Ulysses Grant eventually convinced Lincoln that to win this war, many men on the other side had to die. Capturing their capital city still left men to continue the fight. The infrastructure could stay, but the men had to die. The fight for Kentucky began as a game of "cat and mouse" between Buell and Bragg. The game was played from Alabama to Tennessee and into Kentucky by August 1862. The Army of the Ohio, however, was chasing an army with two heads. One head belonged to Braxton Bragg and the other to Edmund Kirby Smith. The two did not communicate very well and often took direction straight from Jefferson Davis, not the Confederate war department.[21] In August 1862, however, infrastructure was still a prime target. Both Smith and Bragg were racing to capture Louisville, Kentucky. The city sat right on the Ohio River and had important railroad bridges over the river into Indiana.

Control of the Ohio River was also important because it gave Bragg access to Union training camps and staging areas in southern Ohio. This was where the Third trained and entered Virginia in 1861. Louisville was a prize that both armies sought. By August 10, rumors started flying that a Confederate regiment was near the Third camp at Huntsville. At 2:00 p.m., one company of infantry and five companies of cavalry were sent out to confirm the rumors. They returned empty-handed. By August 29, the regiment was ordered to march for Decherd, Tennessee. General Buell took the lead. Unfortunately for the Army of the Ohio, Buell was not popular with either his men or the politicians who gave him the job. Beatty referred to him as "cold, smooth-toned, silent."[22] Upon reaching Decherd, Lieutenant Stephen Carpenter took the Third Ohio to Stevenson for provisions and local intelligence. On the way back to camp, they were surprised by snipers. The only casualties, however, were one dead bushwhacker and one captured horse. They reported that everything was scarce in this area. Although there was no whiskey, there was a good supply of dust and foul air from the sweat of hundreds of pack mules. By September, the Third Ohio was on the move again. Both armies were headed for Louisville. This would make a good supply base for anyone operating in Kentucky.

Major General Don Carlos Buell was considered a cool and aloof man. He did not associate with his men, and the officers generally found him hard to get to know. He developed an excellent plan at Perryville by convincing Bragg to divide his forces. Ironically, this forced Bragg to strike first and strike hard with devastating effect (Library of Congress).

By September 7, the Third had crossed the line into Kentucky. After Shiloh, east Tennessee appeared to be safe.[23] That was important because the border of Tennessee touched most of the Deep South. If the Union could hold the state, Tennessee could launch armies into Missouri, Arkansas, Mississippi, Alabama, Georgia and North Carolina. Tennessee was worth its weight in blood. Kentucky lay to the north. As a border state, it was also important for many reasons. Jefferson Davis hoped to recruit more men for his army from Kentucky. He knew it would be difficult because Kentucky was more Union than he hoped. Davis also anticipated that its border with the Ohio River would help in regaining control of the entire western theater of war. This is where the Third Ohio was headed:

- September 7—Edgefield, Kentucky (Gee's Tavern)
- September 9—Sharp's Branch, Kentucky (near Franklin, Kentucky)
- September 10—Sinking Springs, Kentucky
- September 11—Bowling Green, Kentucky
- September 16—Barren River (camped here)
- September 17—Dripping Springs, Kentucky
- September 18—Prewitt's Knob, Kentucky
- September 19—Horse Well, Kentucky
- September 21-22—Munfordville, Kentucky
- September 23—Nolin, Kentucky
- September 24—Burlington (Bloomington, Kentucky)
- September 25—Cross Salt River at 2:00 a.m.
- September 26–October 3—Louisville, Kentucky

By the end of September, the Third was in Louisville, Kentucky. Getting there wasn't easy. A base was established south of Louisville in Munfordville. The town was critical because it was a station on the Louisville-Nashville railroad line. The Union base was commanded by Colonel John T. Wilder. It was here that the first shots of Perryville were fired. By September 13, Brigadier General Lovell Rousseau believed that Munfordville was in danger. He wired Buell staff officer J.B. Fry, "May I suggest that the forces at Louisville be moved rapidly down on the railroad to Elizabethtown or by mouth of the Salt River, and aid in saving Munfordville and help in the fight that must take place in a few days."[24] In many ways, Munfordville was the last of the "gallant" contests of the Civil War. Although the blood and death of Shiloh were not forgotten, Gettysburg was not even a hint yet for "Bobby Lee." In Munfordville, John Wilder was opposed by Confederate general James R. Chalmers who was impulsive and willing to act without orders from his commander, Braxton Bragg. By contrast to Chalmers, one historian considers Wilder to have "intelligence, imagination, mechanical knowledge and topographical intuition."[25] Nevertheless, Wilder surrendered to Braxton Bragg on September 17, 1862. What happened and how did this impact the Third Ohio? The fight at Munfordville was chaotic. At one point, Chalmers' men got ahead of their own artillery and were shot in the back by the guns of Confederate colonel John S. Scott. To make matters worse, Chalmers was forced to ask Wilder for his extra shovels so he could bury his own dead. In the end, however, Wilder was outnumbered and forced to surrender. In doing so, Bragg captured 4,000 Union troops, 5,000 small arms as well as horses and the mules needed to pull artillery and haul supplies. Bragg paroled the men but left for Perryville after burning the bridge over the Green

River after him. For the Third Ohio, this meant that Kentucky was not "western" Virginia. Kentucky would be a battle, not a skirmish. Still, Lincoln was determined to hold on to his "home" state.

Part of the president's plan involved keeping that state as neutral as possible. The strategy was to first take and hold Louisville. Finally, Buell beat Bragg to the prize, but that was it. Communication between Henry Halleck and many other commanders in the field clearly indicate that the administration believed that Buell had squandered too many opportunities to catch and defeat Braxton Bragg before reaching Louisville. Lincoln was frustrated and sent a message relieving Buell and putting George Thomas in his place. Halleck's aide-de-camp, J.C. McKibbin, took the following message to Buell:[26]

Washington, September 24, 1862

Col. J.C. McKibbin, *aide-de-camp*:

Colonel: As the bearer of the accompanying dispatches you will proceed by the most practicable route to the army of General Buell in the field. The secretary of war directs that if General Buell should be found in the presence of the enemy preparing to fight a battle, or if he should have gained a victory, or if General Thomas should be separated from him so as to not be able to enter upon the command of the troops operating against the enemy, these dispatches will not be delivered.... If while *en route* to General Buell you should ascertain that either of these contingencies will have occurred you will telegraph results and await orders. If neither of these events should occur you will present the dispatches to both General Buell and General Thomas and return to these headquarters. The mission is strictly confidential and the instructions or object of your visit will not be communicated to anyone. If by any accident you should fall into the hands of the enemy you will destroy your dispatches.

Very Respectfully, your obedient servant,
H.W. Halleck,
General-in-Chief

Thomas was caught in the middle and very reluctant to push Buell out. Unfortunately, things only got more confusing. If Buell was chasing Bragg and planning to engage him in battle, Halleck intended that the note not be delivered. McKibbin misunderstood the instructions, and Buell got the message, just before the Battle of Perryville. Subsequent notes to Buell finally restored him to command. The damage may have been done, however. Already accused of being slow, Lincoln's aborted solution reduced Buell to a crawl.

Regrettably, the regular army was an "old boys' club" where seniority and experience controlled promotion. Senior commanders were very reluctant to step on another man's toes. Lincoln knew this and generally accepted a "culture" that often worked against him and the Union war effort.²⁷ Nevertheless, Buell got the message. By October 3, the Ohio regiment was in Taylorsville, Kentucky, but the march was hard. According to Beatty, "Our first day's march out of Louisville was disagreeable beyond precedent. The boys had been full of whisky for three days, and fell out of the ranks by scores. The road for sixteen miles was lined with stragglers. The new men bore the march badly. Rain fell yesterday afternoon and during the night; I awoke at three o'clock this morning to find myself lying in a puddle of water."²⁸

A battle for a critical border state was about to take place. Tactically, what was happening? Who were the key players and what was their thinking? Don Carlos Buell faced off against Braxton Bragg. Ulysses Grant thought that Bragg was "a remarkably intelligent and well-informed man … who had an irascible temper and was naturally disputatious."²⁹ The men of the Third Ohio didn't think much of Buell either. From a Cincinnati journalist watching Buell ride through Elizabethtown: "His dress was that of a brigadier, not that of a major-general. He wore a shabby straw hat, dusty coat, and had neither belt, sash or sword about him…. Though accompanied by his staff, he was not engaged in conversation with any of them, but rode silently and slowly along, noticing what transpired around him…. Buell is, certainly the most reserved, distant and most unsociable of all the generals in the army. He never has a word of cheer for his men or his officers, and in turn his subordinates care little for him save to obey his orders, as machinery works in response to the bidding of the mechanic."³⁰ Colonel John Beatty may have regarded Buell as "cold" and not sufficiently

Confederate general Braxton Bragg was often thought of as the most hated man in the Confederate army. He was a West Point graduate, intelligent but prone to arguing with anyone within arm's reach, including his commanding officers. He was a wealthy man through marriage but died young at the age of 59 in 1876 (Library of Congress).

aggressive, but the general still had a good plan. He had devised a feint to separate Kirby Smith from Bragg. Don Carlos Buell made a smart tactical move when he sent part of his force under General Joshua Sill to hold Kirby Smith in Frankfort, Kentucky. "Buell's feint toward Frankfort, led by Brigadier General Joshua Sill's division ... succeeded admirably. Bragg, being directly confronted, considered this the major Federal effort ... and underestimated the three corps column moving down towards Bardstown."[31] Smith was in Frankfort for the inauguration of Governor Richard Hawes.[32] The hope was that Bragg would believe that Sill was the main body of Buell's army. It worked. Bragg's army was now split. Every textbook on tactics at the time warned against this. Bragg was taking a big risk. Sill confirmed the diversion at Frankfort in his telegram to Washington: "On Friday evening and Saturday morning (October 3 and 4th) the rebels had massed at Frankfort an army estimated at from 12,000 to 20,000. They inaugurated Richard Hawes as Governor at 12 pm. yesterday; Bragg, Smith, Marshall, Heath and Stevenson were there."[33] In contrast, Buell was successful in getting all of his scattered divisions to come together at the same place and at the same time. Buell complained that his army got a late start due to the telegram firing him but later reinstating him. Nevertheless, he told Halleck, "The army march on the 1st ultimo (August) in five columns. The left moved toward Frankfort, to hold in check the force of the enemy which still remained at or near that place."[34]

By early October, the Third Ohio was in Louisville. After forced marches, the men of the Third Ohio took full advantage of the Kentucky whiskey that was available everywhere. Later that day, they left for Taylorsville. The march was difficult because three days of drinking made for a difficult journey. Men often fell out of rank to sleep. Beatty and Keifer had their hands full running after stragglers. Soon after stopping for the night, the sky darkened and rain began to fall. A regiment full of hungover men who were soaking wet and miserable was not a hopeful beginning to what became one of the bloodiest campaigns of the war to date. The colonel in command, John Beatty, woke up at 3:00 a.m. in a muddy puddle. Restless, wet and bored, two men from Captain William Rossman's Company F started wrestling to pass the time. A friendly wrestling match soon turned deadly when one man threw the other who landed on his head and died. After a quick burial, the regiment marched on to Bloomfield. Upon arrival, however, the Third quickly struggled to get Cyrus Loomis' 12-pound battery in place to shell an unexpected rebel force hiding in the woods near town. The woods were scourged with canister shot. Most of the rebels ran away, but a few prisoners were taken. At this point, more

4. Bushwhackers and Scorched Earth

marching and less fighting turned some of the men in the Army of the Ohio against Buell. Some referred to him as a traitor. Most of the men and officers preferred General George Thomas. Regardless of who was in command, the Third was looking for a fight. They were about to get their wish.

By October 7, the regiment was in Mackville where they camped for the night. Everyone felt secure because Bragg had split his forces, and Buell now commanded an army of 55,000 men, almost four times the size of Bragg's. Unfortunately, Buell fell from his horse on the 7th and was forced to quarter himself almost three miles away from the intended battlefield. Nevertheless, the Union attack was planned by October 9. Buell was surprised, therefore, when Bragg launched an unexpected attack on Buell's far-left flank on October 8. That left flank was held by Major General Alexander McCook. This impacted the Third Ohio for several reasons. First, McCook's corps contained the division commanded by Lovell Rousseau. This division included the 17th Brigade of which the Third Ohio was now a part. More significant, however, were the opinions of Colonels Beatty and Garfield. Beatty commented that McCook was "a chucklehead ... deficient in the upper story.... He should not be permitted to retain control of the Corps for a single hour."[35] Rosecrans had come to lean heavily on the advice and support of his adjutant, James A. Garfield, but in this instance, the general held firm. McCook remained in place.

Just before the battle, the men from the Third joked about who might oppose them in battle when they reached Perryville. According to brigade commander Colonel John Beatty, "Robt. E. Lee was the great man of the rebel army in West Virginia. The

Simon Bolivar Buckner was a Confederate major general and 30th governor of Kentucky. In 1862, he surrendered Fort Donelson to Ulysses Grant. He later served as adjutant to Edmund Kirby Smith. The Third Ohio considered Buckner an easier opponent than Lee (Library of Congress).

boys all talked about Lee, and told how they would pink him if opportunity offered. But Simon Bolivar Buckner is the man here on whom they all threaten to fall violently. There are certainly a hundred soldiers in the Third, each one of whom swears every day that he would whip Simon Bolivar Buckner quicker than a wink if he dared present himself. Simon is in danger."[36] Ironically, the man the Third Ohio faced on the morning of October 8, 1862, was a division commanded by Simon Bolivar Buckner.[37]

On October 7, the night before the battle, the fight had already begun. Skirmishing had broken out between Brigadier General James Gilbert's Third Corps and the forces of Confederate general Leonidas Polk.[38] Beatty and his men could already hear the boom of cannon in the distance. Despite the recent rain, most of the rivers and streams in the area were still dry or low on water. Men and horses were thirsty. Their scouts told them that Doctor's Creek and the Chaplin River were full. The problem was, however, that the creeks ran through the town from which the Third could hear the roar and rumble of rebel guns. Perryville was a short march. The field report filed by the brigade commander, William Lytle, describes what happened on the morning of October 8, 1862:

> On Our arrival on the field at 10:30 a.m. a section or more of artillery was thrown forward and opened fire.... My orders being imperative, however, to march I sent an order to Lieutenant-Colonel Burke, commanding to fall in the rear of my brigade, and directed Colonel Beatty, with his regiment (Third Ohio Infantry), to take the advance.
> Colonel W.H. Lytle, commander 17th Brigade, Lovell Rousseau's Third Division, Army of the Ohio[39]

The Third was looking for a fight and now they had one. No more drinking and no more disrespect.

This was a time for support.

5

Men of Iron

No useless coffin inclosed his breast;
Not in sheet or in shroud we wound him,
But he lay like a warrior taking his rest,
With his martial cloak around him.
Slowly and sadly we laid him down
From the field of his fame fresh and gory;
We carved not a line, we raised not a stone,
But left him alone with his glory.

—Colonel John Beatty diary, Interring the
dead after Perryville, October 8, 1862

All hell broke loose, and Parrott guns with canister were the tactical choice of the day.[1]

At the battle of Perryville, October 8, 1862, it is ironic that both Confederate general Braxton Bragg and Union general Don Carlos Buell had been taught by the same tactician from the same textbook. One of the best-read volumes on army tactics in 1862 was written by Confederate lieutenant general William Hardee, *Rifle and Light Infantry Tactics*.[2] On that warm and overcast morning of October 8, the Third Ohio formed a line of battle directly opposite the forces of Hardee himself. The further irony is that the Third Ohio had also been taught tactics from Hardee's book. The men from Ohio were raw recruits who knew little about the manual of arms.[3] The officers of the Third found themselves teaching their men tactical basics. According to Beatty,

> Hardee for a month or more was a book of impenetrable mysteries. The words conveyed no idea to my mind, and the movements described were utterly beyond my comprehension; but now the whole thing comes almost without study. Had the third sergeants in my school to-night. Am getting to be a pretty good teacher. General Mitchell gave the officers a very interesting lecture this evening. The whole division has become a school. Had five lieutenants before me. Lesson: grand guards and other outposts. The General summoned the officers of his division about him and went through the form of sending

out advanced guard, posting picket, grand guards, outposts, and sentinels. During these exercises we rode fifteen or twenty miles, and listened to at least twenty speeches. My horse was very gay, and I had the pleasure of running many races. I learned something, and am learning a little each day. Had the lieutenants in my school again to-night. Lesson: detachments, reconnaissance, partisans, and flankers.[4]

One of the most critical lessons advocated by Hardee was to avoid splitting forces while engaged in an attack on the enemy. On October 8, Braxton Bragg violated this sacred proverb by falling for Buell's ruse of sending Joshua Sill to Frankfort, thus keeping Edmund Kirby Smith detached from Bragg's already small force on the Chaplin River at Perryville.[5] Hardee warned Bragg in a personal note just before the battle, "Permit me, from the friendly relations so long existing

Confederate general William Hardee was camped in Perryville, Kentucky, while Braxton Bragg was in Versailles. Bragg believed that he would be receiving the fight there, but Hardee convinced him that Perryville would be the flash point (Library of Congress).

between us, to write you plainly. Do not scatter your forces. There is one rule in our profession which should never be forgotten; it is to throw the masses of your troops on the fractions of the enemy.... Strike with your whole strength to the right then to the left. I could not sleep quietly tonight without giving expression to these views."[6] Ironically, while Bragg was dividing his forces, Buell had his massive Army of the Ohio intact and spread out over a vast six-mile front. Believing that he had the larger force, Buell spread his army out to force Bragg to spread himself thin to avoid a flanking action. This should have been a decisive victory for the Army of the Ohio. Unfortunately, Buell unwittingly failed to engage the full force of his 55,000 men. The men of the Third Ohio fought hard and did their part but were actually outflanked by Bragg. Soon, North and South would learn some hard lessons from Hardee's *Rifle and Light Infantry Tactics*.

At 2:20 a.m. on the 8th, the Third Ohio Volunteer Infantry Regiment started the ten-mile march to Perryville. John Beatty recalled what happened next:

> Started in the early morning toward Perryville. The occasional boom of guns at the front notified us that the enemy was not far distant. A little later the rattle of musketry mingled with the roar of artillery, and we knew the vanguard was having lively work. The boys marched well and were in high spirits. At ten o'clock we were hastened forward and placed in battle line on the left of the Maxville [sic] and Perryville road; the cavalry in our front appeared to be seriously engaged, and every eye peered eagerly through the woods to catch a glimpse of the enemy. But in a little while the firing ceased, and with a feeling of disappointment the boys lounged about on the ground and logs awaiting further orders. They came very soon. At 11 a.m. the Third was directed to take the head of the column and move forward. We anticipated no danger, for Rousseau and his staff were in advance of us, followed by Lytle and his staff. The regiment was marching by the flank, and had proceeded to the brow of the hill overlooking a branch of the Chaplin river, and was about to descend into the valley, when the enemy's artillery opened in front with great fury. Rousseau and his staff wheeled suddenly out of the road to the left, accompanied by Lytle. After a moment spent by them in consultation, I was ordered to countermarch my regiment to the bottom of the hill we had just ascended, and file off to the right of the road.[7]

The quiet morning was soon interrupted again by the distant sound of artillery. It was now 10:30 a.m., and the Third came to a halt opposite the division commanded by Confederate brigadier general James Gilbert. They were formed approximately 100 yards away, but the sight of them gave the men of the Third some comfort. If there was trouble, help was close. At this point, McCook and Rousseau rode to the front to determine where to form a line of battle. Seeing rebels in the woods ahead of them, Rousseau ordered Cyrus Loomis to bring up two of his Parrott guns and shell the woods. At only 5 degrees elevation, both guns were loaded with canister. When they roared into action, the canister balls tore through trees and bushes like a giant harvester cutting down an early fall crop. When the guns stopped after two hours, the trees were gone and so were the rebels.

Colonel William H. Lytle was in command of the 17th brigade of which the Third Ohio was a part.[8] In his field report, Lytle confirmed Loomis' gun battle. He reported what happened at noon on October 8, 1862:

In compliance with orders about 12 o'clock, I resumed the march, the 3rd Ohio having the right. The impression at the time seemed to be that the enemy had retired. My column was in motion, as directed, when my attention was directed to a scattering fire on the left of the road. It immediately struck me that it proceeded from the skirmishers of the 10th Ohio, which, as I have said, had not yet reported. Riding up to the eminence where our artillery had been posted in the morning, commanding a ravine, an officer of my staff approached me and said he discovered the enemy on the opposite side of the ravine. With my glass I saw heavy masses of rebels apparently deploying into line of battle. The morning was bright and clear. General Rousseau directed me to form line of battle immediately. My column, then in motion and descending the hill into the ravine, was marched by the right-about, and the order was complied with.... We had an artillery duel which lasted perhaps two hours.[9]

Confirmed further by Rousseau in his field report, "I then ordered up Loomis with two of his Parrott guns, and he shelled the woods, the enemy now and then appearing, until finally he was no longer to be seen."[10]

Rousseau took advantage of the lull in fighting to send his brigades down to the Chaplin River to get water. Unfortunately, this was only a rebel ploy to lure the Union troops into the open. As soon as the men from the Third and the other brigades reached the creek, the rebel forces came out and opened fire. Getting water was a wasted effort because when the men got to the creek, it was dry. Private Joseph W. Laybourne, Company D of the Third Ohio, commented, "We had marched ten miles without finding water, and formed line of battle at least a half mile from the creek.... I know that many lay on the field two or three days without water."[11] Without water, and rebel skirmishers reloading, the regiments fell back, and Loomis rammed more spherical case down the barrel of his Parrott guns. The two guns quickly settled the matter. In frustration, Buckner's division assembled cavalry, infantry, and artillery units to charge into the brigades of Lytle and Colonel Leonard A. Harris. According to Rousseau's report, "I then sent an order to Colonel Lytle to form his brigade on the right in good position, and galloped back to place Harris' brigade in position to resist the advance of the enemy ... which was being made in that direction in great force of cavalry, infantry and artillery."[12]

With Buckner's men advancing in large numbers, the men of the 10th Division and the 33rd Brigade were in jeopardy. The 10th was commanded by Brigadier General James S. Jackson and the 33rd by Brigadier General William R. Terrill. The First Corps commander, Alexander McCook, was quickly put at a disadvantage by the death of both Jackson and Terrill. In McCook's report, "The attack on my line now became general. My attention was directed principally to the left, where the attack was most fiercely made. I had no apprehension about my right, as it rested on Gilbert's left. A fierce attack being made on Terrill's brigade, General Jackson being killed at the first fire, this brigade in a few moments gave way in confusion."[13]

At this point, Loomis ran out of ammunition. It was 2:00 p.m. Without artillery support, the 17th Brigade and Third Ohio were in trouble. Nevertheless, if Buckner's division continued, someone had to stop them. The 10th Ohio was already on the crest of the hill watching enemy troops fire into what was left of the 33rd Brigade. They need help, so the Third Ohio was ordered out of the ravine and up the hill. The 15th Kentucky and 42nd Indiana were behind them in support, and the 88th Indiana was held in reserve. By 4:00 p.m., Buckner's men came out of the woods and started for the crest of the hill held by the Third and 10th Ohio Infantry. Almost immediately, Beatty's men knew they were outnumbered. More artillery was brought up and positioned near the Third. Loomis was in position again and had resupplied his battery with more canister. Artillery shelling from both sides was so intense that a barn next to the Third caught fire. Lytle remembered a scene of fierce battle and his wounding and capture:

> I remember that when a barn near the right of the 3rd Ohio was fired by the enemy's shells, the whole line was almost enveloped in smoke.... The 10th was nearly enveloped by the enemy and was obliged to fall back. A most destructive fire was poured on the regiment's front and from the flanks, and while endeavoring to cover its movement to the rear with skirmishers, I was wounded and captured.... It is my impression that after Harris was obliged to retire for want of ammunition, the attack of eight or ten regiments of the enemy were concentrated on my brigade, or rather on the three regiments—the 3rd Ohio, the Fifteenth Kentucky and 10th Ohio—which were the last to retire.[14]

Almost a quarter of a century later, the men of the Third remembered that barn which was owned by Henry Pierce Bottom. "Our headquarters on the field were at Squire Bottoms' house. It was around this house that the fiercest fighting of the battle took place. In the rear was located the barn that was fired by the rebel batteries as it was an obstruction to their view of the right of our regiment. Some of our dead had their legs and arms burned off here."[15] Bottom and his family were hiding in the house while the battle raged all around them outside. One member of the Third Ohio later remembered Bottom's youngest son, coming out of the house with his shotgun and threatening to shoot the men from the Third. However, there is no record of the little boy pulling the trigger. Presumably, someone from inside the house saw what was happening and ran to pull him back to safety. By this time, it was almost 4:00 p.m., and Buell had just gotten word that McCook's First Corps had been under attack all afternoon—without his knowledge. Within two hours, however, it began to get dark. The damage had been done, and Bragg decided to save his army for another day and retreat.

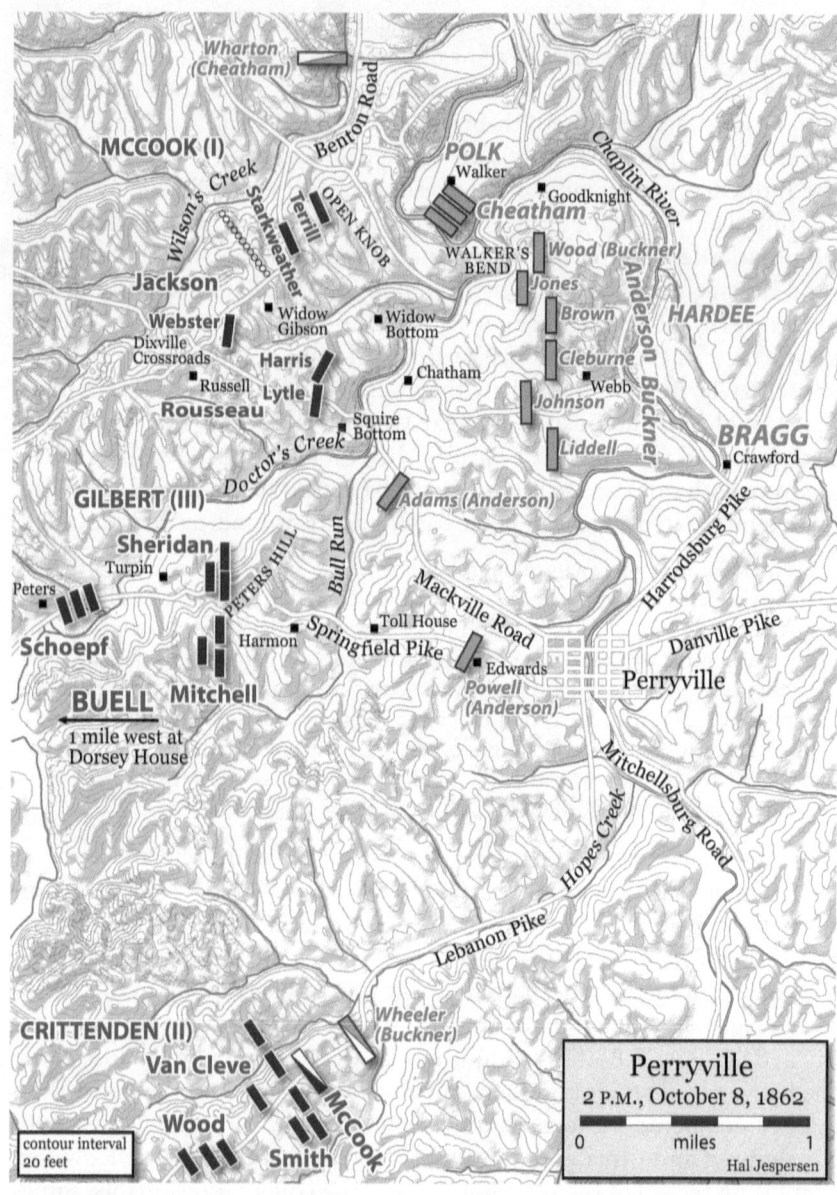

Perryville at 2:00 p.m. demonstrates that Lytle's brigade containing the Third Ohio was immediately opposite the main body of Braxton Bragg's forces. Just north of this position is the Bottom farm whose barn was shelled by Confederate artillery and caught fire. Men from the Third were positioned close to the barn in the afternoon of the 8th. Many were badly burned (map by Hal Jespersen, www.cwmaps.com).

5. Men of Iron

McCook's corps, which included Rousseau's division and the Third Ohio, took the full force of the fighting at Perryville that day. From the *Louisville Courier Journal*: "Gen. L.H. Rousseau's division received the enemy's first attack, and bore the brunt of the battle.... His entire division behaved with great gallantry, and to them more than to any other troops engaged is accorded the honor of repulsing the enemy."[16] For three hours, the batteries of Cyrus Loomis and Captain Peter Simonson roared with canister and shell until they almost overheated. One of the unanticipated problems with the lack of water was the inability to swab down the gun muzzle after every shot. This was necessary to ensure that heat and sparks from the previous discharge did not ignite the new powder charge while loading the gun for another round. David H. Chandler, part of an Indiana artillery battery fighting next to the Third Ohio, confirmed that after just a few shots, their gun muzzles got hot. They didn't have enough water to sponge the barrel. However, around 2:00 p.m., they halted because they could see the enemy advancing through a valley below the Chaplin Hills. Their guns could not be sighted at that lower elevation. For a few brief minutes, there was silence on the battlefield. Rebel forces were attempting to turn the right flank of Rousseau's division. The Third was ordered to climb to the top of the hill to be in a position to fire down on the advancing rebels. After reaching the crest of the hill, however, they were now exposed to artillery fire from rebel guns.

The shrapnel from the spherical shell of these guns tore off the limbs of any man standing below the impact. With the advancing enemy out of musket range, the Third was ordered to lie down in the grass and wait. Buckner's men were still there and getting closer. At this point, the Confederate forces were hidden by a large cornfield that stretched along the bottom of the ravine into which they had moved. Emerging from the cornfield, the Third now had a good shot at the enemy. The colonel commanding recalled,

> In this position, with the enemy's batteries pouring upon us a most destructive fire, the Third arose and delivered its first volley. For a time, I do not know how long thereafter, it seemed as if all hell had broken loose; the air was filled with hissing balls; shells were exploding continuously, and the noise of the guns was deafening; finally the barn on the right took fire, and the flames bursting from roof, windows, doors, and interstices between the logs, threw the right of the regiment into disorder; the confusion, however, was but temporary. The boys closed up to the left, steadied themselves on the colors, and stood bravely to the work. Nearly two hundred of my five hundred men now lay dead and wounded on the little strip of ground over which we fought.[17]

At this point, Colonel Curran Pope of the 15th Kentucky yelled to the men of the Third to come back down from the crest and let the 15th relieve them. By this time, the Third Ohio had fired so many volleys into the rebel ranks that Beatty agreed, and the regiment retired. This is confirmed by a Union veteran from an Indiana regiment that fought next to the Third Ohio. Private George Morgan Kirkpatrick recalled, "The Johnnies were coming right over toward us. They came up to the fence, where we were and before we were relieved, our whole regiment gave them a volley that stopped them until the other three regiments which were in our Brigade could get there. These were the 10th Ohio, 3rd Ohio and the 15th Kentucky, and they got back of us, and fought hard, but about half of them were left there, killed or wounded or captured, and we had to retreat, shooting all the time. Other troops came up and we fell back on a hill. It was so smokey [sic] that we could not see far, so we were ordered to charge down the hill."[18] Instead of charging down the hill, all three regiments retreated to allow fresh troops to take over. The field report filed by Brigadier General Lovell Rousseau adds confirmation: "Hearing of this condition of things, I galloped over to the right and found the brigade formed in line of battle, the right (the Fifteenth Kentucky Volunteers, Colonel Pope) resting on the hill at Clark's House, with Loomis' battery immediately in the rear on an eminence, the 10th Ohio, Lt. Col. Burke, and the Third Ohio, Colonel Beatty, on the left of the road. These regiments had, without support, struggled hard to hold their line of battle for several hours, and were only forced to retire after immense loss and the movements of the enemy above referred to."[19]

Retreat encouraged the rebels to immediately increase their fire. The 15th suffered many losses, including Pope who was wounded in the arm. The officers of both regiments quickly discussed the situation and decided to reform the line of battle with both regiments parallel to each other. While this was happening, the rebel forces believed that both Union regiments were continuing their retreat. This encouraged them to charge. Seeing this, the Third Ohio was ordered to fix bayonets and advance toward the approaching enemy. Years later, the Third reunion minutes reflected, "Just as the 15th Kentucky Volunteer Infantry Regiment came to relieve us, we fixed our bayonets, without orders, and in another minute we would have been down among the Johnnies in a charge, hopeless perhaps, but soldiers like the 3 O.V.I. [Ohio Voluntary Infantry] could not stand long and see their comrades shot down around us without using the only weapon we had left. We would have gone orders or no orders."[20] Just then, the men of the Third heard from Lieutenant Grover of Colonel Lytle's staff to retire. Under cover of the hill, the Third found an ammunition wagon and filled their cartridge boxes. The 17th Brigade commander, William H. Lytle, had been wounded and taken prisoner during the battle. As a result, Colonel Beatty sought his orders from the Ninth Brigade commander, Colonel

Leonard Harris. Before Harris could be found, the battlefield became slowly quiet. The days were shorter in early October, and it was already dark. The men of the Third Ohio camped for the night and waited for battle the next day. Looking around at his men, Beatty was saddened to see so few were left. The Third went into battle at half-strength. They returned with half of that number. According to Beatty, "We bivouacked in a corn-field. The regiment had grown suddenly small. It was a sorry night for us indeed. Every company had its long list of killed, wounded, and missing. Over two hundred were gone. Nearly two hundred, we felt quite sure, had fallen dead or disabled on the field. Many eyes were in tears, and many hearts were bleeding for lost comrades and dear friends."[21] Knowing he had to bury "obstinate devils" who were difficult to discipline but who fought with stubborn courage and bravery, Beatty knew their sacrifices were not in vain. Just then, General Rousseau rode up to the Third in the darkness and let everyone know that "soldiers of the Third Ohio, you stood in that withering fire like men of iron." It was still dangerous because rebel regiments were also camped nearby. In the darkness, the Third could hear musket fire and see the flash of light that comes from enemy pickets. Men on both sides tried to sleep but found it difficult due to the constant whistle of bullets over their heads. Before sunup, however, the whistling noise had stopped, and the enemy camps were empty. No smoke or noise except for the cries of wounded and dying men on the crest of the hill overlooking the Chaplin River.

The men of the Third woke to the sound of shovels digging trenches, not holes. Men were already on the crest of the hill burying the dead. There were too many, however, for an individual grave for each man. Believing that they would soon be chasing after Bragg's army, the men of the Third dug a long trench to save time. The dead were lowered into the ditch and placed neatly side by side.[22] Digging graves was always a difficult job. The day after Perryville, the men of the Third, as well as other regiments, cried as they shoveled dirt and threw rocks. Most of the Confederate dead and dying were left unburied on the field. With crows and buzzards already swarming over the bodies, Henry Bottom finally dug two large pits on his property and dumped all of the rebel bodies into it. They were the lucky ones because the Third found the bodies of several hundred rebel infantry in the woods beyond musket range. Gently nudging the dead with the end of a boot sometimes resulted in an unexpected moan. Unfortunately, some of Hardee's men survived Loomis' canister. Beatty directed the men of the Third to help as many as possible to the doctors and surgeons.

By October 13, the Third Ohio had left Perryville and was camped near Harrodsburg, Kentucky. Rain began to fall, and the regiment had no tents. Most of the Third were sick of learning the manual of arms and the textbook drills they were forced to practice as Beatty and his officers read to them from the Confederate manual on tactics. The action at Perryville changed all of that. According to Beatty,

> Many, perhaps most, of the boys of the regiment disliked me thoroughly. They thought me too strict, too rigid in the enforcement of orders; but now they are, without exception, my fast friends. During the battle of Chaplin Hills (Perryville), while the enemy's artillery was playing upon us with terrible effect, I ordered them to lie down. The shot, shell, and canister came thick as hail, hissing, exploding, and tearing up the ground around us. There was a universal cry from the boys that I should lie down also; but I continued to walk up and down the line, watching the approaching enemy, and replied to their entreaties, "No; it is my time to stand guard now, and I will not lie down."[23] Meeting Captain Loomis yesterday, he said: "Do you know you captured a regiment at Chaplin Hills?" "I do not." "Yes, you captured the Third. You have not a man now who wouldn't die for you." I have been too much occupied of late to record even the most interesting and important events. I should like to preserve the names of the private soldiers who behaved like heroes in the battle; but I have only time to mention the fact that our colors changed hands seven times during the engagement. Six of our color bearers were either killed or wounded, and as the sixth man was falling, a soldier of Company C, named David C. Walker, a boyish fellow, whose cheeks were ruddy as a girl's, and who had lost his hat in the fight, sprang forward, caught the falling flag, then stepping out in front of the regiment, waved it triumphantly, and carried it to the end of the battle. On the next morning I made him color bearer, and undertook to thank him for his gallantry, but my eyes filled and voice choked, and I was unable to articulate a word. He understood me, doubtless.[24]

In General Alexander McCook's final report on the battle at Perryville, he praises the fighting done by Lovell Rousseau's division, which included the Third Ohio Volunteers. McCook concluded his report, "Thus ends my account of the part taken in the battle of Chaplin Hills by my corps, the bloodiest battle of modern times for the number of troops engaged on our side.... The battle was principally fought by Rousseau's division, and if there are or ever were better soldiers than the old soldiers engaged, I have neither seen nor read of them."[25] Braxton Bragg also confirmed the ferocity of the battle in his report of October 12, 1862, to Confederate assistant adjutant General George W. Brent. His report confirmed, "For the time engaged, it was the severest and most desperately contested engagement within my knowledge.... The ground was literally covered with [Buell's] dead and wounded. In such a contest, our own loss was necessarily severe."[26]

What had happened at Perryville became the core of testimony against General Don Carlos Buell for allowing McCook to be attacked without help and finally allowing Bragg and his army to get away without effective pursuit. McCook, Rousseau and the Third Ohio fought the entire right wing of the Army of Tennessee for most of the day. They received little to no support from General Buell who had his entire army with him and greatly outnumbered Bragg and his forces. What happened? Years later, a court of inquiry was set up to answer that specific question. The *Louisville Courier* summed up the mood in Kentucky as well as Washington, however. They bitterly noted that Bragg's entire force was allowed to attack McCook's single corps without support. When reinforcements finally came at the end of the day, Bragg had successfully escaped with his army intact. Where was Buell and why didn't he overtake Bragg and defeat him? On October 13, 1862, the *Courier* reported, "In his attack on General McCook's Corps on Wednesday ... he hurled his army on a single column of our forces unsupported by the rest.... We have no explanation of the reason why, after the retreat of the rebels the whole of Thursday was permitted to pass without our following up our victory by attacking them." On the 15th, the *Louisville Courier* reflected the Union sentiment expressed by many in Kentucky by 1862: "The rebels came in as braggarts and blusterers, and they flee as sneaks and cowards.... Buell has now an opportunity of redeeming Kentucky and rendering a mighty service to his country."

Braxton Bragg invaded Kentucky for several reasons. One of those was the assurance he received from Kirby Smith that there was much Confederate sentiment in Kentucky. Smith bragged that their small army would soon equal the Army of Ohio because loyal Kentuckians would rally to their side. Smith was wrong. When writing to his wife, Bragg complained, "Why then should I stay with my handful of brave Southern men to fight for cowards who skulked about in the dark to say to us, 'we are with you. Only whip these fellows out of our country and let us see you can protect us, and we will join you."[27] The day before the battle, General Buell was thrown from his horse and injured. He set up headquarters three miles from the center of Perryville and made plans to attack Bragg the next day. Water continued to be a problem, however. Because the men had so little, Buell refused to allow a physician to clean his leg wound with water. The gash festered but did not appear to impact Buell's ability to organize and plan for battle. Unfortunately, those divisions he had worked so hard to bring together at Perryville were late in forming an effective line of battle because some were still looking for water. Men needed water to survive the heat, and the mules needed water to pull the heavy artillery caissons and guns that were so effective during the fight. As a result, Buell put off his planned attack to the 9th. With Kirby Smith now on the move from Frankfort but not yet at Perryville, Bragg decided to surprise Buell and launch his own attack on the 8th. Hopefully, Smith would arrive and help with the assault.

After rebel forces pounded Alexander McCook's men and then retreated with their army intact, Don Carlos Buell wrote to General-in-Chief Henry Halleck to explain what went wrong. This communication was brief, but the subsequent Board of Inquiry in Perryville was lengthy. Buell explained, "The left column, under General McCook, came up on the Mackville Road about 10 o'clock yesterday, the 8th. It was ordered into position to attack, and a strong reconnaissance directed. At 4 o'clock I received a request from General McCook for re-enforcements and heard with astonishment that the left had been seriously engaged for several hours, and that the right and left of that corps were being turned and severely pressed."[28]

Buell had no idea that one division from his First Corps had been under heavy attack since early in the morning. How did Buell explain this? What happened? He outnumbered Bragg almost four-to-one, yet Bragg was in control during most of the battle. Finger-pointing began immediately. In November, Secretary of War Edwin Stanton wrote to General-in-Chief Henry Halleck and demanded,

> General: You will please organize a Military Commission to inquire into and report upon the operations of the forces under command of Major-General Buell, in the states of Tennessee and Kentucky, and particularly in reference to General Buell suffering the state of Kentucky to be invaded by the rebel forces under General Bragg, and in his failing to relieve Munfordville and suffering it to be captured; also in reference to the battle in Perryville and General Buell's conduct during that battle, and afterward suffering the rebel forces to escape from Kentucky without loss or capture.[29]

Ironically, part of the problem lay in the fact that the Army of the Ohio was much larger than the Army of Mississippi. General Buell complained that an army this size required a big quartermaster base and a long supply line from that base out to the battle front. To attack Bragg at Perryville, Louisville needed to be heavily supplied. In addition, Perryville was 70 miles away from the base and thus required a long supply train. That train ultimately consumed 40 miles and became an easy target for Morgan and other rebel cavalry raiders. However, it was later determined that Buell had 20 days' rations on hand for his men. The diary kept by John Beatty of the Third Ohio indicates that the regiment was well fed. The Third Ohio had so many chickens that they started to teach them to fight. Just before Perryville, Beatty commented, "The boys have a great many game chickens. Not long ago Company G, of the Third, and Company G, of the Tenth, had a rooster fight, the stakes being fifteen dollars a side. After numerous attacks, retreats, charges, and counter-charges, the Tenth rooster succumbed like a hero, and the other was carried in triumph from the field."[30] Halleck told the Buell inquiry that in addition to a supply line that was unnecessarily long, he should have supplied his men with local provisions. Later, Halleck wrote the inquiry committee, "The fault here as elsewhere was having too large supply trains and in not living more upon the country. He was frequently urged to subsist his troops in this manner."[31] In this regard, Colonel Beatty of the Third Ohio was in agreement. He noted in his diary,

> If we make the country through which we pass furnish supplies to our army, the inhabitants will have less to furnish our enemies. The surplus products of the country should be gathered into the Federal granaries, so that they could not, by possibility, go to feed the rebels. The loyal and innocent might occasionally and for the present suffer, but peace when once established would afford ample opportunity to investigate and repay these sufferers. Shall we continue to protect the property of our enemies, and lose the lives of our friends? It is said that it is hard to deprive men of their horses, cattle, grain, simply because they differ from us in opinion; but is it not harder still to deprive men of their lives for the same reason? The opinions from which we differ in this instance are treasonable.[32]

The battle at Perryville was significant for many reasons. For the Third Ohio, this was the first serious test of their courage under fire. By all accounts, it was Lovell Rousseau's division that took the full force of the rebel attack. The Third suffered the capture of their brigade commander, William Lytle. This was fortuitous for the Third because Lieutenant Colonel John Beatty now assumed command. Beatty and the Third had experienced a complicated relationship up to this point. After Perryville, however, the regiment and their brigade commander were much better coordinated. In addition, Braxton Bragg and the rebel forces in the west learned that Kentucky was no friend of the Confederacy. As a result, Bragg left and went looking for better acquaintances in Tennessee. East Tennessee was Union, but what about Central and West Tennessee?

Thirty years after the Battle of Perryville, the Third Ohio met for their 17th annual reunion. The minutes of that meeting reveal the sacrifice made by the Third on October 8, 1862:

> We know not why Buell allowed Bragg's army to escape, but we know that we took 42 men in the fight and that 31 of them were killed or wounded. We know that at the colors five men brave and true were shot to death and that six men, equally brave and equally true, lost arms or legs or were terribly wounded while holding aloft that shot torn banner. And here, perhaps one of the most dramatic events of the war occurred. Eleven men had fallen at the colors. Sergeant Perry, a magnificent young man of Company D, was holding them aloft when a shell tore off his right arm. He falls and through the smoke of conflict, din of battle and shrieks and groans of the wounded, our flag is seen fluttering to the ground. But there was an unknown hero close by. Gilbert Walker, a blue-eyed boy of sixteen, a member of Company C, the color company saw the

flag as it fell with Sergeant Perry, rushed to it, and hatless, with his long, yellow hair streaming in the wind, he snatched the colors and waved them in defiance at the enemy.[33]

The following year, 1893, Mary Imbrie, the daughter of Captain James Imbrie, read a poem about Perryville to the surviving members of the regiment. It looked ahead to a time when the war would be over.

>Little they think of their bravery, or the
>Battle they have won
>For the Glorious Queen of Liberty; that
>Very day as the sun
>Cast his last look on the hill, Freedom was
>Setting the stars in her crown;
>And one bright star that illumed her
>Brow, one beam of fame renowned,
>Was the Gallant Third Ohio. If this one
>Star of its glory
>Had come short Oh,
>Where the perfect
>Blending light of Freedom's Glory?
>And now brave heart, when thou art weary,
>Freedom's hand remembers thee
>And when this life's war cloud passes,
>Never more to be,
>In the realm of peace eternal, there will
>Be a crown for thee.[34]

By the end of October 1862, the Third knew that Bragg was in Tennessee. As a result, they all knew where their orders would take them. The war wasn't over yet. On October 24, 1862, they were camped out in the open in Lebanon, Kentucky. The beech trees and the stars were clearly visible at night because they had no tents. It was getting colder, and they were headed for Tennessee.

6

Christmas Crept In

In the months between Fredericksburg and Chancellorsville, events swirled round the peculiar pivot where Lincoln moved, and put him into further personal isolation. So often daylight seemed to break—and it was a false dawn—and it was yet night. When hope came singing a soft song, it was more than once shattered by the brass laughter of cannon and sudden bayonets preceding the rebel yell.

—Carl Sandberg, 1925

"Poor old Nashville—dull, dirty, and in mourning! Two-thirds of her stores and business places are shut up. People sour and uncomfortable in appearance."[1]

General Rosecrans arrived in Nashville in early November 1862. He was using this as a base from which he could feed his men and his horses in the pursuit of Bragg. However, Nashville had to be rebuilt to serve Rosecrans' needs. When he arrived, the general saw a city that "looked desolate. War had left buildings dirty and dilapidated, and streets rough and filthy. On an impressive acropolis, the unfinished capitol building had been converted into a fort, a Greek temple with cannon snouts sticking over its parapets. Streets were barricaded with cotton bales or earthworks. St. Cloud Hill was an 'armed fort,' and other forts lay beyond. In wealthy homes, pantries were bare, silver coffee pots empty, and fine China plates held scanty rations. Markets stood abandoned and money was scarce."[2] Rosecrans brought his wounded from Perryville with him to Nashville, but the hospitals were already full. On November 15, the *Nashville Courier Journal* recorded that from the Third Ohio, Daniel Silence from Company I had died,[3] and Corporal William S. Pickering, Company K, was recovering from his wounds. Nevertheless, the men who fought for William Rosecrans appreciated his organizational efforts on their behalf. The *Courier* continued with an editorial on the 15th that "one feature strikes me as forcefully as any other connected with this war—the craving of our intelligent, home-loving army for their mail matter. Gen. Rosecrans appreciates this and it is one among his many other means of gaining the affections of his men. He is a practical hard-working soldier—he knows their wants. He is very careful and examines into his commissary and quartermaster departments, and consequently his men are kept up in supplies and transportation and mail matter."

William Rosecrans had his hands full. How did he come to Lincoln's attention in the first place? With little military experience, Lincoln often allowed himself to be constrained by military tradition. Seniority in command was jealously guarded and protected by army officers, regular and volunteer. If an officer was next in line for command based on his date of original commission, he was generally allowed to take that command, whether he was qualified or not. During the Blackhawk wars of his youth, Lincoln often said that he fought more mosquitoes than Indians. As president and commander in chief, he was technically able to appoint anyone to command. Simply backdate his commission to a point in time where the desired man now outranked other claimants. There may be hard feelings by the one left out, but there was a war to be fought. The best men were needed wherever they may be.[4] When Don Carlos Buell "lost" Perryville and allowed Braxton Bragg to get away, Lincoln looked back to that earliest battle that allowed George McClellan to sparkle and shine. Rich Mountain made "Little Napoleon" look good enough to be called to Washington to command all of Lincoln's armed forces. Was there anyone else from Rich Mountain who might work? What about William Rosecrans? Rumors of his leading troops from the front had found their way back to the Executive Mansion. Unfortunately, Rosecrans was outranked by George Thomas. Not a problem. The War Department was so upset with Buell letting Bragg get away that they gave Rosecrans the embarrassing job of going to Buell in the field and telling him that he was relieved of command. After that, Rosecrans had to face George Thomas who might not accept this paper-shuffling promotion with enough grace to allow Rosecrans to command at all.

Dealing with Buell first, Rosecrans wrote to him and admitted, "I, like yourself, am neither an intriguer nor newspaper soldier.... Propriety will permit me to say that ... you had my high respect for ability as a soldier, for your adherence to truth and justice in the government and discipline of your command."[5] The corps within which the Third Ohio served was commanded by George Thomas. He was upset with the promotion scheme. Rosecrans was skillful enough to write to Thomas and tell him, "My command came to me unsought. Had the government so willed, I would gladly have served under you. Anticipating the question of rank, the War Department antedated my commission. The best interests of the country demand your service with this army."[6] Always a professional and a gentleman, Thomas accepted Rosecrans' offer of corps command center.

As soon as he was in command, Rosecrans immediately began to shake things up. He inherited an army that was beaten and starting to disintegrate into a void full of disrespect, pillaging and intoxication. On November 3, 1862, "Old Rosey" put his foot down hard. Writing to Stanton, he demanded, "I wish authority to muster out of service for flagrant misdemeanors and crimes—such as pillaging, drunkenness and misbehavior in the face of the enemy or on guard duty—on order, subject to the approval of the President."[7] The Third Ohio was on notice and had to be careful. However, Rosecrans was just getting started. He wanted better guns and trained sharpshooters. With no response from Halleck, Rosecrans wrote directly to Stanton. On November 9, he pleaded, "If I have not worn out my welcome, I beseech you for the public service to serve to me revolving arms or breach-loading carbines for my cavalry."[8] With pressure from Lincoln on one side and Rosecrans on the other, Halleck looked for a way out. On November 17, he wired Rosecrans, "We cannot rob Peter to pay Paul."[9] Speaking of payment, Rosecrans also wanted his men to get paid. They were fighting and dying for the Union cause, and they had not been paid. On November 23, he told Stanton that he needed $1 million just to pay one corps through August 31. Back pay that was already three months past due! There was more to come. In General Orders No. 23, issued on November 27, Rosecrans went after the Sutlers.[10] He declared,

"Information having reached these headquarters, to the effect that large quantities of goods of every description are being sold by Sutlers and other parties to citizens, and by them being passed beyond the lines of this army, thereby giving aid and comfort to the enemy, the following regulations will hereafter be strictly enforced":

    I. All army Sutlers are required to join their regiments, and they will not be permitted to sell goods to any but persons connected with the army.

    II. No Sutler will be permitted to ship boots, shoes or any articles of clothing to his regiment unless he first obtain a certificate from the commanding officer of the regiment, stating that such articles and quantities are absolutely necessary for the comfort of his men, and also receive a permit from the Colonel approved by the Brigade and Division commanders for the shipment of such goods to the regiment.

    III. No persons whatever, other than regular Sutlers, will hereafter be permitted to follow this army, or to establish itself within its lines.

IV. In towns or cities, now or hereafter within the lines of this army, no person will be allowed to sell goods needed for the use of the resident citizens.[11]

Rosecrans meant business, and all were on notice. However, while bypassing the chain of command to achieve these results, Halleck finally had had enough. With both eyes bulging to the maximum, scratching two elbows at the same time and squirming with hemorrhoids, Halleck warned Rosecrans on November 27, "If you remain long at Nashville you will disappoint the wishes of the government." He increased the pressure on December 4: "The Government demands action, and if you cannot respond to that demand someone else will be tried."[12] For a man who was impatient and led his men almost recklessly from the front, Rosecrans sent a quick response. At 10:45 p.m. on the 4th, he threatened, "To threats of removal or the like, I must be permitted to say that I am insensible."[13] Halleck wasted no time with his reply. The next day, he backed down with, "My telegram was not a threat, but merely a statement of facts."[14]

Rosecrans wasn't through, however. Without a large cavalry force, he set up a new system of "couriers" to gather the intelligence and make sure that his central command was always informed of the most up-to-date information. In General Orders No. 12, November 12, 1862, "Old Rosy" put his foot down even harder:

General Orders, HDQRS. Fourteenth Army Corps
Department of the Cumberland
Nashville, Tenn. November 12, 1862
No. 12

I. In establishing courier lines, a commissioned officer must be placed in charge of each line, who will be held strictly responsible that the line is kept in perfect order. He will be habitually at the station of most importance, but will frequently ride the whole length of his line to see that it is in order. He will collect all information that will affect the movement and subsistence of troops, and make a written report of the same to the chief of courier lines at these headquarters. This report will embrace information as to what roads and by-paths cross the branch and at what points and how far they extend, and the nature of the road; also the name of any prominent points and individuals on the line, and their distance from one of the extremities. He will report upon the forage, what kind and at what points it can be delivered on the road. These reports will be made as soon as possible after the line is established.

II. The stations will be from 4 to 6 miles apart, according to circumstances, and there should never be less than six men at a station. At each station, there will always be kept 2 horses saddled, ready to move at a moment's notice, with no extra articles on the saddle to impede their movements. The other horses can be groomed and fed whilst the two are saddled. Courier stations will answer the purpose of vedettes on the road in which they are established, always keeping themselves on the alert, and never suffering themselves to be captured. If a capture is inevitable, the dispatch must be destroyed. When a courier is bearing a dispatch, he must move at a fast gallop to the first station on his road, hand the dispatch immediately to the courier ready to move at that station, who will proceed like the one before him. If marked immediate and important, he must move at half the speed of the horse. They will then walk their horses back to the station from which they started. An officer or non-commissioned officer will be at each end of the line to receipt for dispatches.

III. Courier stations will always pick up stragglers and forward them to the nearest general headquarters. This order is imperative.

IV. Couriers will never receive orders from any person except the officer placed immediately over them. If strangers, they must give the most satisfactory evidence of their authority to give them orders.

The General Order was signed by Arthur C. Ducat, lieutenant colonel and acting chief of staff. If Halleck and Lincoln thought they could make Rosecrans move faster, they were mistaken.[15] Shake-up notwithstanding, "Old Rosy" was still required to catch Braxton Bragg. With the weather getting colder, he hoped that would happen soon.

Headquarters Army of Tennessee, Murfreesborough, Tenn., December 1, 1862. Brig. Gen. John H. Morgan, Commanding Cavalry at Baird's [Mills]:

General : The general commanding directs me to say that, when relieved from your present duties, you will proceed with your whole command, by the most practicable route and with the least delay, to operate on the enemy's lines of communications in rear of Nashville. You will assail his guards where your relative force will justify it; capture and destroy his trains; burn his bridges, depots, trestle-work, &c. In fine, harass him in every conceivable way in your power. When practicable, * But see inclosure A to Bragg's report of the battle of Stone's River, send all prisoners to the rear, so as to conceal your operations. When it is necessary, parole them, sending lists by first mail to these headquarters. You are authorized to increase your command to the extent of your captured arms and horses, assigning the men to your old regiments. Do everything to prevent the enemy from foraging north of the Cumberland River, and especially toward Clarksville. If practicable, communicate and co-operate with Brigadier-General [N.B.] Forrest. You are not limited in the extent of your operations, every confidence being reposed in your zeal, discretion, and judgment. You will make weekly reports of your operations, sending with each a return of your command. It is reported that the enemy is obstructing the fords of the Cumberland. Brigadier-General [J.] Wheeler has been ordered to relieve you as soon as Brigadier-General [J.] Pegram can be placed in position with a sufficient command.

> I am, general,* very respectfully, yours,
> GEORGE WM. BRENT,
> Assistant Adjutant-General[16]

While "Old Rosy" brawled with Halleck and fought the cold weather, John Hunt Morgan clashed with a brigade in Ebenezer Dumont's division. John Beatty remembered what happened: "Everything indicates an early movement. Whether a reconnaissance [sic] is intended or a permanent advance, I do not even undertake to guess. The capture of a brigade, at Hartsville, by John Morgan, has awakened the army into something like life; before it was idly awaiting the rise of the Cumberland, but this bold dash of the rebels has made it bristle up like an angry boar; and this morning, I am told, it starts out to show its tusks to the enemy. Our division has been ordered to be in readiness.... The whole army feels deeply mortified over the loss of the brigade at Hartsville; report says it was captured by an inferior force. One of our regiments did not fire a gun, and certainly the other two could not have made a very obstinate resistance. I am glad Ohio does not have to bear the whole blame; two thirds is rather too much."[17]

What happened at Hartsville?

> War Department
>
> Washington, December 9, 1862.
>
> Major General Rosecrans
> *Nashville, Tenn.:*
> The President directs that you immediately report why an isolated brigade was at Hartsville, and by whose command; and by whose fault it was surprised and captured.
>
> H.W. Halleck
> *General-in-Chief*[18]

Abraham Lincoln was commander in chief, but he learned army tactics from books borrowed from the Library of Congress. His secretary, John George Nicolay, would make frequent trips to the library to get the books needed to help Lincoln try and actually direct his generals and their battles—all the way from the Executive Mansion. Rosecrans took exception to this and quickly replied at 11:00 p.m. on the same day, "In reply to your telegram, inquiring why the brigade was stationed at Hartsville, I respectfully state that it was necessary to cover the crossing of the Cumberland River against rebel cavalry, who would essay to attack our road and capture our train."[19]

Why was Hartsville significant, and how did this impact the Third Ohio? Hartsville was strategically located next to the Cumberland River and the Louisville-Nashville Railroad. The only bridge across the Cumberland in this area was in Hartsville. To help secure the area, Major General Thomas Crittenden was stationed in nearby Gallatin. The Louisville-Nashville line ran through Gallatin. That railroad was part of an 8,000-mile system that ultimately connected to every major city in the Confederacy. As a result, Hartsville was effectively the start of the Stones River/Murfreesboro campaign. That battle would ultimately help to secure Tennessee for the Union. Its rivers, railroads, raw materials and Union support in east Tennessee were critical to ultimate Union success. The Third Ohio played a significant combat role in this battle.

With the guerrilla bands like Morgan and others impacting communication and supply, Union armies had trouble fighting the battles that eventually decided the conflict. Under the circumstances, was it too risky to continue chasing Bragg? Rosecrans often complained that he did not have the cavalry necessary to screen his movements, gather intelligence and chase men like Morgan away. He told Halleck that Confederate cavalry outnumbered his small force by a ratio of seven to one. Who was in command at Hartsville, and what happened? If Rosecrans had sufficient cavalry, the surprise at Hartsville might not have occurred. The regiment securing Hartsville was part of the division led by Ebenezer Dumont. The finger was initially pointed at him. Later in the evening of December 7, Rosecrans wired Halleck, "General Thomas dispatches me that one of his brigades, Dumont's, was posted at Hartsville."[20] On December 9, George Thomas confirmed that lack of cavalry was the real issue. He wired Halleck, "That outpost was stronger and better supported than our outpost at Rienzi, 7 miles below Corinth last summer. The difference was in the superiority and number of rebel cavalry."[21]

The issue was more fundamental than that. At least one month before the clash at Murfreesboro, Rosecrans is warning Corps Commander T. Crittenden about Morgan and his threat to the Army of the Cumberland. One month before the attack on Hartsville, General Crittenden is warning Arthur Ducat, adjutant to General Rosecrans, "Without a cavalry force at Hartsville, I fear a single regiment would not be safe here."[22] Where was the Third Ohio at this time? John Beatty confirms that the Third Ohio was sent to Mitchellville on the border of Tennessee and Kentucky. According to Beatty, "We have settled down at Mitchellville for a few days.... We learned over a week ago that the rebels endeavored to enforce the conscription law in this neighborhood."[23]

It was fortunate that the Third Ohio was not at Hartsville. A report published in the *Chicago Tribune* on February 14, 1863, was not complimentary to some of the Ohio regiments who were involved in Hartsville. Colonel Absalom B. Moore, 104th Illinois, was captured at Hartsville and sent to Libby Prison. He smuggled out a letter that was published in the *Tribune* on the 14th. His colorful prose provides a detailed account that is supported by some of the field reports filed at the time. According to Moore,

> Of course, you are aware that I am a prisoner of war and am now confined in a room 78 feet × 43 feet with 125 men composed of officers, citizens, sutlers, thieves, deserters. Highwaymen, and robbers, all thrown together promiscuously, and you can fancy what a comfortable position I am in. We are full of vermin; if we did not slaughter them wholesale every morning, we should be soon eaten up alive. As I assure you that these filthy creepers and Confederate money are the only two things abundant in Dixie. It is useless for me to write about our living in this place as I must reserve that until I see you for I indulge the hope that I shall get out of this place by and by, but when I cannot say....
> On the evening of December 6th, John Morgan with his whole cavalry force of over 4,000 and eight pieces of artillery and two regiments of infantry (the 7th and 9th Kentucky) and Cobb's battery started at 10 o'clock at night eight miles from Lebanon with the infantry mounted behind the cavalry and marched 25 miles that night, crossing the Cumberland five miles below my camp, cut off my videttes, and pushed on for Hartsville. My pickets gave the alarm in time for me to have my men in proper line to receive them. I commenced the attack upon the enemy and fought him for one and half hours. The fight while it lasted was very severe. The 104th Illinois and the 2nd Indiana Cavalry fought nobly, but the 106th Ohio led by their colonel [Gustav Tafel] behaved most shamefully and cowardly. I did my utmost to rally them and also called upon Colonel Stewart of the 2nd Indiana Cavalry to aid me in rallying them, but it was unavailing. They ran with their colonel at their head and were soon captured. The 108th Ohio did much better than the 106th. Indeed, I have no particular fault to find with the 108th as it did not have a single field officer in the regiment; Captains Piepho and Kreider did good service.

Morgan and his cavalry band sneaked up on Moore's pickets and videttes without being challenged. Morgan was a mythological figure who was reported in the press to have worn Union uniforms in disguise to walk right into Union campgrounds to gather intelligence. Although some of the reports were exaggerated, the Hartsville attack was genuine.[24] Morgan dressed his advance scouts in Union army blue uniforms, which allowed them to trot right up to the Union pickets guarding Hartsville and capture them all. After 90 minutes of fighting, Morgan captured almost 2,000 men from several Union regiments. Although uncertain whether it was Morgan or not, the ruse of wearing Union blue uniforms to enable rebel cavalry to sneak up on unsuspecting outposts seems to have caught on. Major General Alexander McCook complained to Rosecrans' adjutant, Julius Geresché, on December 23, 1862, "One of General Sherman's outposts (a sergeant and 9 men) were captured this evening. The vedettes were driven in and gave no alarm. The enemy's cavalry were dressed in our uniform. Detailed report will be sent in the morning."[25] With the Confederacy relying on guerrillas like Morgan to supplement their small army, conscription quickly became necessary.

Conscription laws were enacted in both the North and South during the Civil War. The Confederacy enacted their first draft on April 16, 1862. It mandated all males between the ages of 18 and 35 years to report for military service. The Lincoln administration passed the first conscription law on March 3, 1863. In the North, however, this provoked bloody riots in New York City in July 1863. It also created a system of hiring substitutes as well as bounty hunters who accepted the $300 fee for acting as a substitute and then turned around and accepted additional payments from others seeking substitute help. In the South, the young men were either hiding in the woods or trying to join cavalry bands like those of Forrest and Morgan. If that failed, some simply formed their own band and burned and pillaged wherever they found easy targets. The *Nashville Daily Union* commented on the substitute problem in Richmond, Virginia, on April 16, 1862: "Our chief article of commerce now-a days is a commodity in the market known as 'substitutes.' The article has risen from $100 to $200, again to $500 and from that to $1,000 and $1,500. The cheapest kind now offering commands $500 readily. A wretch named Hill has been making enormous sums, as much as $3,000 to $5,000 a day, by plundering substitutes, some of whom are the scum of the earth.... A friend of mine bought a substitute from Hill for $400. He saw Hill give the poor devil $100 and put the remaining $400 in his pocket. As my friend went out the door, he met a gentleman who had just paid $1,500 for a substitute.... You may infer therefore that [Hill] coins more money than a Yankee distiller."

Up North, substitutes were also bought and sold. If that didn't work, Gideon Welles complained that his navy was overrun with more applicants than he could handle. John George Nicolay, Lincoln's senior secretary, paid $300 to find a substitute to take his place so that he could continue working for the president. Unfortunately, draft riots broke out in New York City when many could not afford the substitute fee. Nevertheless, Abraham Lincoln had a secret weapon denied to Jefferson Davis. He already had an army big enough to stretch its arms from coast to coast. The Confederacy could not cover all of the bases. What the Union infantry managed on land, the navy took up the slack at sea. Monitor-class ironclads protected harbor entrances north and south to an extent that Great Britain finally realized that intervention in the American Civil War was not possible.[26] In addition, the Second Confiscation and Militia Act of July 17, 1862, allowed Lincoln to "employ as many persons of African descent as he may deem necessary and proper for the suppression of this rebellion ... in such manner as he may judge best for the public welfare."[27] Events during the winter of 1862 would soon justify Lincoln's actions.

December 1862 was a hard month for Abraham Lincoln and a fragile Union that hadn't heard of Chancellorsville, Gettysburg or Cold Harbor yet. On December 17, 1862, Colonel John Beatty, Third Ohio, was also anxious about December. In his diary, he recorded,

> The news from Fredericksburg has cast a shadow over the army. We did hope that Burnside would be successful, and thus brighten the prospect for a speedy peace; but we are in deeper gloom now than ever. The repulse at Fredericksburg, while it has disabled thousands, has disheartened, if not demoralized a great army, and given confidence and strength to the rebels every-where. It may be, however, that this defeat was necessary to bring us clearly to the point of extinguishing slavery in all the States. The time is near when the strength of the President's resolution in this regard will be put to the test. I trust he will be firm. The mere reconstruction of the Union on the old basis would not pay humanity for all the blood shed since the war began. The extinction of slavery, perhaps, will.

What happened at Fredericksburg? General Ambrose Burnside was assigned the command that included Fredericksburg. He didn't want the assignment and was surprised when he got it. Fredericksburg was critical because of the railroad that ran direct from there to Richmond. Capture Fredericksburg, send an army and its supplies via rail to the Confederate capital and the war might be over. Unfortunately, the task was much easier said than done. First, the element of surprise was lost when the newspapers plotted and published every ponderous move Burnside made to get his army in place to cross the Rappahannock River. The Washington newspapers had already reported that Burnside had divided his army into three separate corps—one directly opposite Fredericksburg, and the other two on the east and west flanks of the Rappahannock River. If surprise was not already lost for many reasons, all "Bobby" Lee had to do was read an old copy of the Washington *Evening Star* from the 11th, which gave away any hope of surprise: "The energy of quartermasters and commissaries have placed the army in such a condition that no want can be anticipated for some time to come.... A large number of officers are arriving daily from furloughs and resuming their active duties in camp. There have been considerable changes of position by several of the army corps within the past few days, foreshadowing future movements of importance. It is stated today by a reliable observer that the enemy have 180 guns in position on the south side of the Rappahannock, some of which are of heavy calibre."[28] So, not only did Jefferson Davis know the Union army was coming; he was forewarned and ready with high-caliber guns to send them back home. If the report of the 11th was not enough to give away the news, the *Star* left no doubt with their report on the 12th: "A dispatch was received here at 8 o'clock last night stating that the entire left wing, under Franklin, had crossed the Rappahannock, and that late in the afternoon the right wing under Sumner crossed."[29] If for some reason Lee's copy of the *Star* had not arrived at his camp on time, the Richmond *Daily Dispatch* filled in the gaps by reporting on the same day, "Early yesterday morning, intelligence was received in this city that the ball opened in earnest in Fredericksburg, and that from the character of the fight, there was little room for doubt a general engagement would ensue."[30] What else went wrong?

The pontoons that Burnside needed to build the bridge across the river for his troops and artillery to pass failed to arrive in time. This gave rebel sharpshooters positioned behind barricades on Center Street time to get their range. They knew exactly where Burnside's engineers would be preparing to construct that bridge. They had a clear shot at anyone attempting to build a bridge across the river. The construction process turned out to be a bloody disaster because those sharpshooters shot and killed many of the engineers before the pontoons could be anchored to the river bottom. Finally, with enough covering fire, the bridge was built. The next problem, however, lay in the fact that the Confederate troops now occupied an elevated position behind a long, stone wall at the top of Marye's Heights. Making their position even more impregnable was the fact that the approach to the hilltop was an open field. If Union troops attempted to charge the heights, there was no cover during the approach. They could be seen as soon as they left the protection of the center of town. Brigadier General Carl Schurz later told Lincoln, "Through our field glasses we saw them fall by the hundreds, and their bodies dot the ground. As they approached Lee's entrenched position, sheet after sheet of flame shot forth from the heights, tearing fearful gaps in our lines.... Hot tears of rage and pitying sympathy ran down many a weather beaten cheek. No more horrible and torturing spectacle could have been imagined."[31] Fredericksburg made the Union army look weak. Hopefully, Stones River would change that.

On December 20, the Third Ohio was told to be ready to march with five days of rations in their haversacks. The sound of cannon could be heard from their campsite. The Third believed that the Confederate victory at Fredericksburg would not be to their advantage because "Bobby" Lee could now release some of the troops there and transfer them to Murfreesboro. It was Christmas 1862. Guns could still be heard in the distance. A battle was coming. The officers of the Third Ohio put their money together and bought a turkey for dinner. It was difficult to hear the holiday songs the men in the regiment were singing. Every pause was interrupted by the vulgar roar of a rebel Napoleon in the distance. There were no thoughts of Happy New Year! The *Chattanooga Daily Rebel* said it best on January 1, 1863: "Sixty-two is gone; is among the things that were; and the rude January winds, and the shrill notes of war, and the soul-stirring rattle of drums and thunders of artillery usher an unknown and stranger guest in his place."

For the Third Ohio, "Sixty-two" still waited. Late December brought rain, more raids from Morgan, Wheeler, Pegram and now Van Dorn. Christmas crept in and hastily tiptoed out. The Third knew that another contest was waiting for them. They wanted to go home, but their enlistment wasn't up yet. On the other side of the Stones River, men from the South did their best to welcome Christmas. They knew that celebrations were useless and in vain.

In a day or two, the orders would come down to kill or be killed by the men from Ohio and the rest of the northern regiments who fought next to them.

The 1857 model of a 12-pound Napoleon gun, which could fire solid shot, grape, chain, and canister. This gun saw action with the batteries of Cyrus O. Loomis and Peter Simonson at Perryville (Library of Congress).

7

Make the Sign of the Cross and Go In

Soldiers, the eyes of the whole nation are upon you; the very fate of the nation may be said to land on the issue of this days' battle.

Headquarters, Department of the Cumberland, Murfreesboro, Tennessee, December 31, 1862. By command of Major General W.S. Rosecrans[1]

"Come and take it!" responded Braxton Bragg to General Rosecrans' demand for surrender. It had already started to snow in Murfreesboro, Tennessee.[2]

It was midnight and it was cold. The dense fog and muddy roads frozen solid didn't help. Soon, however, the frosty air was warmed by the snarling heat and flame of 64 supply wagons that had been set on fire. The blaze shot 30 feet into the air. The ammunition, chloroform and salted beef had been removed by Wheeler's men. All the rest got torched. The ground was littered with useless debris including empty trunks, saddlebags, and extra uniform tunics. The sparks could be seen for miles, and General William Rosecrans could smell the smoke. He knew this was not a good sign.

All of that smoke and flame came from "Fighting Joe" Wheeler and his rebel cavalry brigade.[3] Those wagons were supplies headed for the Union forces of General Rosecrans, camped just outside Murfreesboro, Tennessee, west of the Stones River. All night, Wheeler rode around and got behind the Union supply train. It was December 29, 1862, and a battle was about to happen. Union general William Rosecrans and Confederate general Braxton Bragg faced each other on opposite sides of the Stone River.[4] The river and the Nashville-Chattanooga railroad ran right through town. The former Tennessee capital and city of 4,000 people were at the center of a contest that some historians consider to have been more significant than Gettysburg. Where was the Third Ohio at this time?

Colonel John Beatty was now in command of the Second Brigade that included the Third. On December 29, 1861, they were on the road to Stewartstown, Tennessee. According to Beatty, "At four o'clock P.M. we were ordered to leave baggage and teams behind, and march to Stewart's creek, a point twenty miles from Nashville. Night had set in before the brigade got fairly under way. The road runs through a barren, hilly, pine district, and was exceedingly bad. At eleven o'clock at night we reached the place indicated, and lay on the damp ground until morning."[5]

Why Murfreesboro and Stones River? Why was this battle so significant?

"Fighting Joe" Wheeler was raised in Georgia and graduated from West Point. During the war, Wheeler helped Morgan and Forrest burn bridges and tear up telegraph lines in Kentucky and Tennessee (Library of Congress).

"It was at Stone's River that the South was at the very pinnacle of confidence and warlike power; and it was here that she was halted and beaten back, never again to exhibit such strength and menace. It was here that the tide of the Confederacy passed its flood, henceforth to recede; here that its sun crossed the meridian and began its journey to the twilight and the dark. Southern valor was manifested in splendid luster on many a field thereafter, but the capacity for sustained aggression was gone. After Stone's River, the Southern soldier fought to repel rather than to drive his foe."[6] How did Tennessee fit into this?

East Tennessee was mountainous and independent like "western" Virginia. The Appalachians, Smokeys and Blue Ridge Mountains helped protect and preserve its independent way of life. It owned few slaves, preferred the Union and wanted no part of a fight that didn't concern it. As the former state capital, however, Murfreesboro had a five-foot gauge rail line that allowed it to connect with every major city and seaport in the "Deep

7. Make the Sign of the Cross and Go In

Stones River is sometimes called the Battle of Murfreesboro. It divided the town of Murfreesboro in a manner that forced both armies to occupy different sides of the river at different times during the battle (Library of Congress).

South." In addition to those connections, the East Tennessee & Virginia Railroad line was the highway that serviced all of those vital links. Control of east Tennessee and its vital rail artery would impact the entire Confederacy. Its ability to move men and supplies would be crippled if Murfreesboro was lost. However, if any of the rail lines were torn up or their bridges burned, there were still plenty of good roads going in all directions from the center of the city. Lincoln was trying to get his foot in the door of the Confederacy. He hoped that east Tennessee would give him a base from which he could launch military operations against the rest of the South. Geographically, Tennessee was critical. Lincoln had to have it. Murfreesboro was the key, and the Third Ohio waited for orders.

The Union commander trying to hold on to east Tennessee was General William Stark Rosecrans. Determined to force him out was Confederate general Braxton Bragg. Bragg's Army of Tennessee and Rosecrans' Army of the Cumberland were approximately the same size: 42,000 effectives. Although their tactical battle plans were similar, their personal disposition and leadership styles were quite different. Bragg was a perfectionist with a sharp, colorful tongue. He was obsessed with his health and more than willing to argue and fight with anyone willing or unwilling to oblige. Before secession, Bragg even took issue with General-in-Chief Winfield Scott. Ultimately charged with insubordination, Bragg was temporarily reduced in rank and fined half of his pay. Nevertheless, in time,

Bragg continued to rise through the ranks. In the Civil War, he commanded the Army of Tennessee at Perryville and Stones River. He fought hard in Kentucky but retreated on October 9, 1862. He moved first to Nashville but then south to Murfreesboro and waited. He knew Rosecrans would not be very far behind. Unfortunately, the Confederate commander selected a terrible defensive position in Murfreesboro and the Stones River. He had the time necessary to select better ground. That did not happen, however. "The position that Bragg selected was not particularly well suited for defense. Most of the area was open farm country without natural barriers. Where there were trees, they grew in thick patches which could conceal the enemy and hamper Confederate cavalry and artillery movements.... Owing to the convergence upon Murfreesboro of so many fine roads by which the enemy could approach," reported Bragg, "we were confined in a selection to a line near enough the point of juncture to enable us to successfully cover them all until the real point of attack should be developed."[7]

The Third Ohio was in General Lovell Rousseau's division, within George Thomas' corps. William Rosecrans, however, took overall command of the Army of the Cumberland. Also possessed of a sharp tongue, he was brave and preferred to lead from the front. William Rosecrans, "Old Rosy," was a West Point graduate but was trained as an engineer, not a tactical infantry commander. After the Third Ohio was activated, Rosecrans led his troops against Confederate forces at Rich Mountain. Pushing back against stiff rebel resistance, Rosecrans personally led Ohio troops into the charge of the enemy works.

As the battle of Stones River was about to unfold, where was the Third Ohio? On December 10, they were three miles outside of Nashville. Knowing that the enemy was camped near Murfreesboro, the Third slowly marched south on the Nashville Pike. By December 21, they could hear cannon booming in the distance. They knew a real fight was coming. By the 25th, officers of the Third began to lament the fact that the rebel forces were able to operate through interior lines of communication. The Third and the rest of Lovell Rousseau's division were on the outside. In theory, interior lines allowed forces to move men and their equipment quickly and safely within that interior space. The reality, however, was often different. Interior lines needed to be protected with skirmishers and enough vedettes to provide security and rapid communication with the command at the center if the interior lines were breached.[8] In addition, if the interior space was also serviced by either railroads or at least macadamized turnpikes, communication and movement were facilitated. However, without this infrastructure, the value of interior lines was greatly diminished. By December 26, brigade commander John Beatty recalled, "This morning we started south on the Franklin road. When some ten miles away from Nashville, we turned toward Murfreesboro, and are now encamped in the woods, near the head-waters of the Little Harpeth. The march was exceedingly unpleasant. Rain began to fall about the time of starting, and continued to pour down heavily for four hours, wetting us all thoroughly. We moved at eight o'clock this morning, over a very bad dirt road, from Wilson's pike to the Nolansville road, where we are now bivouacking. About ten the artillery commenced thundering in our front, and continued during the greater portion of the day. Marched two miles toward Triune to support McCook, who was having a little bout with the enemy; but the engagement ending, we returned to our present quarters in a drenching rain. Saw General Thomas, our corps commander, going to and returning from the front. We are sixteen miles from Nashville, on a road running midway between Franklin and Murfreesboro. The enemy is supposed to be in force at the latter place."[9]

By December 31, 1862, battle lines for both armies were drawn and ready for action. The Stones River battle is unique in many ways. Foremost is the fact that both commanders knew exactly where the "enemy" was located. Normally, cavalry units were used to gather intelligence on location and strength of the enemy they might be fighting. Knowing the exact location of your opponent as well as his effective strength was critical data. Success in battle often depended on this knowledge. After Gettysburg, for example, Robert E. Lee lamented the fact that Confederate cavalry Major General J.E.B. Stuart, Lee's "eyes and ears," had failed to provide him with data necessary to know the true disposition of Union forces on July 2, 1863. This was a moot point on December 31, 1862.

Both armies were positioned parallel to the Nashville Railroad line and the Stone River. The right and left flanks of both armies were positioned southwest to northeast. The Union force consisted of three corps. They were commanded by Generals Thomas Crittenden, Alexander McCook and George Thomas. As they faced the Confederate forces, McCook occupied the right, Thomas the Center and Crittenden the left. Across from them were Confederate corps commanders William Hardee (opposite McCook), Leonidas Polk (opposite Thomas and the Third Ohio) and John Breckenridge (opposite Crittenden).

Tuesday night, December 30, 1862, was flooded with rain and fog. Many in the Third Ohio had secured their bayonets to keep the gun barrel dry. After attaching the bayonet, they turned the gun upside down and rammed the blade into the ground. There would be a fight tomorrow. Powder and gun barrel had to be dry. The men of the Third moved and shuffled all night while their muzzle-loading muskets stood still and waited. They had to be patient. By six o'clock in the morning, the Third Ohio Volunteer

Infantry "marches to the front and forms in line of battle. The roar of musketry and artillery is incessant. At nine o'clock we move into the cedar woods on the right to support McCook who is reported to be giving way. General Rousseau points me to the place he desires me to defend, and enjoins me to 'hold it until hell freezes over,' at the same time telling me that he may be found immediately on the left of my brigade with Loomis' battery."[10]

Due to the rain and fog, Rosecrans decided to postpone his attack. Bragg didn't wait. At first light, he ordered William Hardee to attack the Union right wing of Alexander McCook. With hot-tempered and incessantly swearing Philip Sheridan and the Third Ohio held in reserve in the center, it was immediately clear that McCook needed help and fast! "They hit with pile-driving force, ten thousand of Hardee's rebels stampeding into the Union camps. McCook had sixteen thousand soldiers in his corps, but mentally, and in some cases tactically, they were not prepared to receive an attack. The onslaught was so startling and appalling that Federal soldiers, officers and enlisted men alike, supposed the enemy's assaulting force must be twenty-five thousand or even thirty-five thousand strong."[11]

However, both Sheridan and the Third Ohio faced an open field in front and a thick, cedar forest at the edge of the field. The trees concealed the movements of Hardee's troops. When they emerged, however, they were exposed to heavy fire. Brigade commander John Beatty remembered, "The enemy comes up directly, and the fight begins. The roar of the guns to the right, left, and front of my brigade sounds like the continuous pounding on a thousand anvils. My men are favorably situated, being concealed by the cedars, while the enemy, advancing through the open woods, is fully exposed. Early in the action, Colonel Foreman, of the Fifteenth Kentucky, is killed, and his regiment retires in disorder. The Third Ohio, Eighty-eighth, and Forty-second Indiana, hold the position, and deliver their fire so effectively that the enemy is finally forced back."[12]

General Rosecrans' report stated that Sheridan fought Hardee's men back four times. However, when they finally ran out of ammunition, they were forced to fall back. Lovell Rousseau's division, which contained the Second Brigade and the Third Ohio, were left to face the Confederate charge on their own. Rosecrans wrote, "Sheridan, after sustaining four successive attacks, gradually swung his right from a southeasterly to a northwesterly direction, repulsing the enemy four times, losing the gallant General Sill, of his right, and Colonel Roberts, of his left brigade, when having exhausted his ammunition, Negley's division being in the same predicament, and heavily pressed, after desperate fighting, they fell back from the position held at the commencement, through the cedar woods, in which Rousseau's division, with a portion of Sheridan's and Negley's, met the advancing enemy and checked his movements."[13]

In the confusion of battle, some of Sheridan's, Negley's and Rousseau's brigades received orders to fall back. However, some never received the orders. Those left on the field to face Hardee included the Second Brigade with the Third Ohio. According to brigade commander John Beatty, "I conclude that the contingency has arisen to which General Rousseau referred—that is to say, that hell has frozen over—and about face my brigade and march to the rear, where the guns appear to be hammering away with redoubled fury. In the edge of the woods, and not far from the Murfreesboro pike, I find the new line of battle, and take position. Five minutes after the enemy strike us. For a time—I cannot even guess how long—the line stands bravely to the work; but the regiments on our left get into disorder, and finally become panic-stricken. The fright spreads, and my brigade sweeps by me to the open field in our rear. I hasten to the colors, stop them, and endeavor to rally the men. The field is by this time covered with flying troops, and the enemy's fire is most deadly. My brigade, however, begins to steady itself on the colors, when my horse is shot under me, and I fall heavily to the ground. Before I have time to recover my feet, my troops, with thousands of others, sweep in disorder to the rear, and I am left standing alone. Going back to the railroad, I find my men, General Rousseau, Loomis and in fact, the larger part of the army. The artillery has been concentrated at this point, and now opens upon the advancing columns of the enemy with fearful effect, and continues its thunders until nightfall. The artillery saved the army. The battle during the whole day was terrific."[14] While the Third Ohio was helping to fend off Hardee's attack, General Rosecrans behaved just as he did at Rich Mountain: he ignored danger and led from the front. This helped to inspire his officers but put Rosecrans in danger. "As they rode swiftly along the irregular front, Rosecrans and his staff made conspicuous targets. An enemy battery opened upon them, and as shells whistled close, all but Rosecrans ducked to the saddle bows. When Garesché begged him not to expose himself, Rosecrans dug his spurs into his horse and replied, 'Never mind me. Make the sign of the cross and go in.' The only way to be safe he told them was to destroy the enemy."[15]

The first day of the Stones River/Murfreesboro battle was critical to Lincoln's ultimate goal of restoring the Union. The battle continued with more rebel attacks. However, Braxton Bragg knew he had failed. The Union lines held and continually pushed back all Confederate assaults. The Third Ohio, along with other regiments in Lovell Rousseau's division, was essential in holding back constant waves of rebel infantry. As night fell and men from both sides collapsed in exhaustion and relief, the scene in the open fields was shocking. Private Sam Watkins, Company H, First Tennessee Volunteers, recalled, "I cannot remember now of ever seeing more dead men and horses, and captured cannon, all jumbled together, than the scene of blood and carnage and battle on the Wilkerson Turnpike. The ground was literally covered with blue coats dead."[16] Continuing to expose himself to danger by leading his troops from the front, General Rosecrans ended the day without a scratch, but his adjutant Julius Garesché was not so lucky. While riding with Rosecrans along the base of the Nashville rail line, an eight-pound, unexploded Hotchkiss shell from a rebel gun whizzed past the general and struck his adjutant.[17] Garesché's head was blown off. Major Frank S. Bond was riding behind Rosecrans and Garesché. Writing to Garesché's son after the war, Bond remembered, "The solid part of one of those Hotchkiss Shells struck your father squarely on the temple, carrying away all that part of his head above the chin. For an instant I did not realize what had occurred, as the body preserved its equilibrium in the saddle while the horse continued in motion at rather a fast walk, but it very shortly leaned towards the left, taking the horse out of the line, and then fell from the saddle to the ground."[18] Rosecrans' only comment was, "I am very sorry, but we cannot help it. Brave men die in battle."[19] Nevertheless, Rosecrans' uniform was wet with blood and brains. As the general calmly continued, the rest of his party passed the headless body with blood and foam pouring out from what was left. The body was quickly buried on the spot.

Each day of combat required a detailed report by the commanders, from brigade to corps. Based on their efforts on December 31, the Third Ohio Volunteer Infantry regiment was singled out for praise by Major Generals George Thomas and Lovell Rousseau. In Thomas' report filed on January 15, 1863, the Third Ohio is referenced by "Beatty's brigade," which included the Ohio regiment (see the Appendix). The general wrote, "December 31, between 6 and 7 am, the enemy, having passed a heavy force on McCook's right during the night of the 30th, attacked and drove it back, pushing his division in pursuit *en echelon* ... until he had gained sufficient ground to our rear to wheel his masses to the right and thrown them on the right flank of the center.... To counteract this movement, I had ordered Rousseau to place two brigades, with a battery, to the right and left of Sheridan's division.... About 11 o'clock General Sheridan reported to me that his ammunition was entirely out, and he would be compelled to fall back to get more.... In the execution of this last movement, with the cooperation of Scribner's and Beatty's brigades ... gallantly held its ground against overwhelming odds."[20]

January 1, 1863, was a quiet day for the Third Ohio. Brigade commander Colonel John Beatty recalled, "At dawn we are all in line, expecting

7. Make the Sign of the Cross and Go In

every moment the re-commencement of the fearful struggle. Occasionally a battery engages a battery opposite, and the skirmishers keep up a continual roar of small arms; but until nearly night there is no heavy fighting.

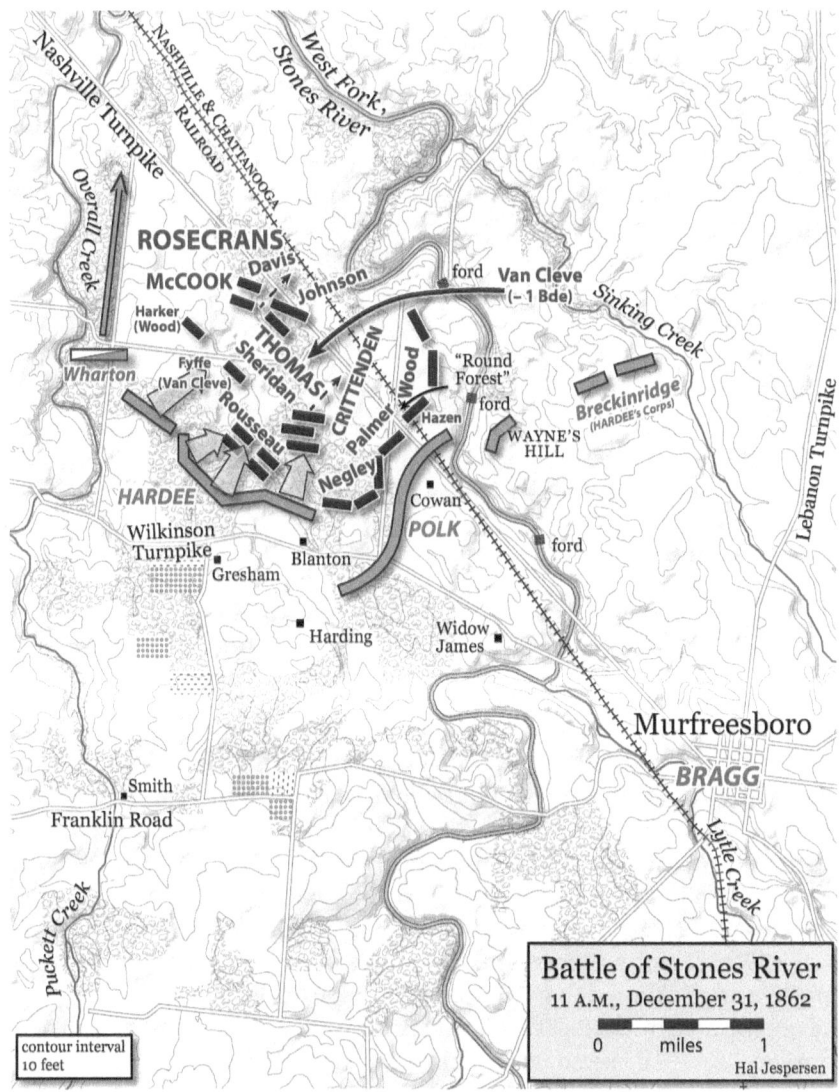

Stones River at 11:00 a.m. shows the river running through Murfreesboro resulting in Union and Confederate forces searching for position on both sides of the river. Rousseau's division containing the Third Ohio is opposite William Hardee. Rousseau was ordered to "refuse the line" and fall back at 90 degrees to avoid a flanking action by Hardee (map by Hal Jespersen, www.cwmaps.com).

Both armies want rest; both have suffered terribly. Here and there little parties are engaged burying the dead, which lie thick around us. Now the mangled remains of a poor boy of the Third is being deposited in a shallow grave. A whole charge of canister seems to have gone through him. Generals Rosecrans and Thomas are riding over the field, now halting to speak words of encouragement to the troops, then going on to inspect portions of the line. I have been supplied with a new horse, but one far inferior to the dead stallion. A little before sundown all hell seems to break loose again, and for about an hour the thunder of the artillery and volleys of musketry are deafening; but it is simply the evening salutation of the combatants. The darkness deepens; the weather is raw and disagreeable. Fifty thousand hungry men are stretched beside their guns again on the field. Fortunately I have a piece of raw pork and a few crackers in my pocket. No food ever tasted sweeter. The night is gloomy enough; but our spirits are rising. We all glory in the obstinacy with which Rosecrans has clung to his position."[21]

On New Year's Day, both armies rested and buried their dead. According to Colonel John Beatty of the Third Ohio, "At dawn we are all in line, expecting every moment the re-commencement of the fearful struggle. Occasionally a battery engages a battery opposite, and the skirmishers keep up a continual roar of small arms; but until nearly night there is no heavy fighting. Both armies want rest; both have suffered terribly."[22] However, Rosecrans had another idea. He decided to cross over to the east side of the Stones River to get behind Bragg's army and draw rebel forces away from the men who had suffered so much the previous day, Thomas and McCook. At 3:00 a.m. on January 1, Rosecrans sent Colonel Samuel Beatty (no relation to John Beatty) from Crittenden's corps across the Stones River to occupy the heights above Bragg's position with artillery. Meeting slight resistance, the scene was set for more action on January 2. Rosecrans would mount his artillery on a small hill which would give him a good shot at Bragg's flank. The high ground gave Rosecrans an advantage, which Bragg could not contend—or so he thought. When Bragg told Major General John Breckenridge to push the Union artillery off the hill, Breckenridge claimed that it would be suicide for his men. The situation was aggravated by the fact that Breckenridge hated Bragg, and Bragg hated everyone else. "The personal animosity between the two men was perhaps aggravated by their appearances and personalities. Breckinridge, with his long mustache and striking profile, was possibly the handsomest general in the Southern army. Bragg, with his bushy beard and wrinkled face, was undoubtedly the ugliest. While the dashing Breckinridge was the epitome of a Southern gentleman, Bragg's blunt, critical style made him a hard man to like and an easy man to hate."[23] Bragg still insisted that Breckenridge take the hill. Breckenridge reluctantly agreed but selected 4:00 p.m. as the time to begin the attack. Knowing that it was winter and it would be dark by 5:00 p.m., he believed the Union men would not be able to counterattack after dark. With some luck, it might work. Unfortunately, Breckenridge's comment about suicide was accurate. When his men moved toward the hill, Union artillery fired double canister at 100 rounds per minute. General Thomas' "sanitary" report describes what happened next: "January 2, about 7 a.m. the enemy opened a direct and cross fire from his batteries in our front.... About 4 p.m. a division of Crittenden's corps ... was attacked by an overwhelming force of the enemy, and, after a gallant resistance, compelled to fall back."[24]

January 3 was not so quiet for the Third Ohio, however. Commanding the Ohio regiment, Colonel Beatty recalls, "The rebels hold a strip of woods in our immediate front, and we get up a lively skirmish with them. Our men, however, appear loth to advance far enough to afford the necessary protection to the workers. Vexed at their unwillingness to venture out, I ride forward and start over a line to which I desire the skirmishers to advance, and discover, before I have gone twenty yards, that I have done a foolish thing. A hundred muskets open on me from the woods; but the eyes of my own brigade and of other troops are on me, and I cannot back out. I quicken the pace of my horse somewhat, and continue my perilous course. The bullets whistle like bees about my head, but I ride the whole length of the proposed skirmish line, and get back to the brigade in safety. Colonel Humphrey, of the Eighty-eighth Indiana comes up to me, and with a tremor in his voice, which indicates much feeling, says: 'My God, Colonel, never do that again!' The caution is unnecessary. I had already made up my mind never to do it again. We keep up a vigorous skirmish with the enemy for hours, losing now and then a man; but later in the day we are relieved from this duty, and retire to a quieter place."[25]

Early in the morning on January 3, "Fighting Joe" Wheeler was at it again. With rebel forces losing their confidence and unsure of the outcome of this great battle, Wheeler and his cavalry tried to weaken Rosecrans by disrupting his supply train. In the past, this had seriously hurt Union forces by depriving them of the extra ammunition and commissary supplies necessary to continue the fight. To draw Union pickets away from Wheeler and allow him to pillage and burn unrestricted, rebel sharpshooters did their best to keep Rosecrans' men occupied. However, Lovell Rousseau had had enough and ordered two regiments to go after the snipers. According to the Third Ohio commander, "About nightfall General Rousseau desires me to get two regiments in readiness, and, as soon as it becomes quite dark, charge upon and clean out the woods in our front. I select the Third Ohio and Eighty-eighth Indiana for this duty, and at the appointed time we form line in the open field in front of Guenther's battery, and as we start, the battery commences to shell the woods. As we get nearer the objective point, I put the men on the double quick. The rebels, discovering our approach, open a heavy fire, but in the darkness shoot too high. The blaze of their guns reveals their exact position to us. We reach the rude log breastworks behind which they are standing and grapple with them. Colonel Humphrey receives a severe thrust from a bayonet; others are wounded, and some killed. It is pitch dark under the trees. Some of Guenther's shells fall short, and alarm the men. Unable to find either staff officer or orderly, I ride back and request him to elevate his guns. Returning, I find my troops blazing away with great energy; but, so far as I can discover, their fire is not returned. It is difficult, however, in the noise, confusion, and darkness, to direct their movements, and impossible to stop the firing. In the meantime a new danger threatens. Spear's Tennesseans have been sent to support us, probably without any definite instructions. They are, most of them, raw troops, and, becoming either excited or alarmed at the terrible racket in the woods, deliver scattering shots in our rear. I ride back and urge them either to cease firing or move to the left, go forward and look after our flank. One regiment does move as directed; but the others are immovable, and it is with great difficulty that I succeed in making them understand that in firing they are more likely to injure friends than foes. Fortunately, soon after this, the ammunition of the Third and Eighty-eighth becoming exhausted, the firing in the woods ceases, and. as the enemy has already abandoned the field, the affair ends. I try to find General Rousseau to report results, but cannot; and so, worn out with fatigue and excitement, lie down for another night."[26]

The action of the Third Ohio is confirmed by reports from General George Thomas and General Lovell Rousseau. Thomas' report of January 15, 1863, states, "About 6 p.m. two regiments from Col. John Beatty's brigade, Rousseau's division, cooperating with two regiments of Spears' brigade, of Negley's division, covered by the skillful and well-directed fire of Guenther's Fifth U.S. Artillery and Loomis' First Michigan Batteries, advanced on the woods and drove the enemy not only from their cover, but from their intrenchments, a short distance beyond."[27]

General Lovell Rousseau said it best, however. He put the Third Ohio in the appropriate perspective when he concluded in his report of January 11, 1863, "On the evening of Third, instant, I asked permission of General Thomas to drive the enemy from our front on our left front, to which he gave his consent. Just before night I directed the batteries of Guenther and Loomis to shell the woods with six rounds per gun, fired as rapidly as possible. This was very handsomely done and ended at dusk, when the Third Ohio Regiment, Lieut. Col. O.A. Lawson and the eighty-eighth

Indiana, Col. George Humphrey, both under command of the brigade commander, Col. John Beatty, moved promptly up the woods. When near the woods they received a heavy fire from the enemy, but returned it vigorously, and gallantly pressed forward. On reaching the woods, a fresh body of the enemy, attracted by the fire, moved up on their left to support them. On that body of the enemy, Loomis' battery opened with shell. The fusillade was very rapid, and continued for, perhaps, three-quarters of an hour, when Beatty's command drove the enemy at the point of the bayonet and held the work in the woods, and, when ousted, about 30 men were taken prisoners behind the works. This ended the battle of Murfreesboro."[28]

January 4 was quiet. The Third Ohio heard no noise from the rebel side of the Stone River. As a result, Rosecrans moved his entire army across the two river fords to occupy the former rebel camps. Historians have called the Battle of Stones River/Murfreesboro one of the bloodiest of the entire Civil War. It rivals both Antietam and Gettysburg. Some divisions lost 30–40 percent of officers and infantry. The Third Ohio was lucky in losing only 27 percent of the regiment. Rosecrans' final report stated that he lost 20 percent of his entire army. He writes at one point, "If there are many more bloody battles on record ... or if there has been more true fighting qualities displayed by any people, I should be pleased to know it."[29] The amount of ammunition necessary to force the rebels from the field was considerable. This is significant because on December 31, Rosecrans had only one more day of ammunition and food supplies left for his army. Joseph Wheeler and his men had caused enough damage to Union supply lines that the outcome of the battle was in serious doubt at that point. Rosecrans' report indicates that it took 20,000 cannonballs to kill 728 rebels, and 2 million musket balls to hit 13,832 Confederate infantry and officers. He estimated that it required 27.4 cannon shots to hit one rebel, and 145 musket balls to hit their mark as well. Assuming that Braxton Bragg paid the same compliment to "Old Rosy," the four-day battle must have been a smoky and thunderous firestorm of brave and frightened men and horses. On January 5, Third Ohio commander Colonel John Beatty went out to the battlefield to gather data necessary for a report that had been requested by General Rousseau. He remembered, "I ride over the battle-field. In one place a caisson and five horses are lying, the latter killed in harness, and all fallen together. Nationals and Confederates, young, middle-aged, and old, are scattered over the woods and fields for miles. Poor Wright, of my old company, lay at the barricade in the woods which we stormed on the night of the last day. Many others lay about him. Further on we find men with their legs shot off; one with brains scooped out with a cannon ball; another with half a face gone; another with entrails protruding; young Winnegard, of the Third, has one foot off and both legs pierced by grape at the thighs; another boy lies with his hands clasped above his head, indicating that his last words were a prayer. Many Confederate sharpshooters lay behind stumps, rails, and logs, shot in the head. A young boy, dressed in the Confederate uniform, lies with his face turned to the sky, and looks as if he might be sleeping. Poor boy! What thoughts of home, mother, death, and eternity, commingled in his brain as the life-blood ebbed away! Many wounded horses are limping over the field. One mule, I heard of, had a leg blown off on the first day's battle; next morning it was on the spot where first wounded; at night it was still standing there, not having moved an inch all day, patiently suffering, it knew not why nor for what. How many poor men moaned through the cold nights in the thick woods, where the first day's battle occurred, calling in vain to man for help, and finally making their last solemn petition to God!"[30]

By the time Beatty got back to camp, rain had turned to sleet. The temperatures were colder than it had been throughout the battle. Most of the rank and file were quiet. Their thoughts were either on home, the comrades they lost in the fight or on God. Sitting around campfires, some men spoke, but most stared at the flames and tried to erase terrible thoughts from their minds. In the distance, laughter could be heard coming from General McCook's tent. Rousseau, Crittenden and McCook drank the whiskey that had been saved to celebrate what they had hoped would be a Union victory. Colonel Beatty turned in surprise when he heard someone singing "Mary Had a Little Lamb." In the midst of so much pain, death and miraculous survival, anything was possible.

Stones River avenged the Union loss at Fredericksburg. Abraham Lincoln and General-in-Chief Henry Halleck were happy. On January 5, 1863, Lincoln sent a wire to Rosecrans:

Executive Mansion
Washington, January 5, 1863

Maj. Gen. W.S. Rosecrans
Murfreesborough, Tenn.:

Your dispatch announcing retreat of enemy has just reached here. God bless you and all with you! Please tender to all, and accept for yourself, the nation's gratitude for your and their skill, endurance and dauntless courage.

A. Lincoln[31]

After the Battle of Stones River, politics became the axle supporting the weight of endless war. Two days later, some of the Tennessee newspapers began to print copies of Abraham Lincoln's Emancipation Proclamation. Although the crest of rebel "power" was just months away at Chancellorsville, the Confederacy was crippled after Stones River. It wasn't the battle per se that caused the damage; it was an accumulation of many factors. East Tennessee and the vital rail line was now secure. While the battle was going on, Union cavalry were already marching toward Kentucky. Clashes at Blountsville and Bristol, Tennessee, were reported in the local newspapers. The so-called Anaconda Plan of navy secretary Gideon Welles and Winfield Scott was starting to strangle the Confederacy. Fewer and fewer Confederate and British privateers were getting through the Union blockade of key Southern ports. Saltpeter for gunpowder was becoming scarce. Before the battle, on October 31, the *Washington Evening Star* published an article about contraband and smugglers bringing medical supplies through Union lines posted in Centerville, Virginia. An older woman named Mrs. Turner, a younger woman named Miss Buckner and a preacher named Buck Bailey were caught smuggling morphine and quinine. The women were suspicious because they wore unusually large hoop skirts. Inside the skirt of Mrs. Turner was discovered 300 ounces of quinine. The Confederacy was getting desperate.

By January 14, 1863, the Third Ohio had marched to Columbia, Tennessee. After 36 hours of marching in the cold rain, the men were tired, hungry and threatening mutiny—again! On the 15th, it began to snow, and the Third was ordered back to Murfreesboro. Overall, the new year, 1863, started with changes that would transform and reshape the nation.

At the 1877 reunion of the Third Ohio, a poem was read to the veterans assembled. It concluded,

> *Three days of bloody carnage, and not a man there knew*
> *On which side went the battle, whether for the wrong or true;*
> *Till cannons spoke their thunder, and the air was black with smoke,*
> *When Bragg was driven across the river with his army crushed and broke.*
>
> *You remember, comrades, that last charge when Beatty led the way,*
> *Over the dead and dying that all around you lay,*
> *With the 88th Indiana and Ohio's gallant third?*
> *You drove the yelling Johnnies as a farmer drives his herd.*[32]

The Third Ohio stood and fought at Stones River. They never ran. Will they fight another day soon? If not Braxton Bragg, who will oppose them? They would find out soon enough.

8

A Bluff Beats a Straight

"*All is fair in love and war*," joked Confederate lieutenant general Nathan Bedford Forrest to Union brigadier general Abel Streight on May 15, 1863.[1] The next day, Streight was headed to Libby Prison in Richmond, Virginia. The Third Ohio rank and file were briefly locked up on Belle Isle. Who was Forrest? What happened?

The new year, 1863, would bring changes to the nation and the Third Ohio. The *Chattanooga Daily Rebel* entertained its readers on January 1, 1863, with stories of both John Hunt Morgan and Nathan Bedford Forrest. "John Morgan treated the Yankees to a Christmas visit, at Glasgow, killing and capturing a large number. The next day he burned all the bridges between Munfordsville and Elizabethtown, Kentucky, and destroyed fifteen miles of the Louisville and Nashville Road ... from West Tennessee we have stirring accounts of the movements of Forrest and VanDorn.... On the 19th Forrest destroyed the railroad connection near Humboldt, cutting off the Yankee supplies."[2]

The Third Ohio didn't realize it in January, but they would soon be fighting with one of the most aggressive men in the South. Nathan Bedford Forrest was a natural risk-taker who had amassed a personal fortune of almost $2 million. He made his money in cotton and slavery. Just before the war, he harvested 1,000 bales of cotton per year. In slaves, Forrest bought cheap and sold high. When the market began to suffer, he rented his slaves out to other plantations looking for more hands to pick cotton. "Nathan Bedford Forrest, a slave trader by profession, high-tempered and capable of disemboweling an enemy with a penknife one day, and arranging a religious revival the next. Hater of whiskey and smut, [Forrest] had few rivals as a cavalry leader."[3]

Abel Streight was a book publisher from Indiana and colonel of the 51st Indiana Volunteer Infantry Regiment. Ironically, Streight, Forrest and Morgan were cut from the same bolt of cloth. "The desire for quick decisive action and hatred for the slower more conservative way of doing things were dominant factors in Streight's personality. Unfortunately, Streight's active nature, when uncontrolled, had a tendency toward rashness—an open invitation to disaster."[4] As a result, Abel Streight put pressure on his friend and new chief of staff, Army of the Cumberland, James Garfield. On March 5, 1863, he wrote Garfield, "I hope you will continue to favor me with your influence to induce the General [Rosecrans] to give me a suitable command for the purpose of penetrating the interior of the South."[5] By March 1863, Vicksburg and Gettysburg hadn't happened yet. Nevertheless, fighting within the Lincoln administration started to generate headlines.

Nathan Bedford Forrest was considered a natural leader and promoted to brigadier general in 1862. Although poorly educated, he was a successful risk-taker in business and became very wealthy by the start of the war. Forrest and his relentless cavalry finally caught Abel Streight and the Third Ohio in Alabama in 1863 (Library of Congress).

Always seeking to find fault with the North and ignore the problems facing the Confederacy, the *Chattanooga Daily Rebel* headlined page 1, January 1, 1863, with, "The Cabinet Embroglio." The issue concerned Secretary of State William Henry Seward and Secretary of the Treasury Salmon Portland Chase. The men hated each other, and both were threatening to resign. Seward ran against Lincoln for the 1860 Republican presidential nomination and lost. He never forgot it and decided to become the de facto president instead. Within one year, however, Seward wrote to his wife, admitting, "Executive skill and vigor are rare qualities. The President is the best of us."[6] Not so Chase. The treasury secretary was constantly trying to politically undercut and chase Lincoln throughout his presidency. Chase was a brilliant and effective treasury secretary, but he was desperate to become president. His beautiful daughter Kate was always hosting parties and gatherings with the rich and powerful to further her father's goal.[7] Chase believed that Seward was unduly influencing the president.

So, behind the scenes, Salmon Chase began feeding a group of senators with inside information on the functioning of the cabinet and what he perceived was the excessive influence of Seward on Lincoln. When the president called all parties together at the Executive Mansion to lay all of the facts on the table, Chase backed down. Lincoln was an intuitively savvy and skillful politician who knew how to handle people in the back room.[8] Nevertheless, the *Chattanooga Daily Rebel* printed all of the "dirt" they could find on the Lincoln presidency. It gave the South hope. The new year, however, brought war and death to the Third Ohio. After Perryville and Stones River, they remained in Murfreesboro and helped to strengthen its fortifications against another visit from Braxton Bragg. After winter turned into spring, the Third was on the move again but in a new direction.

On April 7, 1863, the Third Ohio was selected to be part of a special cavalry force charged with disrupting communication and supplies to the Army of Tennessee. If they had any extra time on their hands, they were also instructed to cut the Virginia and Tennessee Railroad line and thus decapitate the Confederacy and perhaps end the war. If they wanted more adventure, they could try to challenge and defeat the devil himself, "Devil" Forrest. Between John Hunt Morgan, the "Wizard of the Saddle," "Fighting Joe" Wheeler, the "Paradoxical Cavalier" (John Pegram) and Nathan Bedford Forrest (Devil Forrest), the Army of the Cumberland had its hands full. Rebel cavalry was able to threaten the rear guard and supply lines of Rosecrans' army wherever it went. From the rear, rebel cavalry captured thousands of Union prisoners and

Brigadier General Abel Streight was a book publisher from Indiana who was appointed colonel of the 51st Indiana Infantry in 1861. He leaned on his friend, Adjutant James Garfield, to get orders from General Rosecrans to try and disrupt the critical Southern rail junction at Rome, Georgia. This resulted in Streight's Raid in 1863 (Library of Congress).

8. A Bluff Beats a Straight

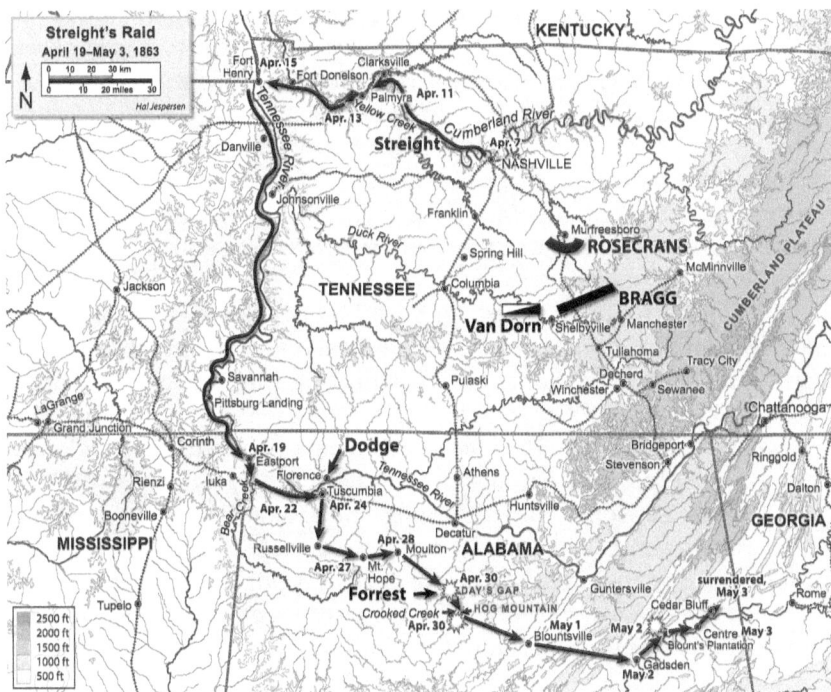

Streight's Raid encompassed a long route over water and land. It stretched from Nashville to Forts Henry and Donelson on the Cumberland River. The men of the Third Ohio continued past the Shiloh battlefield and through much of northern Alabama. They almost reached their goal of Rome, Georgia, before their capture by Confederate general Nathan Bedford Forrest (Library of Congress).

burned hundreds of supply wagons valued in the millions. On the eve of the Battle of Stones River, Forrest left Union troops with only one day of ammunition. Without resupply, Rosecrans would either be forced to surrender or retreat. The threat to Abel Streight and the Third Ohio came from "Devil Forrest." Forrest would prove to be a challenge for the Third Ohio. Even worse, the regiment was about to have a new leader.

John Beatty was promoted to brigadier general in March 1863 but was still very much attached to his original regiment, the Third Ohio. The new orders for the regiment were top secret to the extent that their brigade commander, John Beatty, didn't know of their plans. His old regiment would go on without him, however. According to Beatty on April 7, 1863, "The incident of the day, to me at least, is the departure of the Third. It left on the two P.M. train for Nashville. I do not think I have been properly treated. They should at least have consulted me before detaching my old regiment. I am informed that Colonel Streight, who is in command of the expedition, was permitted to select the regiments, and the matter has been conducted so secretly that, before I had an intimation of what was contemplated, it was too late to take any steps to keep the Third. I never expect to be in command of it again. It will get into another current, and drift into other brigades, divisions, and army corps. The idea of being mounted was very agreeable to both officers and men; but a little experience in that branch of the service will probably lead them to regret the choice they have made. My best wishes go with them."[9]

With this, the Third Ohio Volunteer Infantry Regiment parted with the officer and leader in whom they had placed their faith and the safety of their lives. Where were they going? According to Abel Streight, "On April 7, 1863, I received orders from General Rosecrans to proceed with the Provisional Brigade—about 1,700 officers and men, composed of my regiment (the Fifty-First Indiana); Seventy-third Indiana, Colonel Hathaway; Third Ohio, Colonel Lawson; Eightieth Illinois, Lieutenant Colonel Rogers, and two Companies of the First Middle Tennessee Cavalry, Capt. D.D. Smith—to Nashville, and to fit out as speedily as possible for an expedition to the interior of Alabama and Georgia, for the purpose of destroying the railroads and other rebel property in that country."[10]

Knowing that going almost anywhere in America at this time was faster over water than by land, the Third was directed to take a steamboat up the Cumberland River to Palmyra, Tennessee. According to Third Ohio, Company A sergeant Henry Breidenthal, "April 7: All was bustle this morning early as we proceeded to leave camp. After leaving, we were placed upon the cars, and after a few hours of rough riding, we were halted two miles south of Nashville, and are bivouacked for the night.... April 10: This four PM, a forward movement was ordered. We were placed on boats the steamers *Nashville*, *Hazel Bell*, and *Aurora*. We found the lower deck crowded with mules—the odor of which was not agreeable to our 'oil-factories.'"[11] From there, they were to march to Fort Henry to secure horses and mules for the expedition. The steamboat trip was an eye-opener, however. According to Breidenthal on April 11, "We saw numerous wrecks of steamboats, which the rebels have recently captured of us and destroyed."[12] According to Streight, "As soon as everything was ready to proceed down the river to Palmyra, where we arrived on the evening of the 11th, and disembarked at once. I sent the fleet, consisting of eight steamers, around to Fort Henry, under the command of Colonel Lawson, Third Ohio, and furnished him with four companies of the Fifty-First Indiana Volunteers as guard."[13] Palmyra looked desolate to the Third Ohio, however. They saw a town that had been looted and burned as fair compensation for their collaboration with the rebels.

The Third Ohio ran into their first serious problem at Fort Henry. Instead of the horses they were promised, they discovered that they would be riding mules during the hundreds of miles that would take them through Middle Tennessee, Alabama and Georgia. However, Streight was familiar with northern Alabama and believed that mules would be better suited for the rugged terrain.[14] Things soon got worse, however. Some of the mules had distemper. Others were too old to walk at all. Some died before the expedition even left Fort Henry. Quartermaster for the Streight brigade was John B. Doughty. With only $3,000 to spend on mounts, good horses were too expensive and out of the question. Foraging parties that scoured the countryside for better animals found enough mules and horses to replace the old and lame ones. Unfortunately, none of the new mounts were shod. They were all "barefoot." Streight's brigade continued to scour the area for horses but found few. Hearing that they were coming caused the locals to turn their stock loose. Nevertheless, what became known as the "Jackass Cavalry" was forced to move on, mounted or on foot. Continuing up the Tennessee River, the Third arrived at Fort Henry on April 16. According to Sergeant Breidenthal of the Third, "We arrived at Fort Henry at midnight.... I went up to see the fort which General Tilghman was forced to surrender after sixty minutes bombardment. Its position is good, commanding a long reach of the river and shows undoubted evidence of having felt 'Uncle Sam's Foote.'"[15]

Fort Henry was one of two forts safeguarding passage on the Tennessee River. The fort was hastily constructed and commanded by Brigadier General Lloyd Tilghman. "Lloyd Tilghman was slim and dark-skinned, with a heavy, carefully barbered mustache and chin-beard, an erect, soldierly bearing, and piercing black eyes intensifying what one observer called a 'resolute, intelligent resolution of countenance.'"[16] On January 28, 1862, Brigadier General Ulysses Grant wired his commander Henry Halleck, "With permission, I will take Fort Henry on the Tennessee and establish and hold a large camp there."[17] Tilghman had a small force to defend the fort, and his men were armed with old, flintlock Tower muskets and shotguns.[18] Those piercing, black eyes wouldn't help either. The only thing he had in his favor was the intense rivalry between Henry Halleck, George Thomas and Don Carlos Buell. All were Union generals operating in the western theater of the war and each jealous of each other's successful engagements in the war thus far. In addition to personal jealousy, however, Tilghman also had the river mined with "torpedoes." These were explosive devises that were anchored to the river bottom with chains. Recent heavy rain had added the benefit of submerging the contact probe of the mine just below the surface of the water.

Coordinating with Ulysses Grant was Admiral Andrew Foote.[19]

While Grant attacked from land, it was Foote's job to attack from the water and squeeze the fort between his monitor-class ironclads and Grant's infantry. If any of Foote's monitors bumped into one of the probes, however, that would be the last such embrace enjoyed in this life. On the river, flag officer Andrew Foote assembled a small fleet of ironclad and timber-clad ships.[20] Grant and Foote, however, had no trouble putting ego aside to plan a combined attack on the fort. With Grant marching on the fort from the north and Foote from the river, they hoped to easily reduce the fort. Before opening fire, however, Grant boarded one of Foote's ships and ordered it to steam close to the fort and draw fire. He wanted to determine the effective range of the guns in Fort Henry. He didn't have to wait. A soon as he got within range, Tilghman opened up on Grant. Quickly steaming back to safety, Grant and Foote knew what to do. On February 6, after only one hour of bombardment, Tilghman surrendered. On April 18, the Third Ohio continued steaming up the Tennessee River. By the 19th, they were passing Pittsburg Landing. It was here just two weeks prior that Grant defeated Albert Sydney Johnston and Pierre Beauregard near the Shiloh Methodist Church. By the 20th, the Third finally caught up with a brigade led by Major General Grenville Dodge. The plan was to use Dodge to screen the countryside ahead of Streight's march. Dodge would be responsible for chasing Morgan, Pegram and Forrest away. Dodge had been successful in frustrating the guerrilla band led by Earl Van Dorn. Nathan Bedford Forrest might be a challenge, however. If Dodge was successful, this would allow Streight to continue with his mission and destroy the extensive railroad connections in Rome, Georgia. By the 23rd, Breidenthal of the Third noted, "General Dodge's command passed us early this morning for Tuscumbia.... In places, we saw evidence of severe skirmishing, dead horses, defaced and burned houses, etc. We saw corn six inches high and it looked healthy, but wheat and rye looked very bad, and very, very scattering."[21] The inability for either army to supply their troops in a timely and consistent manner forced both sides to forage for themselves. As a result, the once-productive countryside in Kentucky and Tennessee were fleeced and robbed of everything edible. Chickens, cows and hogs couldn't run fast enough. The corn and wheat got picked, and the houses got burned. This was war.

Streight and Dodge reached Tuscumbia, Alabama, at 5:00 p.m. on April 24. It took 15 hours to travel 40 miles. At Tuscumbia, Streight talked with Major General Grenville Dodge to plan strategy and tactics.[22] Streight was charged with burning bridges and tearing up rail lines, not fighting if it could be avoided. That was Dodge's job. However, the closing paragraph of Special Field Order #94 made it clear that "should you be surrounded by rebel forces and your retreat cut off, defend yourself as long as possible, and make the surrender of your command cost the enemy as many times your number as possible."[23] Later on the 24th, the Third could hear the sound of cannon in the distance. Grenville Dodge was doing his job and clearing the way for Streight. Dodge had run into Confederate general Phillip Roddey. Like Dodge, Roddey's job was to screen and gather intelligence for Forrest. Roddey commanded a mounted infantry regiment, however. His men were armed with rifled muskets, but they fought dismounted. On April 26, Streight and the Third Ohio left Tuscumbia and started for Moulton, Alabama. Dodge knew that Forrest was in the area. Everyone was on high alert. They had good reason because later on the 26th, Company F of the Third Ohio was attacked by Forrest's men. According to Henry Breidenthal of the Third, "Our advance guard was ambushed by a company of bushwhackers, but fortunately we received no injury, we all dismounted, and leaving every fourth man to hold the stock, we started and deployed out to flank them, but they 'lit out' as soon as soon as they delivered two rounds."[24] At Perryville, the Third was constantly thirsting for water. Now the spring rains had arrived and the roads were muddy. Under these conditions, even an old mule was a blessing. Streight's march was slow because many of the men had no mount, and marching in the mud was a challenge. Nevertheless, "Devil Forrest" came after Streight. Dodge had already engaged Forrest before the rebel cavalry got too close. After camping in Moulton, Streight's brigade started for Blountsville via Day's Gap on April 28. At this point, Forrest and his men were getting impatient and wanted more action. On the 29th, the Third Ohio sent out a scouting party. According to Breidenthal of the Third, "As one of our foraging parties was going out, one mile from camp, they came unexpectedly on a squad of ten rebels, fired into them, scattering and capturing several prisoners."[25]

The final combat experience of the Third Ohio Volunteer Infantry Regiment occurred during the three frantic, rowdy months of "Streight's Raid." Riding on mules that refused to run, Streight and the Third Ohio were constantly pursued and hounded by a much faster cavalry brigade led by Confederate general Nathan Bedford Forrest. Abel Streight and the Third Ohio never achieved their objective because Forrest and his men rode horses that were faster than Streight's stubborn, barefoot mules. Although not a fair fight, Streight and the Third gave battle, spiked Confederate guns and ambushed "Devil Forrest" and his cavalry all over northern Alabama and almost into north Georgia. The fact that Streight outnumbered Forrest three to one didn't bother the rebel cavalry, however.

By April 29, 1863, Streight reported, "We marched the next day [the 29th] to Day's Gap, about 35 miles, and bivouacked for the night.... We destroyed during the day a large number of wagons belonging to the enemy, laden with provisions, arms, tents, & c."²⁶ The "Jackass Cavalry" was successful because they always traveled with their own skirmishers in the rear to protect against attack. On the morning of the 30th, the Third heard the sound of heavy artillery in the rear of their column. The skirmishers had been attacked by scouts from Forrest's cavalry. This time, however, the rebel brigade was led by the "Devil's" younger brother William.²⁷ His private band of highwaymen was nicknamed the "Forty Thieves." They were neither volunteer nor regular army. The younger Forrest commanded a group of bandits and privateers who paid themselves with whatever they could steal or grab from the local population. Rushing for Day's Gap to try and outrun Forrest, Streight was concerned because the gap was flanked by other mountain passes that might allow Forrest to surge ahead and strike Streight head-on. The Third might emerge from the protection of the steep walls of Day's Gap and run right into a roadblock of mountain howitzers and rifled muskets. The only option was to stand and fight. Union scouts had already discovered that Forrest was already gaining on both right and left flanks. They were ready to pounce as soon as Streight came out of the gap. Nevertheless, Streight and his men kicked and screamed at the mules to run as fast as they could to get ahead of Forrest and find a suitable place to make a stand. The area was thinly wooded and denied Forrest the protection of the trees and rocks that would keep his men safe. The plan was to secure the high ground at the crest of Sand Mountain. It worked!

It was an ideal defensive position. The mules were moved out of musket range and the howitzers loaded with double canister. Forrest and his men emerged from gaps to the left and right of Streight. At first, all they could see were the two guns and their crews manned by the Third Ohio's Major James Vananda. Streight hoped to lure Forrest up to the crest of Sand Mountain and into the hidden ranks of the rest of his brigade lying out of sight. As Forrest ordered his men to charge, Streight and his brigade suddenly stood and opened up on the surprised rebels.

> We continued to pour a rapid fire into [Forrest's] ranks, which soon caused them to give way in confusion; but their re-enforcements soon came up, when they dismounted, formed, and made a determined and vigorous attack. Our skirmishers were soon driven in, and about the same time the enemy opened upon us with a battery of artillery.²⁸

The artillery fire acted as a shield to allow the enemy artillery to be brought to within a few hundred yards of Streight and the Third. This was going to be the turning point in the battle.

> During their advance they had run their artillery to within 300 yards of our lines, and as soon as they began to waver I prepared for a charge. I

ordered ... the Third Ohio, Colonel Lawson, and the Eightieth Illinois, Lieutenant-Colonel Rodgers, forward rapidly, hoping to capture the battery. The enemy, after a short but stubborn resistance, fled in confusion, leaving two pieces of artillery, two caissons, and about 40 prisoners, representing seven different regiments, a large number of wounded and about 30 dead on the field. Among the former was Captain [William H.] Forrest, a brother of General Forrest.[29]

As soon as Straight saw Forrest's men break and run, he decided to charge and finish them off. According to Henry Breidenthal of the Third Ohio, "We burned the wagons as per arrangement; but before our whole column had filed out into the road, the rebels, who had come up, had got a battery of two pieces in position, and began playing upon us pretty sharply, but fortunately doing us no injury. Our command was then forwarded briskly on three miles upon the crest of a ridge, near Day's Gap, where we were dismounted and formed in a line of battle in the best kind of order and waited for the approach of the enemy. We had not long to wait, for they came thundering on, and planted their two pieces of field artillery but a few hundred yards from our line of skirmishers, and commenced to open on us with shell and shot, but without much effect as their range was too high to reach us in our sheltered position. Our little mountain howitzers were brought to bear upon them with good result, for they fell back and tried our left wing, but were signally repulsed by the Fifty-First and Seventy-third Indiana with considerable loss on their side. They then reformed, making a feint upon the right wing where the Eightieth Illinois was posted, while they at the same time made a demonstration on our center, where our battery and part of the Fifty-first Indiana and Third Ohio were, and were met with a murderous fire that sent them back. The Third was then ordered to fix bayonets and charge on their battery and at the command every man sprang to his feet and skipped off on a run, gun and hat in one hand, yelling like so many Mohawks, taking their battery of two pieces and one limber and some horses without firing a gun, the rebels taking to their heels and horses and 'light-out.' The enemy was so surprised at our appearance in force (for they did not suppose that our whole force had halted and formed so soon) that they fled. We pursued them a few hundred yards, and were recalled, taking the pieces and placing them in position by the side of ours, and manning them. We were then reformed on our old ground as we anticipated a renewal of the attack. We then threw out a heavy line of skirmishers and videttes; but with the exception of a few scattering shots, no further demonstration was made against us at this place."[30]

After a battle that lasted almost five hours, Streight decided it would be best to move quickly before Forrest was able to receive reinforcements. The mules were brought back and loaded. A rear guard of skirmishers was posted, and the Jackass Cavalry was on the march again. The Third Ohio was posted as a "chain guard" in front to protect against an attack from that position. Later, Sergeant Henry Breidenthal of the Third Ohio recalled the day when his regiment charged down the side of Sand Mountain and drove the infamous "Devil Forrest" back through the gap: "Let me say here that the movement just ended, lasting one hour, was one of the most brilliant affairs that I have yet witnessed, especially the bayonet charge upon the enemy, where everyone went in with a vim, and those having the strongest legs getting their [sic] first and those with the strongest lungs making the most noise."[31] The charge of the Third Ohio produced chaos in Forrest's camp. Some of his horses were killed. The other surviving mounts were so panic-stricken by the noise and smoke of battle that they became tangled in their chains and leather traces. Untangling that mess took enough time to allow Streight and his men to escape.

It didn't take long, however, before Forrest caught up again. Only 10 miles south of Day's Gap, Forrest started shooting at Streight's rear guard. They were near Black Warrior River and were forced to stop and make a stand. This time, however, Streight was armed with the two mountain howitzers as well as two other heavy guns captured from Forrest. The rebel force was able to charge from both right and left flanks. According to Streight, however, "With a good effort of Major Vananda, of the Third Ohio, we were able to repulse them."[32] Not wishing to push his luck, Streight got the mules loaded and the men ready to march. Unfortunately, the ammunition for the two captured rebel guns had run out. It was ordered to spike the guns before leaving. Men from the Third quickly inserted rat tail files into the gun vents and hammered them into place. Now they were useless and could no longer threaten Streight's brigade. Leaving both guns in the middle of the road, the brigade moved out as quickly as stubborn mules would allow.

With faster mounts, however, Forrest caught up with Streight and the Third very quickly. It was 10:00 p.m. and the moon was bright. The approaching enemy was clearly visible in the distance. This cat-and-mouse game was starting to wear down the Union cavalry. So the 73rd Indiana was placed in a row of bushes about 20 yards from the side of the road. They were backed up by the Third and the rest of the brigade. They should be able to slow Forrest down and give Streight time to make his escape. Yard by yard, Forrest's cavalry galloped closer to Streight's hidden brigade. Forrest paid no attention to the fact that the rest of the Union force was moving at a walk. This was unusual. The 73rd was told to wait until the head of the rebel cavalry was past the bushes—and then open fire. "The head of his column passed without discovering our position. At this moment the whole regiment opened a most destructive fire, causing a complete stampede of the enemy."[33] Confederate private Thomas D. Duncan remembered the scene: "Then [Streight] placed his men in ambush and drew us into a deadly trap.... After losing a number of men, we ... recoiled from the front of flame; and on our retreat the enemy pursued us so closely that we lost two of our field pieces."[34] Streight and the Third were urging their mules on as fast as their tender feet would go. As a result, they missed an opportunity to see Nathan Bedford Forrest explode in rage at his men. He wanted his two guns back. After lashing the back of some of his men with the flat of his sword, the brigade mounted and took off after the "Jackass Cavalry."

Streight took advantage of his success and made a dash for Blountsville, about 40 miles away. The countryside was empty. No houses and no feed for the exhausted animals. When crossing over Hog Mountain, Forrest caught up with Streight again. Henry Breidenthal from the Third Ohio remembered May 30, 1862: "Finally, the brigade reached the safety of Blountsville at ten o'clock the next morning. It had been a long night, and a hard ride."[35] What had begun as a mission to burn bridges and tear up railroad track had turned into a race for their own survival. The bridges could wait. Fortunately, Blountsville supplied corn for the mules, food for the men and ammunition for the guns. It was clear at this point that the mules were no match for Forrest's horse cavalry. In addition to stubborn mules, Streight was also hauling supply wagons which further slowed them down. The mountain howitzers were designed to be disassembled and loaded on pack animals. As a result, the decision was made to burn the supply wagons and load everything else on the mules and make a run for it. According to Breidenthal, they burned "four thousand dollars' worth of good flour, five hundred stand of arms and the ferry boat."[36] In addition to burning every bridge they crossed on their way east, they also burned the ferry boat that crossed the Coosa River. Streight and the Third got close to Gadsden, Alabama, when they were faced with trying to cross a swollen branch of the Black Warrior River. Forcing stubborn mules across without getting the ammunition wet was going to take some planning. They were still west of the town and desperate to get over the river before Forrest caught up. A skirmish line was placed at the edge of the river to allow the main body of Streight's brigade to cross. On the other side, the artillery was set up to protect the crossing of the skirmishers. It was 5:00 p.m. when all had crossed and entered Gadsden. By the next morning, May 2, it was clear that Forrest would not give up. His men could be seen searching the riverbank where they could cross without dismounting and swimming the horses. Forrest was frustrated and his anger began to show. He knew Streight was close but on the other side of the river. He needed to get across fast. Farther down the Gadsden-Blountsville road, some of Streight's men spotted a lone farmhouse. The first thing they saw was the well that would help keep them and their mounts alive. Watching them from inside were Lavinia Sansom and her two daughters, Emma and Jennie. They lived by themselves because Lavinia's husband died in 1859, and her son Rufus was in a field hospital in Gadsden. Emma remembered, "We were at home on the morning of May 2, 1863, when about eight or nine o'clock a company of men wearing blue uniforms and riding mules and horses galloped past the house and went on towards the bridge.... By this time, they came in [the house] to search for firearms and men's saddles. They did not find anything but a side saddle, and one of them cut the skirts off that.... Just then someone from the road said, 'you men bring a chunk of fire with you, and get out of that house.' They all soon hurried down to the bridge, and in a few minutes we saw smoke rising, and knew they were burning the bridge."[37]

After Streight and his men got across the river, one of the skirmish guard left to protect the regiment as they crossed the river was mistakenly left behind. Emma watched from the house as a company of scouts from Forrest's regiment came chasing after the stranded Yankee. He couldn't run fast enough. After tying him up, Forrest went to the Sansom house and asked if anyone knew another place to cross the river. Emma immediately said that she knew where her cows crossed and would show "Devil Forrest" how to get there. Grabbing Emma by the arm, Forrest pulled the young girl on to the back of his horse. Emma pointed, and off they went to find the shallow ford across the Black Warrior River. After the ford was found and Forrest's men had all crossed, the "Devil" took Emma home and thanked her for her help. At this point, Streight and his men were trying to get to Blount's Plantation. They hoped to find food and water there. Forrest caught up quickly, however. "Forewarned of the Reb's approach, Streight had deployed his men to insure that Forrest received a hot reception. The terrain selected by Colonel Streight for this delaying action possessed a number of advantages. The Gadsden-Rome road, the axis of Forrest's advance, was extended to a depth of about 20 yards. As the road near the ridge where Streight had established his battle line, it veered abruptly to the left. One hundred yards beyond it turned sharply to the right and ascended the ridge, where the federals were deployed. Open field lay to the right and to the left of the thickets which flanked the road. Streight's skirmishers had thrown down a worn fence, using the rails to erect a barricade across the road at a point where it veered to the left. The federals hoped to force the Confederates into the open field to the right of the road. Sharpshooters were posted in the scrub timbers on both sides of the road, ready to rake the oncoming greyclads. Soldiers from the 51st and 73 Indiana, supported by the two mountain howitzers held the center of Streight's line; the 80th Illinois assumed responsibility for the right flank and the 3rd Ohio for the left."[38]

8. A Bluff Beats a Straight

Although Forrest's men were repeatedly thrown back, Streight lost one of his best men, Colonel Gilbert Hathaway from the 73rd Indiana. In addition, the Third Ohio lost 27-year-old Private Charles Stafford. He died of his wounds on May 2, 1863. Rome, Georgia, and the primary target of Streight's Raid was still 50 miles away. To get there, the Provisional Brigade had to cross the Coosa River. While searching for Dyke's Bridge to get across, they discovered the Iron Mountain Iron Works near Cedar Bluff, Alabama. If they couldn't tear up the Western and Atlantic Railroad, at least they could cripple an iron foundry that made the steam engines that supplied Confederate armies all over the South. According to Sergeant Henry Breidenthal of the Third Ohio, "We then filed to the left and took the road leading to [the Iron Works], and came to it in a short time, where we dismounted and placed a guard over the animals, and the rest of us proceeded to destroy the mammoth establishment. It was designed originally for smelting iron, but has within the last year, been undergoing great additions, until they almost had it completed for manufacturing a variety of munitions of war, such as cannon, shell, etc. and was worth several millions to them. But through the agency of fire, applied by us, with the heavy cooperation of the negroes, who threw the first brands into their own sleeping berths, we soon had the 'heaven and earth' illuminated with the conflagration of one of Dixie's most valuable establishments."[39]

A resident from Gadsden, John Wisdom, rode into Rome, Georgia, like Paul Revere to warn the residents that a Union brigade was coming to town. Forewarned, Rome was ready. If Streight and the Third Ohio thought Nathan Bedford Forrest was a problem, they hadn't reached Rome yet. Streight would first need to get across the Coosa River. Rome was ready with cotton bales at the end of the bridge. Wedged in between the bales were two cannons loaded with "buck and ball."[40] As the sun came up on Sunday, May 3, 1863, the "Jackass Brigade" was looking for a bridge to cross the Chattooga River. Streight wanted to send out scouts to screen their approach to Rome. They had to find Dyke's Bridge to make the crossing. They found it and crossed. The scouts were on their way to Rome. They would screen the final approach of the entire brigade. Burning the bridge behind them as they got close to Cedar Bluff, Streight thought he might complete his mission after all. His men were tired, and the mules were ready to quit. They had come a long way and successfully fought the "Devil" himself for every mile of their route across Alabama. Nathan Bedford Forrest had been a constant threat to the communications and supply of Union armies in the Deep South since the start of the war. He had cut telegraph lines and railroad tracks. Wagons loaded with Florida beef, coffee, ammunition and chloroform brightened the Tennessee and Alabama landscape with flames set by Forrest's men. Hopefully now, bluecoats would either starve or die in pain. Either way, he didn't care as long as they left and went home.

By 9:00 a.m. on Sunday morning, Streight and his brigade stopped near Cedar Bluff, Alabama. They were tired, but so was Forrest. According to Breidenthal, "The boys were so overcome with drowsiness that they would sleep on their animals; for we had not slept more than six hours in the last seventy-two, and had fought three general engagements and had rode one hundred and fifty miles."[41] Nevertheless, Forrest and his men finally caught up with Streight and the Third Ohio. As the men of the "Jackass Cavalry" sat next to their campfires cooking breakfast, they saw someone on horseback riding their way. Lying on their stomach and waiting, the Third watched as Confederate captain Henry Pointer rode up and asked to speak with Streight. Speaking for "Devil Forrest," Pointer demanded surrender to avoid further bloodshed. At this point, Streight's brigade was very low on ammunition. The powder for their howitzers had accidentally gotten wet while crossing the Black Warrior River. They had little with which to fight. Streight called his officers together and talked about what to do. Watching from a distance, Forrest bluffed Streight by moving cannon and men from one flank to another around Streight to give the Provisional Brigade the impression that Forrest's army was bigger than it might otherwise have appeared. Forrest was bluffing Streight with a small group of 400 men. Streight was actually the larger force with approximately 1,400 effectives. Streight's report simply stated, "At about noon, May Third, we surrendered as prisoners of war."[42] According to Sergeant Henry Breidenthal, Company A, Third Ohio Volunteer Infantry Regiment, "At about nine a.m. we were marched out into a field and there stacked arms. One of the boys, learning of the surrender, took his Henry rifle, a present from General Beatty, and broke it and stuck it in a mud hole. I bent mine as did others so they would shoot, like old Blackburn's rifle, around a tree or a hill! We then remounted and started for Rome."[43]

In Rome, Confederate troops ensured that Streight's men and officers were well treated. Before the officers and men were separated, Captain Charles David Anderson, Sixth Georgia Infantry, spoke to Abel Streight and joked, "Cheer up Colonel, this is not the first time a bluff has beat a straight."[44]

Between June 3, 1863, and June 23, 1864, life was less exciting for the Third Ohio. On May 15, 1863, they were paroled and sent to Maryland. From there, they went to Camp Chase in Columbus, Ohio. On August 1, 1863, the Third started for Chattanooga where they remained on garrison duty until June 1864. On June 9, 1864, the regiment was back where they started: Camp Dennison. They were mustered out on June 23, 1864.

Epilogue

The first Third Ohio regimental reunion was held in Cardington, Ohio, on September 14, 1876. By the 51st reunion in 1927, only two members of the regiment were in sufficient health to meet at the home of Mr. and Mrs. Williams, 4th Street, Columbus, Ohio. Although the history of the three-year regiment began on June 12, 1861, the story of the Third Ohio continued until February 2, 1928, with the death of George Coffey, the last of the Third Ohio to fight in Streight's Raid, 1863. During 52 years of reunions, the minutes of those meetings reveal a vivid picture of the men and the sacrifices of the Third Ohio Volunteer Infantry Regiment. Although many consider Stones River to have been a more significant engagement than Perryville, it was the battle at Perryville, Kentucky, that always crept into the conversation during the reunions. The Third Ohio generally held their annual meetings during the first week of October to coincide with the October 8 date of the battle. October 8 was "Perryville Day" to the surviving members of the regiment. In 1885, Third Ohio Association president John Beatty requested that the 1886 reunion be held on the Perryville battlefield. The minutes of the 1885 meeting end with, "A motion was then made that the 15th Ky. Vol. Inft. be invited to meet with us at Perryville."[1] It was the 15th Kentucky that stood with the Third Ohio at 4:00 p.m. on October 8 while the men from Buckner's division almost surrounded them. The men from Ohio did not forget and wanted to share the memories with them over 20 years later.

On October 10, 1878, Third Ohio reunion president John Beatty recalled the fighting at Perryville and Stones River:

> We pass in rapid review that terrible midsummer march from Decherd Station Tennessee back to Louisville Kentucky. Comrades, we stood together at Perryville, and as our ranks were thinned by scores, we closed up to the right and the left on those colors, stopping perhaps long enough to receive the last message or hand pressure from a dying comrade; but standing there in that hell of fire, shot and shell, till all that remained of our proud regiment would not make two fair Companies. No wonder that Rousseau said, "Soldiers of

the Third Ohio, you stood in that withering fire like men of iron." After Perryville, on to Nashville again; still further on, at Stone River, we met the old foe once more. Do you remember our midnight charge? How in the darkness we aimed at the flash of the enemy's guns, and how scores of us went down torn, wounded, bleeding, dying? It is sixteen years since we first met, and here is gathered the remnant of us. But alas! How many are gone? Some lying in unknown graves in the mountains of West Virginia, the hills of Kentucky, the plains of Tennessee, Alabama, Georgia, and Mississippi. And to the mothers, fathers, brothers and sisters of our dead, I wish to say in the name of our comrades, we feel for you? And Oh, if this meeting has caused the hidden springs of grief to reopen, be assured you aged parents, you brothers and sisters, that every one of the killed of the Third Ohio Regiment, died with his face to the foe, nobly doing his duty, died as an American soldier loved to die, midst the rattle of musketry, the roar of artillery, the crash of shells, with that proud flag floating above him.[2]

During that half century after the Civil War, the minutes of the Third Ohio reunion meetings reveal many themes. Throughout the many post-war years, the love and respect consistently shown to John Beatty is clear in the minutes and the newspaper articles discussing the latest reunion. As the years passed, the Third voted on a resolution condemning the assassination of President William McKinley.

However, this writer believes that the most significant post-war activity as reflected consistently in the reunion minutes was the invitation by the men of the Third Ohio to the survivors of the 54th Virginia to the eighth reunion on July 25, 1883. The two regiments originally met after the capture of the Third by Nathan Bedford Forrest after Streight's Raid. On Monday, May 4, 1863, the rank and file of the Third were marched through the streets of Rome, Georgia. When Forrest and his cavalry were in charge, the Ohio regiment was well treated. However, Forrest was soon reassigned, and the citizens of Rome took over. Henry Breidenthal remembered, "They offered several insults, but we did not accept them, but exhibited our indifference and independence by standing aloof upon our dignity with one exception. Some man had bawled out, 'So you came to take Rome and Rome took you,' which one of the boys retorted with, 'The Hell you did! I can see it in that light, for when our two hundred and fifty advance came within range of the city, not one of your skulking citizens could be found, and had we orders to take this place, we would have taken it. You talk of taking us! Forrest took us; you took nothing! You belong to the Royal Stand-backs who are the last in and the first out when there is fighting to be done.'"[3] However, things got worse very soon. The 73rd Indiana fought alongside the Third in Streight's Raid. They remembered, "Next day, May 4th, [we] marched to Rome and were corralled in an open lot, with no shelter whatever from the broiling sun. On [our] march,

[we] were reviewed by citizens who lined the road curious to see the 'Yankees,' this being the first command to penetrate so far into their country. Many of them were very insolent and disagreeable."[4] At 8:00 p.m. on May 7, the Third left for Richmond on railcars. According to Henry Breidenthal of the Third, "The trip to Richmond, in overcrowded and bare box cars was broken only by the arrival in Knoxville where [we] had the good fortune to be placed under the guard of the 54th Virginia Infantry. [The guards] kindly divided their rations with our starving boys. This was a most gracious thing to do and proved that even out of Sodom some good might come."[5] Twenty years later, the Third Ohio reciprocated the kindness of the 54th Virginia. According to the minutes of the July 25, 1883, reunion, "The 54th Virginia Regiment, C.S.A. [Confederate States Army], was in camp near the place where the Third were placed, and they came over to see the 'Yankees.' They soon discovered that our boys were very hungry, and although on half rations themselves, they gave them all they had to eat.... The generous action could not fail to generate kindly feeling on the part of the prisoners, and they promised to reciprocate if ever the opportunity occurred.... Three years ago [1880], Aidin Burt conceived the idea of hunting up the Virginia Confederates, and after writing frequently for two years, succeeded in finding some of them, and the committee on invitation asked them to meet with the Third O.V.I. at Columbus during the reunion last week.... The best speech ever any ex-Confederate ever made was that of Comrade B.F. Moorehead. Being called on to make a speech, Mr. Moorehead rose up with Mr. Burt's little girl in his arms and her arms around his neck and said, 'Gentlemen, I cannot make a speech, but I assure you that my feelings toward you are the same that I have for this little girl.' It is such speech as this that healed up the breach in the nation."[6]

After the turn of the century, death and poor health limited the number of Third Ohio veterans who could come to the reunions. When President McKinley was shot on September 6, 1901, there were only 17 members of the Third Ohio able to get together. Nevertheless, they passed a resolution at their September 11 meeting that was sent to Congress regarding the assassination. It read, "Therefore be it resolved that the Third O.V.I. assembled in its 26th annual reunion, denounce the attempted assassination of President William McKinley and consider the act one of the most cowardly acts of modern times."[7] On the 11th, McKinley still clung to life. Three days later, he died.

The final chapter in the life of the Third Ohio may not have been written at Cedar Bluff. In 1893, the program for the Third Ohio reunion listed the battles in which the regiment participated. The engagement that followed Streight's Raid on the program cover was *Pursuit and Capture of*

Morgan. The Third Ohio Volunteer Infantry Regiment was responsible for the capture of the "Wizard of the Saddle," John Hunt Morgan himself? Neither Abel Streight's reports nor Henry Breidenthal's diary mentions this. The 1893 reunion mentions this for the first time. It is not referenced in any of the other Third Ohio records before or since this program statement. Nevertheless, the files containing the papers on the 1893 meeting contain a newspaper article titled, "The Great Raid: Or the True Story of the Capture of John Morgan." It was written by Major Lewis H. Bond, commander, 88th Ohio. The known facts of Morgan's last raids establish that he crossed the Ohio River in July 1863 in an attempt to divert General William Rosecrans' push to disrupt the vital railroad connections at Chattanooga, Tennessee. On July 26, 1863, Morgan and 400 of his men were caught and surrendered in Salineville, Ohio. What does any of this have to do with the Third Ohio? After the surrender of Streight's brigade at Cedar Bluff, the men were quickly paroled on May 15, 1863. At this point, some of the men remained with the original Third Regiment at Camp Chase in Columbus, while others from the Third were combined with the remnants of various other regiments into a brigade commanded by Brigadier General James M. Shackleford. According to Whitelaw Reid in his *Ohio in the War*, volume 2, "The regiment took an active part in the pursuit and capture of John Morgan and his rebel Raiders, being among the number that finally captured him."[8] Reid provides no other details. However, according to Lewis Bond, some members of the Third Ohio were involved in the capture of Morgan. He begins his story, "My experience as commander of the 3rd Ohio Regiment, while it was engaged in the pursuit of Morgan's command, enables me to speak of facts from personal knowledge which have not hitherto been published. [It was on the 7th of July, 1863] that my personal participation in the Morgan Raid began.... The men I commanded were splendid soldiers, inured of fatigue and danger.... Within six hours after we crossed the Muskingum we engaged the Confederate rear guard. Morgan sent in a flag of truce. This was a ruse to buy time so he could escape.... Finally, the Third Ohio had gained the enemy's front without any cooperation from any other force, and the Confederate Chieftain finding himself hemmed in on all sides, had announced his surrender."[9] Bond claimed that Morgan refused to surrender his sword to a major. He would only hand it over to General Shackleford. As a result, according to Bond, Shackleford got the credit. Although difficult to confirm Bond's story, it seems likely that some members of the original Third Ohio were part of another integrated brigade and participated in the capture of John Hunt Morgan. The Third Ohio Volunteer Infantry Regiment per se, however, ended their Civil War combat experience at Cedar Bluff at noon on May 3, 1863, and were mustered out after their three-year enlistment ended on

Epilogue 145

June 23, 1864. The last two members of the Third Ohio passed away in 1928, 65 years after the end of their enlistment. On January 4, 1928, the Columbus newspapers carried an article, "Thomas J Haughey, aged 88, civil war veteran and life-time president of the Third Ohio Volunteer Infantry succumbed Wednesday at the home of his son, Clarence Haughey, 433 South Sixth Street." One month later, on February 2, 1928, "Civil War Veteran is Taken by Death: George W. Coffey succumbs after only few days duration. George W. Coffey, 90, veteran of the civil war dies at 6:30 p.m. Thursday at the home of his daughter, Mrs. I.D. Wingate.... Mr. Coffey enlisted in the Union army in May, 1861. He was in the column led by A.D. Streight which had a noted campaign against Nathan Forrest and was also at Murfreesboro. He was at one time a prisoner in the famous Belle Isle prison in the James River at Richmond." Some of the principal players in this colorful story include the following:

John Beatty: 1828–1914. In April 1861, Beatty raised Company I, Third Ohio. He was promoted to colonel in 1861, lieutenant colonel 1862 and promoted to brigadier general in 1863 after service in Perryville, Stones River and Tullahoma. He also saw service at Chickamauga and Missionary Ridge. Beatty resigned in 1864 and went back to banking. He started in business with his younger brother William as a banker in 1852, and became president of the Citizens Savings Bank of Columbus, 1873–1903. He served as a House Representative in the U.S. Congress from 1868 to 1873. Beatty also served as a presidential elector for Lincoln in 1860 and James Blaine in 1884. He was a Republican and was unsuccessful in running for governor in 1882. Beatty supported John C. Fremont for president in 1856. He voted for 15th Amendment and campaigned for Garfield in 1880. He was against the high McKinley protective tariff and against silver to back currency. Despite this, Beatty favored William Jennings Bryan for president in 1900. Beatty wrote four fiction novels as well as the published memoirs that helped frame this book. He also served on several battlefield preservation committees. By 1907, the reunions were being held at Beatty's home, 49 Lexington Avenue, Cleveland, Ohio. Beatty said it was necessary due to his health. He died in 1914.

Joseph Warren Keifer: 1836–1932. Graduated from Antioch College and became a lawyer in 1853. He served in the U.S. House Representatives, 1877–1885. He was elected speaker, 1881–1883. During the war, Keifer served as Lieutenant colonel, Third Ohio, and later 110th Ohio, colonel commanding. He saw action at Rich Mountain, Cheat Mountain and Second Winchester (June 1863). He was sent to New York City in 1863 to suppress the Draft Riots. He was wounded at the Wilderness while in command of Second Brigade, James Rickets' Third Division, Sixth Corps. Keifer was in brigade command at Cedar Creek, Virginia, 1864, and was promoted to brevet brigadier general, on December 12, 1864. He served with the Second Brigade, Third Division, Sixth Corps at Petersburg and Appomattox. He was wounded four times and promoted to major general on April 9, 1865. Keifer practiced law after the war and served as a trustee of Antioch College. He practiced law with three of his sons until 1923. In Congress, he voted in favor of civil rights for blacks and supported the 14th and 15th Amendments, like John Beatty. Unfortunately, he later opposed civil service reform. Later, Keifer served as a major general during the Spanish American War. From 1905 to 1911, he served in the U.S. House of Representatives again. He also worked as president for the Lagonda National Bank, Springfield, Ohio. During the reunion held at the Perryville battlefield on October 8, 1886, Keifer echoed Lincoln and commented, "When the Third crossed the Ohio, it was not to abolish slavery, but to protect it."

Lovell H. Rousseau: 1818–1869. Born in Kentucky. His father owned slaves, but they were sold to pay family debts after the death of his father. Rousseau became an attorney in 1841 in Indiana. He married the daughter of his law partner in 1843. Rousseau served briefly in the Indiana State House in 1844. He was a captain in a volunteer regiment during Mexican War and earned distinction during the Battle of Buena Vista. He went back to the Indiana senate after the war, but then moved to Kentucky and served in the Kentucky senate. He raised two Kentucky volunteer regiments. He was promoted to colonel, Fifth Kentucky Volunteers in 1861 and breveted as major general at Shiloh, Stones River and Tullahoma. Rousseau served briefly in the U.S. House of Representatives, 1864–1866. In 1866, he had a running disagreement with Iowa congressman Josiah Grinnell over the new Freedmen's Bureau. Thousands of slaves were now free. However, their "rights" and means of livelihood were serious issues. Grinnell was an abolitionist who favored more power to the bureau; Rousseau opposed it. His opposition, however, was based on the potential abuse that such a bureau might exercise. Grinnell chided Rousseau on the House floor and questioned his military record. Rousseau demanded an apology, which Grinnell refused. Rousseau attacked Grinnell outside the Capitol building with his cane. He was heard yelling at Grinnell, "You damned puppy ... whipped now like a dog." Rousseau was reprimanded by the House but resigned in protest—and was quickly reelected to the same seat in Congress. However, he decided to return to the practice of law. Secretary of State William Seward asked Rousseau to represent the United States in accepting the transfer of Alaska from Russia to the United States. On his return from Alaska, Rousseau was assigned command of the Department of Louisiana. His consistent winter coughs and colds, however, caught up to him in January 1869. He died that year in New Orleans.

George Thomas: 1816–1870. He was born in Virginia but fought for the Union. His father owned slaves, and the family fled during the Nat Turner rebellion. This turned Thomas against slavery. He graduated from West Point and was a roommate of William T. Sherman. Thomas was rapidly promoted to major general. He had distinguished combat experience in Florida during the Seminole Wars and in Mexico. In the Civil War, he served at Perryville, Stones River, Chickamauga, Missionary Ridge, Chattanooga and Nashville. He earned the nickname "Rock of Chickamauga" for his service in that battle. Many historians consider George Thomas to have been the best of the Union generals. He was later criticized for being slow, but so was Buell, Rosecrans and many others. However, this criticism often came from men like Ulysses Grant and William Sherman. Both men survived the war long enough to be able to rewrite history and cover their own mistakes. Major Donn Piatt, adjutant general and colorful observer/writer of the war, said, "Grant felt uneasy and ashamed in the presence of Thomas, and both Grant and Sherman were troubled with the thought that truth and justice would award to their subordinate in office the higher position on the honor roll." After the war, Thomas remained in the service. He worked to frustrate the efforts of the Ku Klux Klan. President Johnson offered him the rank of lieutenant general and wanted to make Thomas general-in-chief. In 1869, he was assigned command of the Department of the Pacific. He died of a stroke in 1870. Later, President James Garfield commented to John Beatty of the Third Ohio that had not Thomas died in 1870, he would probably have become president.

John Hunt Morgan: 1825–1864. Morgan was born in Alabama but grew up on a farm near Lexington, Kentucky. Morgan attended Transylvania College but was suspended for dueling. He saw combat at Buena Vista in Mexico. After that war, he raised an infantry regiment, the Lexington Rifles. His sister married A.P. Hill. Morgan became a slave owner. Like many in Kentucky, he did not favor secession. After his wife died 1861, Morgan was promoted to colonel, Second Kentucky Cavalry Regiment. His was promoted again to brigadier general in 1862 and remarried in December, 1862. Some have suggested that Morgan lost interest in his raids after his second marriage. The *Nashville Daily Union* noted Morgan's second marriage on December 4, 1862: "Morgan, we are informed, was married a few days ago to a young lady in Murfreesboro.... We send our best sympathies to Mrs. Morgan. She has the sympathies of every decent man, in her new position. Unless the Devil has a spouse, we don't know of a being who can realize her dreadful fate." Nevertheless, Morgan continued his successful raids against Union supply trains. In July 1863, he was captured while on a raid in Ohio and sent to the Ohio Penitentiary. Before long, however, he dug a tunnel and escaped. Morgan continued his raids into 1864. Finally, he was shot in the back and killed while running through a grape arbor to get away from Union scouts in Greenville, Tennessee, on September 4, 1864.

Nathan Bedford Forrest: 1821–1877. He enlisted as a private in the Confederate army and was ultimately promoted to general. Forrest was born in Tennessee, a state in which the Third Ohio saw action at Stones River. He had no formal military training but soon proved to be a natural leader and was promoted to brigadier general in 1862. He was the first Grand Wizard of the Ku Klux Klan. Forrest received a poor education as evidenced by some of the written communications that still exist. However, he was a good businessman, a risk-taker in business and became one of the largest slave dealers. He bought and sold as well as rented out his slaves to farmers to help with their work. He bought and managed several cotton plantations and became one of the richest men in the South. Forrest was involved in some of the most critical battles of the Civil War, including Fort Donelson, Shiloh, Stones River, Streight's Raid, Chickamauga, Fort Pillow and Nashville. However, he is often most remembered for the massacre at Fort Pillow, Henning, Tennessee, April 12, 1864. Forrest's men demanded the surrender of the fort. Refusal to surrender resulted in Confederate troops seizing the fort. At that point, many surrendered, while others tried to flee. In both cases, Union troops, black and white, were slaughtered by Forrest's men. Almost 400 Union soldiers were killed. Forrest was branded a war criminal in the Northern press. Ultimately, Forrest survived the war and died of apparent complications from diabetes in 1877.

John Pegram: 1832–1865. After Pegram's capture and subsequent exchange after the Battle of Rich Mountain, he returned to the army and was promoted to colonel. In 1862, he was chief engineer on the staffs of Generals Beauregard and Bragg and later chief of staff to General Kirby Smith. In November 1862, he was promoted to brigadier general and assigned to the command of a cavalry brigade of Tennesseans, which he led in the Battle of Murfreesboro, and at Chickamauga he commanded a division of Forrest's cavalry corps. He was transferred to the Army of Northern Virginia and given command of an infantry brigade. Thomas disliked politics and declined. Battle of the Wilderness was where he was wounded. He took part in the Shenandoah Campaign against Sheridan, and when Jubal Early's Confederate forces returned to the Petersburg lines, he commanded a division throughout the winter. On January 19, 1865, he married Hetta Cary in Saint Paul's Church, Richmond. Jefferson Davis sent his personal carriage to transport the couple to the church. Their honeymoon was at Pegram's headquarters near Petersburg. In the action at Hatcher's Run, February 6, 1865, he was struck near the heart by a musket ball and was killed. Three weeks later to the day, General Pegram's coffin occupied the spot in Saint Paul's Church where he had stood to be married. The minister who performed the wedding ceremony also performed the funeral service.

William S. Rosecrans: 1819–1898. He was born in Ohio, and graduated from West Point. Although he had little formal education, he did well at West Point. He got the nickname "Old Rosy" at the Academy. He graduated with James Longstreet. After graduation, Rosecrans stayed at West Point and taught engineering. He also converted to Roman Catholicism at this time. He did not participate in the Mexican War and continued to teach engineering. He resigned in 1854 to go into the coal oil business, and became very successful. In November 1862, Colonel John Beatty noted in his diary, "I predict that in twelve months Rosecrans will be as unpopular as Buell. After the affair at Rich Mountain, the former was a great favorite. When placed in command of the forces in Western Virginia the people expected hourly to hear of Floyd's destruction; but after a whole summer was spent in the vain endeavor to chase down the enemy and bring him to battle, they began to abuse Rosecrans, and he finally left that department, much as Buell has left this." In 1864, his former chief of staff James Garfield wired him to ask if he would consider being Lincoln's vice president. Rosecrans wired back a note in the affirmative, but Garfield claimed he never received the wire. Mustered out of service in 1866 and breveted major general, Rosecrans was appointed U.S. minister to Mexico, 1868–1869. He served in the U.S. House of Representatives, 1880–1884. "[Rosecrans] possessed virtues and excellencies, some to an heroic degree. He was blessed with a brilliant, resourceful mind, and prodigious energy. No General, North or South, surpassed him in personal leadership.... He made enemies needlessly and unwisely.... He was critical and impatient in slipshod performance in others.... He could be short of temper and long of tongue." Rosecrans made a lifelong enemy of Ulysses Grant. This did not help ensure Rosecrans' legacy.

Braxton Bragg: 1817–1876. Born in North Carolina. It was rumored that his mother Margaret Crosland Bragg was released from jail in time to give birth. She was allegedly in jail for the murder of a slave for rudeness. He never mentioned his mother in his later letters. Bragg was educated at West Point. He received three brevet promotions during the Mexican War. Bragg resigned from the army in 1855 and bought a sugar plantation with 100 slaves. Bragg married a wealthy woman, Elise, and paid $156,000 for a plantation with 1,600 acres. He became a very successful sugar planter. planter, and his wife later became a close adviser. In an army that enjoyed their drink, Bragg forbade alcohol in his command. He returned to the army in 1861 and was promoted to major general. He was promoted again to corps commander at Shiloh in April 1862. Bragg is credited with forcing the surrender of Union forces at Munfordville, August, 1862. He became commander of the Army of Mississippi and renamed it the Army of Tennessee. He was a good administrator but a mediocre field commander. Historians have been critical of Bragg. Bruce Catton said, "Braxton Bragg was as baffling a mixture of high ability and sheer incompetence as the Confederacy could produce." He suffered from rheumatism and migraine headaches. He died relatively young at the age of 59 in 1876.

Issac Harrison Morrow: 1812–1925. Although Morrow spent many years after the war defending his bluster and inaction with the Third Ohio, he was still regarded well enough to be invited to the 25th reunion of the Third held in Cardington, Ohio. It was attended by John Beatty, Warren Keifer and Orris Lawson. On October 14, 1889, at the age of 77, Morrow married Edith Gilmore of Toledo. The bride was 19 years old. This was Morrow's second marriage. A newspaper account of the wedding stated, "She possesses more than ordinary beauty, and has been a great traveler, having made four trips through Europe." In addition to his political interests, Morrow also served as a fire chief in Columbus after the war.

Don Carlos Buell: 1818–1898. Born in Ohio he was thought of as an introvert and teased by peers while growing up. Buell graduated from West Point and was soon fighting in the Seminole and Mexican American Wars. He was a disciplinarian who was court-martialed for striking an enlisted man with his sword. In Mexico, Buell was breveted three times for bravery. He was a lieutenant colonel by the start of the Civil War and promoted to brigadier general in April 1861. Buell took command of the Army of the Ohio in November 1861. He considered himself the hero of Shiloh. Grant was ambivalent in his opinion and said that Buell was too slow but also very brave. Buell was severely criticized after letting Bragg escape after Perryville. In the commission that was set up to investigate, Buell was allowed to cross-examine the witnesses against him. He defended his actions with skill. The commission declined to punish Buell. After the Civil War, he and his wife lived in Indiana and Kentucky. Buell served as president of the Green River Iron Company. The death of his wife in 1881 was hard on Buell. He died in poverty in 1898. Unfortunately, he wrote no memoirs of his service during the war.

Abel Streight: 1828–1892. Streight was born in New York and became a book publisher in the late 1850s. He was appointed colonel of the 51st Indiana Infantry in 1861. Streight is best known for Streight's Raid in 1863. After he and the Third Ohio surrendered to Forrest in 1863, Streight was sent to Libby Prison in Richmond. Streight had $3,400 on him when searched after surrender. In prison, he constantly wrote to Confederate authorities about poor conditions. In October 1863, he helped organize a mass uprising of prisoners. However, one of the plotters gave the plan away. In December 1863, he attempted to bribe a guard to facilitate an escape. However, this was a trap that had been set by the rebel guards. Having failed twice, Streight helped dig a tunnel in 1864. Unfortunately, he was now too big to fit through, so he took his clothes off, and on February 9, 1864, he crawled to safety. Over 100 officers and enlisted men came out to freedom through that tunnel. Streight made it to Washington on March 1, 1864. He returned to his regiment and was promoted to brigadier general in March, 1865. He resigned one week later. Streight was elected to two terms as Indiana state senator. He was buried in his front yard in Indianapolis. His wife Lavinia Streight said after he died, "I could never keep track of him when he was alive, now I can keep my eye on him."

Ormsby Mitchell: 1810–1862. Born in Kentucky, Mitchell went to West Point and was a classmate of Robert E. Lee and Joseph Johnston. After graduation, Mitchell became an assistant professor of math at West Point for three years. He later became an attorney and professor of mathematics, philosophy and astronomy at Cincinnati College. His passion, however, was astronomy. He personally raised the money to build the Cincinnati Observatory. He went to Europe to fund the best lens for the telescope. John Quincy Adams delivered the speech when the observatory was dedicated. Mitchell served as a brigadier general of Ohio volunteers and briefly commanded the Department of the Ohio. He was involved in seizing the locomotive, *The General*, in north Georgia in 1862. Before it was caught by rebel forces, *The General* and its crew tore up rail and telegraph lines all over northern Georgia, thus disrupting effective command by Confederate forces in the area. The engagement was made into a movie called *The Great Locomotive Chase*. Mitchell assumed command of the Department of the South. He was based in Hilton Head, South Carolina, but soon died of yellow fever in October, 1862. Mitchell was a disciplinarian and clashed with the Third Ohio. He referred to them as "Obstinate Devils."

Newton Schleich: 1827–1879. Born in Lancaster, Ohio, he became a successful lawyer and editor of the *Ohio Eagle*. In 1853, he was elected militia captain and later served as a two-term Ohio senator. In 1861, he announced the firing on Fort Sumter in the Ohio Senate chamber. By April 1861, he was appointed brigadier general in the Ohio militia. Schleich was involved in the fraudulent bidding for army supplies that created great scandal in the early part of the war. He commanded a small brigade containing the Third and Fourth Ohio Regiments, which saw service at Middle Fork Bridge and Rich Mountain. McClellan realized that Schleich had no military skill and replaced him with Joseph Reynolds before Cheat Mountain. Schleich resigned on July 30, 1861. Very quickly, however, he started working on another commission. He used his own money to organize another brigade, the 61st Ohio Volunteer Infantry Brigade. He wasn't popular with the 61st either. Soon, he was accused of nepotism by giving posts to friends and relatives in his brigade. Nevertheless, whenever fighting occurred, Schleich made himself scarce. He finally resigned on September 20, 1862, and resumed his law practice.

Appendix A

Chronology (Annotated): Third Ohio Volunteer Infantry Regiment

Note: This chronology ends on May 3, 1863, when the Third Ohio Volunteer Infantry Regiment was captured by the regiment commanded by Confederate general Nathan Bedford Forrest. After their prisoner exchange, the Third continued to serve, but they performed in a guard and maintenance capacity until mustering out on June 23, 1864. Their combat service was over, however, on May 3.

1861

June 22	Bellaire, Ohio
June 23	Grafton, "western" Virginia. The Third was the first Ohio regiment to cross the Ohio River into Virginia. They came to Grafton by train.
June 26	Clarksburg, "western" Virginia (by train, arriving at midnight)
June 28	Camp at Elk Creek
July 2	March to Buckhannon, "western" Virginia (near Middle Fork River Bridge)
July 4	McClellan reviews the troops.
July 5	Captain Orris Lawson goes to secure Middle Fork Bridge.
July 6	Colonel Beatty and Third Ohio go to Middle Fork Bridge to drive off rebel skirmishers who had surrounded Lawson and his men
July 8	Third Ohio regiment advances to secure Middle Fork Bridge
July 9	Roaring Creek camp. McClellan headquarters established at base of Rich Mountain
July 11	Third Ohio forces rebel pickets back to allow Rosecrans to pass
July 13	Huttonsville, near Cheat Mountain
July 14	Light skirmishing with rebels. Third reconnaissance at top of Cheat Mountain
July 27	John Beatty, colonel of the Third, meets with Brigadier General Schleich whom Beatty considers a "rampant demagogue."

August 4	Third and Loomis' battery support Colonel George Wagner who is fighting a rebel force of 3,000 near Cheat Mountain
August 14	Third captures Captain Julius DeLagnel of the Rich Mountain battle
August 18	Elk Water Creek, "western" Virginia
August 21	Picket from the Third shoots own man who didn't know the password
September 12	Battle of Cheat Mountain
September 19	Continued skirmishing near Cheat Mountain
September 20	Cheat Mountain, killed Colonel John A. Washington, great grandnephew of George Washington
October 3	Continued fighting on Cheat Mountain
October 6	Logan's Mill
October 8	Third Ohio assigned to new brigade under Brigadier General Ebenezer Dumont
November 1	Louisville, Kentucky. Camped and resupplied
December 1	Louisville, Kentucky
December 12	Elizabethtown. Third now assigned 17th Brigade, Third Division, Ormsby Mitchell
December 18	Bacon Creek
December 28	A spy is discovered in the ranks.
December 31	General Don Carlos Buell reviews the troops.

1862

January 5	Beatty straps drunken, disrespectful man from the Third to a tree
January 26	Nolan Creek, Kentucky. Rebels get to the rear and skirmish with the Third
January 28	Charges filed against Colonel Morrow by Colonel Beatty
February 1	Bacon Creek, Kentucky. Colonel Morrow agrees to resign
February 10	Colonel Marrow leaves the Third Ohio
February 10	Munfordville, Kentucky
February 13	Bell's Tavern, Kentucky
February 16	Bowling Green, Kentucky
February 27	Nashville, Tennessee
March 8	John Hunt Morgan raids the camp of the Third. Slaves come into camp seeking freedom. This became a political difficulty for Lincoln.
March 18	Murfreesboro, Tennessee
March 31	Major Keifer goes to Nashville to repair burned bridges
April 2	Shelbyville, Tennessee
April 5	Third called "Obstinate Devils" by General Ormsby Mitchell
April 7	Destroyed trains on the Nashville and Chattanooga Railroad. Took 15 prisoners
April 10	Fayetteville, Tennessee

Chronology (Annotated)

April 15	Huntsville, Alabama (forced march, 65 miles in two days)
April 20	Decatur, Alabama
April 23	Pickets of the Third attacked by 300 rebels
April 27	Burned a bridge over the Tennessee River
April 28	Bellefonte, Alabama
April 29	Skirmish at Widow's Creek, near Bridgeport, Alabama
May 2	Huntsville: Paint Rock skirmish
May 13	Elk River, Alabama
May 17	Skirmish with forces of John Hunt Morgan after Morgan destroyed supply train
June	Third Ohio remains in the Huntsville area for the month
July 3	Beatty returns from sick leave. Complains his horse is too fat
July 14	Beatty complains that General Buell is too soft.
July 29	Huntsville, rebel cavalry skirmish with Third Ohio at midnight
August 7	Rebel bushwhackers kill General Robert McCook.
August 10	Third goes out to gather intelligence on rebel forces nearby
August 29	Decherd, Tennessee. Third ambushed on return from Stevenson, Tennessee
September 4	Murfreesboro, Tennessee
September 5	Nashville, Tennessee
September 7	Edgefield, Tennessee
September 11	Bowling Green, Kentucky
September 25	Louisville, Kentucky
October 3	Taylorsville, Kentucky
October 4	Bloomfield, Kentucky
October 7	Maxville, Kentucky (*sic*)
October 8	Battle of Perryville
October 13	Harrodsburg, Kentucky
October 24	Lebanon, Kentucky
November 9	Sinking Spring, Kentucky. Third now assigned to Thomas' 14th army corps
November 11	Mitchellville, Tennessee
November 15	Tyree Springs, Tennessee
November 30	Nashville. Third placed in reserve division under Rousseau
December 2	Nashville, Tennessee
December 16	General Negley's forage train attacked
December 21	Confederate cannon and musketry heard all night
December 25	More Confederate artillery heard all night
December 29	Artillery continues
December 30	Murfreesboro, Tennessee
December 31	Stones River fighting starts

Appendix A

1863

January 1	Fighting at Stones River. Third Ohio told to stay "until hell freezes over"
January 6	Stones River battle ends
February 4	Confederate guns heard all night in aftermath of Stones River
February 5	Forage train of the Third attacked
March	Third Ohio engaged in digging defensive trenches in March
April 7	Nashville (by train)
April 8	Murfreesboro, Tennessee
April 10	Men shot in the morning for desertion at Stones River
April 13	General Thomas congratulates Beatty for brigadier general promotion
April 15	Skirmish at Franklin, Tennessee
April 21	Streight's Raid (Day's Gap, raid began), Alabama
April 30	Hog Mountain, Alabama
May 1	Blountsville, Alabama
May 2	Black Creek, Alabama
May 2	Blount's Plantation, Alabama
May 3	Cedar Bluff, Alabama

Appendix B

Roster: Third Ohio Volunteer Infantry

* *The Official Roster of the Soldiers of the State of Ohio in the War of the Rebellion 1861–1866* (aka The Ohio Roster Commission) does not list the ages of the following men: Barber, Hallett; Benedict, Hiram; Blair, James A.; Boston, John; Dudley, William; Fowler, Lyman D.; Henry, John W.; Mitchell, John G. [adjutant]; Mitchell, John G. [captain]; Mortram, John; Peck, William L.; Reed, Dexter; Smith, Robert; Teetors, Thomas B.; Underhill, John; Whiting, John DeWitt [captain]; Whiting, John DeWitt [1st Lieut.]; Willets, Wendell P.; Williams, William; Williamson, Jacob L.; Wood, William H.; Wright, George C.; Wright, James. When these men signed up for their three-year enlistment, they did not enter an age on the enlistment form. When the Commission published the roster in 1886, it didn't check the ages. F & S = Field and Staff.

Abbott, Ephraim P.—Co. E, 30, Captain
Adams, Robert H.—Co. F, 27, Private
Albert, Daniel G.—Co. K, 21, Corporal
Aldrich, Sidney J.—Co. I, 25, Corporal
Alexander, Robert—Co. H, 38, Private
Allen, Charles—Co. E, 29, 1st Lieut.
Allen, David—Co. A, 19, Private
Allen, Henry—Co. E, 24, Corporal
Allison, Hezekiah D.—Co. E, 26, Private
Alloway, William R.—Co. C, 21, Private
Amsden, Henry R.—Co. F, 18, Private
Anderson, David—Co. K, 34, Private
Anderson, James—Co. E, 29, Corporal
Anderson, William S.—Co. F, 25, Sergeant
Anthony, John—Co. B, 22, Private
Anthony, John—Co. H, 19, Private
Applegate, John J.—Co. E, 20, Private
Archer, William—Co. H, 20, Private
Armstrong, John J.—Co. I, 22, Private
Armstrong, William H.B.—Co. H, 27, Private
Asher, Albert—Co. H, 18, Private
Ashley, Seaman—Co. I, 22, Private
Aten, George B.—Co. K, 24, Sergeant
Atkins, John—Co. G, 25, Private
Auginbaugh, C.C.—Co. K, 25, Private
Auginbaugh, W. A.—Co. K, 20, Private
Avery, Joseph—Co. H, 18, Private
Ayers, Wesley—Co. I, 19, Private
Babbitt, Edward—Co. H, 20, Private
Backus, Joseph—Co. H, 21, Private
Badger, Elisha S.—Co. E, 31, Private
Bafford, Benjamin—Co. B, 21, Private
Bafford, William—Co. B, 24, Private
Bahlman, Joseph—Co. G, 22, Corporal
Bailey, George W.—Co. A, 23, 2nd Lieut.
Baird, John—Co. G, 18, Private
Baker, John C.—Co. K, 18, Private
Baker, John W.W.—Co. D, 23, Private
Ball, Allen W.—Co. H, 20, Private
Ball, George A.—Co. H, 18, Sergeant
Barber, Hallett—Co. I, Private
Barcaffer, John P.—Co. D, 47, Sergeant

Barcus, Henry F.—Co. K, 19, Corporal
Barcus, John G.—Co. K, 22, Private
Barnes, Oliver P.—Co. B, 24, 1st Lieut.
Barnes, William H.—Co. B, 24, Private
Barney, Henry—Co. G, 22, Private
Barrie, James W.—Co. B, 27, Sergeant
Bartholomew, John S.—Co. E, 24, Private
Bartlett, Isaac S.—Co. C, 19, Private
Battin, Asa H.—Co. K, 32, Captain
Baugh, Peter—Co. D, 38, Corporal
Baughman, Joshua—Co. A, 19, Private
Beach, Thomas W.—Co. F, 33, Private
Bean, Edmond—Co. C, 22, Private
Bean, John—Co. K, 19, Private
Beatty, John—F & S, 32, Colonel
Beatty, John—Co. I, 32, Private
Beckett, David C.—Co. F, 24, Sergeant
Beebe, William H.—Co. C, 23, Private
Behr, Rudolph—Co. G, 21, Private
Bell, Leroy S.—Co. H, 30, Captain
Bellville, George—Co. G, 19, Private
Bender, Henry D.—Co. G, 22, 1st Sergt.
Benedict, Charles W.—Co. B, 24, Corporal
Benedict, Charles W.—Co. I, 18, Private
Benedict, Hiram—Co. I, Private
Benedict, Jonathan—Co. I, 20, Private
Bennet, Henry K.—Co. A, 25, Private
Bennett, Simon C.—Co. I, 22, Sergeant
Benson, Amos—Co. K, 20, Private
Berkshire, William—Co. E, 26, Corporal
Bertch, Matthew—Co. B, 26, Private
Best, William—Co. E, 24, Private
Biggett, John—Co. K, 23, Corporal
Binkley, Charles N.—Co. E, 25, Private
Birnbryer, August—Co. G, 22, Private
Black, Nicholas—Co. G, 23, Private
Blair, James A.—Co. I, Corporal
Bliner, Henry C.—Co. G, 26, Private
Blue, Joel G.—Co. I, 21, 1st Lieut.
Board, Charles T.—Co. F, 21, Private
Board, James—Co. F, 19, Private
Bobie, Ellis—Co. B, 25, Private
Bodell, Louis—Co. H, 18, Private
Bodell, William—Co. H, 37, Private
Bolinger, Michael—Co. B, 37, Private
Bonner, Benjamin—Co. G, 21, Private
Boston, John—Co. I, Private
Bovard, Charles W.—Co. K, 19, Private
Bowers, Albert A.—Co. H, 22, Corporal
Bowers, Jacob—Co. F, 19, Private
Boyce, Andrew J.—Co. K, 22, Private
Boyce, Charles R.—Co. K, 26, Corporal
Bradley, George W.—Co. E, 21, Private
Bradley, Thomas—Co. K, 26, Private
Brady, Patrick—Co. H, 26, Corporal
Brady, Samuel—Co. D, 26, Private
Brandenburg, David W.—Co. F, 19, Private
Brannon, Mathew—Co. K, 20, Private
Bray, Daniel—Co. H, 26, Private
Breidenthal, Henry—Co. A, 28, Sergeant
Brewer, August—Co. G, 21, Private
Briggs, Elisha C.—Co. B, 23, Sergeant
Brigham, James B.—Co. B, 42, Corporal
Brigham, James B.—Co. B, 45, Private
Brincefield, William J.—Co. F, 19, Private
Broadbeck, Benjamin—Co. K, 25, Private
Broadbeck, William—Co. A, 20, Private
Bronson, Jesse—Co. G, 19, Corporal
Brooks, James—Co. K, 34, Private
Brothers, Francis M.—Co. D, 20, Private
Brown, George W.—Co. B, 47, Private
Brown, Henry F.—Co. H, 19, Teamster
Brown, Henry S.—Co. A, 24, Private
Brown, John—Co. K, 18, Private
Brown, Manassa—Co. G, 24, Private
Brown, Rodolph M.—Co. C, 20, Private
Brownlee, Horace,—Co. C, 20, Corporal
Bruce, William R.—Co. F, 33, Sergeant
Brumbaugh, Daniel W.—Co. B, 42, Private
Brush, Albert S.—F & S, 24, Q.M.S.
Brush, Albert S.—Co. B, 27, Corporal
Bryan, John—Co. F, 19, Private
Bryon, Charles—Co. C, 29, Captain
Buchanan, Clinton C.—Co. A, 20, 1st Sergt.
Buchannan, Robert—Co. C, 23, Private
Bulger, James—Co. E, 21, Corporal
Bunker, Bryon—Co. I, 20, Private
Burdick, William H.—Co. H, 28, Private
Burgess, James H.—Co. D, 21, Private
Burley, Frank—Co. F, 20, Private
Burns, James—Co. H, 21, Private

Roster: Third Ohio Volunteer Infantry

Burns, John—Co. A, 28, Private
Burns, Nathaniel—Co. K, 20, Private
Burt, Arden—Co. I, Private
Burt, George N.—Co. C, 27, Private
Bush, David L.—Co. A, 26, Private
Bush, David L.—Co. H, 24, Sergeant
Butler, Joel C.—Co. E, 24, Private
Butler, Simon P.—Co. B, 28, Private
Byers, Charles H.—Co. B, 28, Private
Byers, John M.—Co. E, 28, Private
Caffee, George W.—Co. H, 19, Sergeant
Caffee, William W.—Co. H, 22, Private
Callahan, Theodore C.—Co. I, 27, Private
Calvert, Saulsberry W.—Co. C, 18, Private
Campbell, Harvey—Co. K, 19, Private
Campbell, Hezekiah—Co. F, 21, Private
Campbell, James—Co. B, 48, Private
Campbell, James—Co. K, 21, Private
Campbell, Joseph J.—Co. K, 23, Corporal
Campbell, Wallace—Co. F, 18, Private
Cannon, Charles—Co. G, 21, Sergeant
Capple, Theodore—Co. E, 22, Private
Carey, John P.—Co. E, 24, Private
Carl, James—Co. D, 23, Private
Carley, Marcus A.—Co. C, 19, Corporal
Carlton, Robert—Co. D, 18, Private
Carpenter, Francis M.—Co. D, 20, Private
Carpenter, Stephen D.—Co. D, 23, 1st Lieut.
Carrigan, John N.—Co. D, 27, Private
Cartman, William—Co. G, 19, Private
Cartwright, Levi H.—Co. I, 28, Private
Case, Charles B.—Co. B, 22, Private
Casey, John B.—Co. I, 28, Wagoner
Casey, William—Co. I, 22, Corporal
Cashner, Simon J.—Co. A, 25, Private
Cassidy, Edmund—Co. E, 18, Private
Cather, James—Co. C, 18, Private
Cathers, Iowa—Co. C, 22, Corporal
Chambers, James J.—Co. B, 22, Private
Chamblain, Louis C.—Co. A, 22, Private
Chase, William—Co. G, 39, Private
Christine, Frank—Co. B, 21, Private
Clark, George W.—Co. H, 26, Private
Clason, Thomas S.—F & S Asst. Surgeon
Click, Jacob W.—Co. D, 21, Private
Clouse, David—Co. H, 20, Private
Cockrell, John N.—Co. E, 22, Private
Cody, Carlos H.—Co. H, 22, Private
Cody, Charles C.—Co. K, 21, Private
Coe, John W.—Co. E, 22, Private
Coff, George—Co. A, 20, Private
Coffey, George W.—Co. D, 23, Corporal
Coleman, John C.—Co. C, 19, Private
Colville, George W.—Co. H, 23, Private
Condon, James J.—Co. A, 22, Private
Conkle, James—Co. F, 18, Private
Conklin, Henry—Co. I, 36, Private
Conner, John—Co. B, 24, Private
Conner, John—Co. F, 24, Private
Conner, Milo A.—Co. K, 23, Private
Connor, John—Co. E, 23, Private
Conway, John—Co. A, 22, Corporal
Conway, William—Co. I, 19, Private
Cook, John E.—Co. C, 26, Private
Cook, William H.—Co. C, 20, Private
Coon, Benjamin F.—Co. D, 18, Private
Cooper, George B.—Co. K, 23, 1st Sergt.
Cooper, George H.—Co. E, 29, Private
Cordrey, James—Co. B, 38, Private
Cornell, Nelson—Co. F, 18, Private
Corte, John—Co. G, 24, Private
Corwin, Thomas, Jr.—Co. F, 26, Sergeant
Cottle, James—Co. G, 27, Private
Courtwright, Lyman M.—Co. I, 18, Private
Cover, Thomas J.—Co. E, 25, Private
Cox, Hiram—Co. E, 19, Private
Cramer, Maurice W.—Co. C, 31, Private
Crammer, William H.H.—Co. H, 20, Private
Crane, Benjamin B.—Co. E, 26, Private
Cranston, Earl A.—Co. C, 20, 1st Lieut.
Crawford, Benjamin—Co. G, 19, Private
Crippen, Earl C.—Co. C, 23, Private
Crooks, John H.—Co. E, 19, Private
Crozier, James—Co. E, 25, Corporal
Crumbaker, James A.—Co. E, 21, Sergeant
Cunard, Henry E.—Co. I, 23, Captain
Currier, Lewis M.—Co. B, 22, Private
Currier, Scuyler—Co. B, 43, Private
Curry, James—Co. G, 19, Private
Curry, William A.—F & S, 22, Sr. Major
Curry, William A.—Co. G, 22, 1st Lieut.
Cusins, Benjamin O.—Co. C, 25, Private

Dailey, James—Co. B, 21, Private
Dale, Francis P.—Co. H, 22, 2nd Lieut.
Dalphin, Joseph—Co. D, 26, Private
Dana, Joseph M.—Co. C, 39, Captain
Darling, George W.—Co. H, 36, Private
Darlington, Reese E.—Co. H, 23, Sergeant
Daugherty, Thomas—Co. F, 20, Private
Davis, Alfred—Co. K, 20, Private
Davis, Cartwright C.—Co. C, 21, Private
Davis, Casper—Co. G, 29, Private
Davis, Fielding S.—Co. F, 22, Private
Davis, John W.—Co. D, 19, Corporal
Davis, Matthew—Co. B, 22, Private
Dawson, Hugh—Co. K, 26, Private
Dawson, William A.—Co. K, 20, Private
Dearth, Doctor—Co. B, 24, Private
Debutts, Richard E.—F & S, 24, Cf. Bugler
Debutts, Richard E.—Co. G, 24, Musician
Delackso, Edward—Co. C, 32, Private
Dell, Frank P.—Co. C, 26, Private
Demorest, John P.—Co. B, 30, Private
Demuth, Jesse A.—Co. H, 25, Private
Denivan, John—Co. D, 22, Private
Denning, William—Co. F, 19, Private
Dennis, Robert J.—Co. B, 26, Corporal
Deremer, Abram—Co. C, 36, Private
Desert, John F.—Co. K, 22, Corporal
Dever, John—Co. K, 21, Sergeant
Dever, Stephen—Co. K, 20, Private
Dever, William—Co. K, 25, Private
Devore, Adam—Co. I, 20, Private
Dick, Frank—Co. G, 25, Private
Dilley, John B.—Co. A, 20, Private
Dilts, Calvin—Co. G, 44, Private
Dipert, William W.—Co. I, 22, Private
Doan, Edward—Co. C, 24, Private
Dobson, Aaron—Co. K, 23, Private
Dobson, Hugh—Co. K, 18, Private
Dobson, Josiah—Co. K, 23, Private
Dolby, Hiram—Co. K, 22, Private
Donahue, John J.—Co. K, 19, Private
Donovan, David—Co. H, 20, Private
Dooley, Callihill—Co. G, 19, Private
Dooley, William—Co. G, 23, Private
Doty, Francis M.—Co. I, 19, Private
Doudna, Ephraim—Co. A, 22, Private
Douglas, Randolph—Co. K, 18, Private
Doyle, Daniel C.—Co. I, 25, Private
Drake, James—Co. H, 27, Private
Driscoll, Alexander—Co. G, 23, Private
Driscoll, Cornelius—Co. G, 22, Private
Driscoll, Edward M.—Co. G, 26, Captain
Droste, John F.—Co. G, 19, Private
Duden, James B.—Co. A, 25, Corporal
Dudley, William—Co. K, Private
Duff, James M.—Co. E, 30, Private
Duffey, Thomas—Co. B, 21, Private
Duncan, James—Co. I, 20, Private
Duncan, John A.—Co. I, 25, Private
Durbin, Thomas—Co. F, 21, Private
Early, George G.—Co. I, 19, 1st Sergt.
Earnest, Parker—Co. G, 23, Private
Ebert, Jerome B.—Co. F, 26, 1st Lieut.
Echart, Philip A.—Co. F, 22, Private
Edson, Daniel B.—Co. B, 43, Private
Eichenlaub, Frederick—Co. G, 20, Private
Eipper, Henry—Co. D, 20, Private
Elliott, John C.—Co. F, 41, Private
Ellis, Jonathan—Co. A, 20, Private
Ellis, Leven B.—Co. A, 28, Private
Emmons, Isaac T.—Co. D, 24, Private
English, Edward—Co. G, 20, Private
Ensanch, Daniel—F & S, 32, Hos. St'd
Ensanch, Daniel—Co. I, 32, Private
Erwin, W.H.H.—Co. D, 21, Private
Etzer, Charles A.—Co. B, 33, Private
Evans, William—Co. C, 27, Private
Everett, Isaac—Co. K, 18, Private
Everson, Ira—Co. F, 29, Private
Ewing, John—Co. K, 24, Private
Ewing, Levi W.—Co. E, 25, Private
Ewing, Robert S.—Co. E, 22, Private
Fadely, William G.—Co. K, 19, Private
Falconer, John W.—Co. F, 20, Corporal
Falls, William D.—Co. E, 22, Private
Farley, Joseph—Co. I, 23, Private
Ferguson, Joseph—Co. A, 31, Private
Fields, John W.—Co. A, 26, Private
Figley, Joseph D.—Co. C, 19, Private
Filser, George P.—Co. E, 23, Private
Finch, David S.—Co. G, 23, Private
Finch, Henry A.—Co. A, 22, Private
Finch, Robert—Co. B, 23, Private
Finch, Robert M.—Co. I, 18, Private
Finch, Thompson S.—Co. A, 31, Private
Findley, Joseph D.—Co. A, 21, Private
Finley, James W.—Co. K, 30, Private

Finley, Levi L.—Co. E, 18, Private
Fish, George W.—Co. F, 27, 2nd Lieut.
Fisher, Alfred—Co. I, 28, Private
Fisher, Daniel M.—Co. D, 23, Private
Fisher, William A.—Co. E, 23, Corporal
Fithian, Philip—Co. G, 30, Captain
Fix, Bernard H.—Co. E, 23, Corporal
Fix, Joseph—Co. E, 24, 1st Sergt.
Flaig, Francis H.—Co. E, 23, Private
Flannigan, Israel—Co. H, 21, Private
Flemming, Joseph—Co. H, 29, Private
Flinn, Horace J.—Co. A, 20, Private
Forney, Elias A.—Co. A, 29, Private
Fowler, Lyman D.—Co. I, Private
Foye, Winthrop H.—Co. E, 22, Sergeant
Francis, John R.—Co. H, 40, Private
Francis, Sebastian E.—Co. G, 33, Sergeant
Frank, Jacob—Co. G, 22, Private
Frazee, Nathan A.—Co. E, 21, Private
Frazier, Joseph D.—Co. E, 32, Private
Frazier, Joseph W.—Co. E, 27, Corporal
Frazier, Samuel A.—Co. A, 19, Sergeant
Freeman, Lewis L.—Co. C, 20, Private
French, Charles—Co. G, 26, Private
French, Erasmus—Co. A, 19, Private
French, Samuel L.—Co. B, 23, Sergeant
Froman, John—Co. F, 19, Private
Galbraith, William—Co. I, 25, Private
Galbreath, Jerome—Co. F, 28, Private
Gallantine, Jasper N.—Co. C, 19, Private
Galligher, Frank—Co. G, 27, Private
Gannon, Thomas—Co. D, 19, Private
Garberson, Job—Co. I, 19, Private
Gardner, William—Co. A, 34, Private
Garver, John—Co. F, 21, Private
Garvey, John—Co. H, 25, Private
Geiger, Frederick—Co. E, 19, Sergeant
Gibson, Charles—F & S, 24, Sr. Major
Gibson, Charles C.—Co. D, 24, Private
Gibson, Henry—Co. H, 22, Sergeant
Gibson, James M.—Co. C, 22, Private
Gibson, John—Co. H, 19, Private
Gilchrist, Jabez—Co. C, 20, Private
Gillen, Patrick—Co. C, 31, Private
Gilliland, Wilson S.—Co. A, 19, Private
Ginevan, Reuben H.—Co. D, 28, Corporal
Ginevan, William E.—Co. D, 18, Private
Glenn, Robert—Co. I, 19, Private

Godfrey, Charles H.—Co. E, 29, Corporal
Gold, Robert H.—Co. K, 21, Private
Gordon, William C.—Co. F, 34, Private
Grabill, Newton A.—Co. D, 21, Private
Graham, Charles—Co. G, 38, Private
Granger, James—Co. A, 23, Private
Grasser, Ernest—Co. H, 21, Private
Grasser, William—Co. H, 18, Private
Gray, Daniel S.—Co. B, 28, Private
Gray, George—Co. C, 22, Private
Gray, Peter—Co. B, 48, Private
Greaves, William—Co. E, 21, Sergeant
Griffith, Robert—Co. B, 36, Private
Grifty, James—Co. C, 21, Private
Grim, Frederick—Co. E, 20, Private
Grooms, John F.—Co. E, 34, Private
Grosvenor, Daniel A.—Co. C, 22, Private
Grosvenor, Edward—Co. C, 25, Sergeant
Haas, Alfred S.—Co. A, 21, Private
Hackathorn, George—Co. K, 22, Private
Hackathorn, Henry—Co. K, 22, Private
Halfhill, Reason—Co. A, 22, Private
Hall, David M.—Co. E, 26, Private
Hall, Francis—Co. A, 33, Private
Hall, John—Co. F, 32, Corporal
Hall, John T.—Co. A, 29, Private
Hall, Joseph L.—Co. B, 31, Private
Hall, Moses W.—Co. F, 21, Private
Halter, Benjamin W.—Co. B, 23, Private
Hamilton, Harry—Co. G, 19, Private
Hammond, James—Co. D, 29, Sergeant
Handley, Michael—Co. B, 43, Private
Hanna, William L—Co. A, 24, Private
Hanna, William L.—Co. C, 22, Private
Hanning, Wm. H.—Co. C, 22, Private
Happ, Henry—Co. D, 31, Private
Harbaugh, Daniel—Co. H, 21, Corporal
Harbert, Robert—Co. I, 24, Private
Harcourt, Henry E.—Co. B, 21, Corporal
Hardey, Albert R.—Co. A, 18, Private
Harkness, William A.—Co. E, 18, Private
Harrington, Daniel—Co. H, 24, Private
Harris, David H.—Co. E, 22, 2nd Lieut.
Harris, James—Co. E, 25, Private
Harris, Jesse—Co. I, Private
Harris, Joseph W.—Co. D, 18, Private

Roster: Third Ohio Volunteer Infantry

Harrison, David—Co. F, 22, Private
Harrison, Richard—Co. H, 22, Private
Hart, Charles—Co. G, 30, Private
Hartley, John—Co. A, 28, Private
Hartley, John—Co. G, 28, Private
Harvey, Samuel H.—Co. B, 26, Private
Haughen, Joseph—Co. K, 19, Private
Haughen, William—Co. K, 22, Private
Haughey, Frank A.—Co. H, 23, Private
Haughey, Henry—Co. H, 23, Sergeant
Haughey, Thomas—Co. H, 19, Private
Haughn, Alonzo—Co. B, 22, Private
Haver, Lewis P.—Co. E, 20, Sergeant
Hawk, William H.—Co. C, 21, Corporal
Hayes, Leonard—Co. A, 20, Private
Hayes, Robert B.—Co. A, 20, Corporal
Headley, Harrison—Co. K, 20, Private
Healey, John F.—Co. H, 25, Private
Heigley, Jacob—Co. D, 28, Private
Heil, Peter C.—Co. A, 21, Corporal
Heinkey, Balthaser—Co. D, 20, Private
Henning, John A.—Co. E, 23, Private
Henry, George A.—Co. G, 28, Private
Henry, James Q.—Co. E, 24, Private
Henry, John W.—Co. I, Private
Henry, Simon K.—Co. E, 21, Private
Herald, Amos J.—Co. D, 22, Private
Herr, Aaron—Co. D, 24, Corporal
Herr, Martin M.—Co. D, 22, Sergeant
Hibbitts, J. Harvey—Co. K, 22, Corporal
Hibbs, Albert G.—Co. A, 19, Private
Hicks, Thomas D.—Co. E, 28, Private
High, Joseph—Co. A, 29, Private
Hiskett, Charles S.—Co. I, 23, Private
Hiskett, John M.—Co. I, 20, Sergeant
Hodkins, Charles—Co. A, 30, Private
Hoffman, Absalmon G.—Co. D, 20, Private
Holland, Nathaniel—Co. K, 25, Sergeant
Holmes, Benjamin—Co. G, 21, Private
Horn, Richard—Co. G, 23, Private
Hornberger, Christian—Co. F, 20, Private
Hoss, George—Co. D, 23, Corporal
Hoss, John—Co. D, 27, Private
House, Elitha D.—Co. A, 24, Captain
Houseman, William—Co. H, 23, Private
Houseman, William—Co. I, 23, Private
Howell, George W.—Co. G, 19, Private
Huber, Henry—Co. A, 27, Private
Hudson, Henry H.—Co. K, 21, Corporal
Hughes, James M.—F & S, 38, Cf. Bugler
Hughes, James M.—Co. H, 30, Private
Hughes, Richard—Co. H, 19, Corporal
Hulings, Charles—Co. F, 22, Sergeant
Hunt, John T.—Co. A, 23, Private
Hurst, William J.—Co. K, 24, Sergeant
Hyatt, Andrew—Co. H, 22, Private
Hyre, Absalom—Co. D, 18, Private
Imbrie, James M.—Co. K, 25, Captain
Ingman, William—Co. H, 29, Private
Irwin, Samuel—Co. C, 29, Private
Irwin, Uriah W.—Co. K, 28, Sergeant
Israel, Peter—Co. E, 32, Private
Jackson, William—Co. H, 22, Private
Jacobs, David—Co. K, 20, Private
Jamison, Levi—Co. F, 24, Private
Jarvis, George P.—Co. C, 19, Private
Jeffries, John J.—Co. K, 20, Private
Jeramlaman, Nicholas—F & S, 24, Sr. Major
Jeramlaman, Nicholas—Co. I, 24, Sergeant
Jewett, John E.—F & S, 20, Q.M.S.
Jewett, John E.—Co. E, 21, Sergeant
Jewett, Nathan—Co. H, 26, Private
Johns, Edward H.—Co. E, 24, Private
Johns, Samuel R.—Co. F, 20, Corporal
Johnson, Arthur—Co. K, 19, Private
Johnson, Daniel P.—Co. A, 19, Private
Johnson, James H.—Co. K, 19, Private
Johnson, John R.—Co. E, 30, 2nd Lieut.
Jones, Daniel A.—Co. B, 30, Private
Jones, David H.—Co. C, 18, Private
Jones, Frederick W.—Co. E, 24, Private
Jones, John E.—Co. C, 19, Private
Jones, John R.—Co. K, 23, Private
Jones, Lewis B.—Co. E, 19, Private
Jones, Riley—Co. D, 28, Corporal
Jones, Samuel—Co. B, 22, Private
Jones, William—Co. H, 24, Private
Jordon, Hezekiah—Co. E, 21, Private
Junkins, Joseph R.—Co. K, 19, Private
Kaiser, John—Co. B, 24, Private
Kearns, George—Co. I, 18, Private
Keeler, Henry—Co. I, 25, Private
Keely, Thomas M.—Co. E, 24, Sergeant
Keifer, J. Warren—F & S, 26, Lieutenant Colonel

Keller, George W.—Co. D, 23, Private
Keller, John J.—Co. D, 22, Private
Kendall, William W.—Co. I, 19, Corporal
Kennedy, William H.—Co. F, 21, Sergeant
Kessinger, David I.—Co. E, 26, 1st Lieut.
Kessinger, David L.—Co. C, 26, 1st Lieut.
Keys, William H.—Co. A, 33, Private
Keys, William N.—Co. G, 32, Private
Kibble, Louis—Co. D, 38, Private
Kiddy, Charles—Co. K, 20, Private
Kille, Abram C.—Co. E, 42, Private
Killie, Lewis A.—Co. E, 21, Sergeant
Kimble, Samuel—Co. F, 18, Private
King, James—Co. G, 19, Private
King, Michael D.—Co. B, 22, 2nd Lieut.
Kinney, Erastus H.—Co. F, 23, Private
Kinsey, Thomas—Co. F, 19, Private
Kipp, Harrison—Co. G, 20, Private
Kirk, Isaac—Co. K, 21, Private
Kirkpatrick, James—Co. D, 22, Private
Klingler, Lewis—Co. G, 20, Private
Knapp, John—Co. G, 18, Private
Knaub, Henry C.—Co. D, 18, Private
Knepper, William—Co. K, 21, Private
Knight, Albert King—F & S, 21, Sr. Major
Knight, Albert King—Co. H, 21, Private
Knuckle, Lewis—Co. C, 30, Private
Koberger, Harry F.—Co. A, 19, Private
Konan, Paul—Co. F, 36, Private
Kreckleton, William—Co. H, 21, Private
Kreuse, Thomas W.—Co. G, 20, Sergeant
Kurle, David J.—Co. G, 28, Sergeant
Laird, John P.—F & S, 20, Prin. Mus.
Laird, John P.—Co. H, 20, Private
Lamme, Gustavus B.—Co. D, 19, Private
Lamson, James—Co. B, 49, Private
Land, Thomas—Co. B, 28, Private
Lane, James T.—Co. C, 18, Private
Langley, Lewis F.—Co. E, 22, Sergeant
Lank, John—Co. G, 25, Private
Latsco, Stephen—Co. I, 34, Corporal
Laughlin, Benjamin—Co. F, 36, Private
Laur, John—Co. A, 25, Private
Law, George—Co. K, 39, Private
Lawler, William—Co. G, 21, Private
Lawrence, James—Co. G, 44, Private
Lawrence, John—Co. G, 20, Private
Lawrence, Richard C.—Co. F, 28, Private
Lawson, Henry—Co. A, 18, Private
Lawson, Orris A.—F & S, 36, Colonel
Lawson, Orris A.—Co. A, 33, Captain
Laybourne, Joseph W.—Co. D, 19, Private
Lees, James—Co. H, 20, Private
Leflar, George W.—Co. F, 18, Private
Lemley, Wesley—Co. H, 18, Private
Lepage, Adam—Co. A, 22, Private
Leper, Robert—Co. K, 21, Private
Light, David H.—Co. C, 18, Private
Light, William C.—Co. C, 21, Private
Linch, Richard—Co. G, 20, Private
Linch, William—Co. G, 23, Private
Lindsey, James W.—Co. E, 26, Private
Linehan, John—Co. D, 18, Private
Linton, James—Co. G, 24, Private
Litz, Abram E.—Co. C, 19, Private
Livington, Aaron—Co. B, 41, Private
Lloyd, James R.—Co. A, 22, Private
Lobaugh, Samuel—Co. B, 22, Private
Lockemeyer, Henry—Co. G, 24, Private
Lohnes, John P.—Co. D, 20, Private
Long, Daniel J.—Co. I, 19, Private
Long, James E.—Co. H, 18, Private
Long, Paul—Co. I, 18, Private
Loring, John W.—Co. F, 30, Corporal
Louis, Cyrus B.—Co. D, 18, Private
Loveland, James—Co. H, 22, Private
Lowe, John—Co. D, 19, Private
Lowery, James O.—Co. C, 22, Private
Lowery, Thomas F.—Co. C, 19, Private
Lunceford, John J.—Co. H, 21, Corporal
Lyle, Arthur—Co. G, 18, Private
Lyles, Charles W.—Co. A, 20, Private
Lyon, John F.—Co. C, 31, Sergeant
Lyon, Lewis A.—Co. C, 26, Private
Lyons, James—Co. H, 22, Private
Mahanna, Bradley—Co. A, 21, Private
Maize, Levi—Co. A, 21, Private
Mann, Jasper—Co. I, 18, Private
Mann, John—Co. C, 26, Private
Mann, Michael—Co. I, 21, Private
Maple, Benjamin—Co. K, 24, Private
Maple, William—Co. K, 21, Private
Marsh, Samuel J.—Co. D, 19, Private
Marshall, Martin—Co. K, 19, Private

Marshall, Robert—Co. D, 33, Private
Martin, George W.—F & S, 18, Q.M.S.
Martin, George W.—Co. K, 18, Private
Martindale, James—Co. H, 39, Private
Martindale, Samuel—Co. H, 36, Private
Mason, George W.—Co. B, 21, Private
Massey, Edward—Co. G, 25, Private
Matheny, Joshua—Co. E, 27, Private
Mathews, John—Co. I, 26, Corporal
Matthew, Martin V.B.—Co. E, 18, Private
Matthews, John T.—Co. C, 23, Corporal
Maxwell, Charles A.—Co. D, 19, 2nd Lieut.
Maxwell, John F.—Co. D, 22, Private
Maxwell, Melville—Co. I, 21, Private
Mayhew, Levi M.—Co. F, 24, Wagoner
McCarrol, James H.—Co. A, 25, Private
McCarten, William—Co. F, 23, Sergeant
McCartney, James—Co. K, 37, Private
McCartney, W. H.—Co. B, 24, Corporal
McCarty, Cornelius—Co. C, 24, Private
McCarty, Henry—Co. H, 22, Private
McClanathan, John—Co. G, 19, Private
McCleary, William H.—Co. B, 28, Private
McCobrie, William V.—Co. G, 27, Sergeant
McCoy, John—Co. F, 23, Private
McCracken, A.P.—Co. F, 29, Private
McCracken, David R.—Co. H, 24, Private
McCreary, John—Co. H, 18, Private
McCroba, Morgan—Co. A, 22, Sergeant
McCullough, Hugh—Co. F, 19, Private
McCullough, John R.—Co. K, 23, Private
McCullough, Thomas—Co. K, 17, Private
McCurdy, William—Co. B, 26, Private
McCutcheon, Oliver G.—Co. E, 27, Private
McDonald, Charles A.—Co. K, 25, Private
McDonald, George O.—Co. B, 30, Corporal
McDonald, James—Co. H, 23, Private
McDonald, John H.—Co. K, 19, Private
McDugall, Leonidas—Co. H, 38, Captain
McFadden, Frank—F & S, 19, Com. Ser.
McFadden, Frank—Co. E, 19, Private
McGaffick, Edward—Co. K, 18, Private
McGath, John D.—Co. A, 23, Private
McGill, John A.—Co. C, 19, Sergeant
McGinley, James—Co. K, 18, Private
McGraw, William—Co. G, 47, Private
McIlvain, George W.—Co. A, 28, Sergeant
McKenzie, John—Co. K, 26, Private
McLain, Daniel—Co. K, 20, Private
McMeans, Robert R.—F & S, 41, Surgeon
McMillen, Edwin—Co. G, 18, Private
McMillen, William—Co. G, 20, Private
McPherson, Joseph—Co. E, 21, Private
McPherson, Robert—Co. H, 28, Private
McRoberts, John B.—Co. B, 29, Captain
McRown, Charles B.—Co. B, 21, Corporal
McSweegin, James D.—Co. K, 23, Corporal
McWhirk, Gilbert B.—Co. G, 21, Sergeant
Meacham, Francis W.—Co. A, 24, Private
Meegan, Edward—Co. E, 19, Private
Meeker, Benjamin J.—Co. I, 19, Private
Menough, John W.—Co. K, 21, Private
Meredith, Leverett—Co. H, 18, Private
Merrill, Bela G.—Co. I, 23, Private
Merrill, Charles R.—Co. I, 20, Corporal
Merrill, George W.—Co. I, 25, Corporal
Mesner, Levi—Co. C, 22, Private
Metz, Frank—Co. G, 22, Private
Miller, Edward—Co. D, 28, Private
Miller, Emile—Co. G, 21, Private
Miller, Fred A.—Co. I, 18, Private
Miller, John A.—Co. A, 26, Corporal
Miller, Jonathan—Co. I, 20, Private
Milliken, William—Co. F, 18, Private
Mills, Ashford—Co. H, 40, Private
Mills, J. Thomas—Co. H, 22, Private
Mills, Thomas J.—F & S, 22, Hos. St'd
Mills, William—Co. G, 39, Private
Misler, Andrew—Co. A, 25, Private
Mitchell, John G.—F & S, Adjutant
Mitchell, John G.—Co. C, Captain
Moats, David V.—Co. H, 25, Private
Moats, Morgan J.—Co. H, 19, Private
Mochler, Edward—Co. H, 34, Private
Moore, Charles M.—Co. H, 20, Private
Moore, Jacob—Co. C, 18, Private

Roster: Third Ohio Volunteer Infantry

Moore, John A.—Co. B, 23, Private
Moore, John D.—Co. G, 24, Private
Moore, Joseph B.—Co. E, 23, Private
Moore, Joseph D.—Co. I, 27, 2nd Lieut.
Moore, Mitchell—Co. K, 30, Private
Moore, Mordecai J.—Co. K, 37, Private
Moore, Shelby K.—Co. I, 18, Private
Moore, William H.—Co. B, 25, Private
Moran, James—Co. H, 24, Private
Morehead, Alexander—Co. B, 24, Wagoner
Morey, Stillman—Co. I, 22, Private
Morgan, Calvin—Co. F, 20, Private
Morgan, James A.—Co. E, 25, Private
Morgan, John C.—Co. H, 26, Private
Morris, Andrew—Co. A, 29, Private
Morris, John L.—Co. H, 23, Private
Morrison, Henry—Co. C, 23, Private
Morrow, Issac H.—F & S, 40, Colonel
Mortram, John—Co. I, Private
Moss, John—Co. C, 26, Private
Munson, Albert—Co. H, 18, Private
Munson, William A.—Co. E, 22, Corporal
Murdock, George W.—Co. E, 32, Private
Murdock, James A.—F & S, 20, Q.M.S.
Murdock, James A.—Co. K, 20, 2nd Lieut.
Murray, Joseph D.—Co. G, 26, Private
Musselman, Charles F.—Co. E, 25, Private
Musselman, William H.—Co. E, 19, Private
Musser, Albert—Co. G, 20, Private
Myers, John—Co. A, 36, Private
Nash, John T.—Co. A, 22, Private
Naylor, John B.—Co. G, 23, Private
Neer, Mahlon—Co. D, 20, Private
Neer, Matthew—Co. C, 26, Private
Neil, John—Co. B, 21, Private
Nesler, Andrew—Co. A, 25, Private
Nessley, Wellington—Co. K, 21, Private
Nevils, Samuel—Co. B, 28, Corporal
Nevitt, Thomas A.—Co. A, 19, Musician
Nevitt, Thomas A.—Co. I, 17, Private
Neyman, Hudson L.—Co. A, 20, Private
Nicholas, Elias C.—Co. I, 20, Sergeant
Nichols, Caleb—Co. E, 27, Private
Nichols, Granville—Co. A, 27, Private
Nichols, John M.—Co. H, 20, Private
Nicholson, Samuel—Co. E, 23, Private
Nicols, Isaac R.—Co. E, 41, Private
Nixon, William—Co. K, 18, Private
Noble, Homer C.—Co. C, 18, Private
Noble, Walter C.—Co. H, 36, Corporal
Norman, William—Co. H, 38, Private
Norris, James R.—Co. K, 18, Private
Norris, John—Co. D, 21, Private
Norvelle, James—Co. H, 30, Private
O'Conner, Frank—Co. G, 20, Private
O'Connor, James—Co. E, 19, Private
O'Connor, James—Co. G, 23, Private
O'Hara, Mahlon M.—Co. B, 22, Corporal
O'Harra, Stewart—Co. K, 21, Private
O'Keeffe, Daniel—Co. G, 24, Private
Oakley, Elijah—Co. B, 28, Private
Officer, John C.—Co. E, 19, Private
Oliver, Smith M.—Co. I, 18, Private
Oliver, William G.—Co. I, 18, Private
Ornsdoff, John W.—Co. H, 20, Private
Otstot, John H.—Co. A, 30, Private
Palmer, Charles S.—Co. G, 32, Private
Palmer, Charles T.—Co. A, 33, Private
Palmer, Henry C.—Co. G, 26, Private
Palmer, John A.—Co. H, 21, Corporal
Palmer, John D.—Co. C, 18, Private
Parker, Charles C.—Co. E, 24, Private
Parkinson, Joseph—Co. A, 22, Private
Parks, Henry—Co. H, 27, Private
Parmeter, Samuel B.—Co. C, 20, Corporal
Parry, Daniel P.—Co. F, 22, Private
Patten, Edward—Co. F, 21, Sergeant
Patterson, Adam—Co. A, 24, Private
Patterson, John M.—Co. K, 21, Private
Patterson, Wesley L.—Co. B, 29, Captain
Paul, Oscar J—Co. D, 18, Private
Peck, James H.—Co. D, 19, Private
Peck, William L.—F & S, Surgeon
Peirce, Curby—Co. K, 19, Corporal
Pence, Isaac—Co. H, 23, Private
Pendergrass, Josephus—Co. C, 21, Private
Penney, Orsmus,—Co. H, 21, Private
Percella, John—Co. A, 23, Private
Perry, Herman—Co. D, 45, Private
Perry, William O.—Co. C, 29, Private
Peters, Mowry I.—Co. D, 19, Private
Pettit, Wesley—Co. K, 20, Private

Phelps, Francis R.—Co. I, 21, Private
Phillips, Charles—Co. G, 24, Private
Phillips, Henry—Co. G, 22, Private
Pickering, Levi C.—Co. C, 18, Sergeant
Pickering, William B.—Co. C, 19, Private
Pickering, William S.—F & S, 25, Com. Ser.
Pickering, William S.—Co. K, 21, Corporal
Pierce, John G.—Co. A, 28, Private
Pinkerton, William L.—Co. B, 21, 1st Sergt.
Piper, Samuel B.—F & S, 24, Adjutant
Piper, Samuel B.—Co. A, 24, 1st Lieut.
Pohlman, John—Co. G, 20, Private
Pollett, Daniel—Co. F, 23, Private
Poncer, George—Co. H, 23, Private
Poncer, Henry—Co. H, 21, Private
Porter, John V.—Co. A, 35, Private
Portier, William—Co. D, 29, Private
Post, David—Co. F, 22, Private
Post, Peter—Co. F, 20, Private
Potter, Charles E.—Co. B, 35, Private
Potts, Robert—Co. G, 44, Wagoner
Powers, Edward—Co. A, 24, Private
Powers, Philander—Co. I, 18, Private
Prairs, W.H.H.—Co. E, 24, Private
Prasser, Jonah—Co. C, 30, Private
Pretzinger, Solomon—Co. F, 22, Private
Price, John—Co. B, 43, Private
Priest, Benjamin—Co. E, 21, Private
Pruden, Silas—Co. C, 21, 1st Lieut.
Quick, Jasper M.—Co. D, 18, Private
Quick, William G.—Co. D, 21, 1st Sergt.
Race, Wesley S.—F & S, 34, Asst. Surgeon
Rainey, Joseph M.—Co. B, 21, Corporal
Ramer, Henry—Co. B, 21, Private
Ranner, Reese W.—Co. F, 31, Private
Ream, Tobias—Co. A, 21, Private
Reasoner, John—Co. I, 20, Corporal
Redhead, Benjamin—Co. H, 40, Private
Redhead, William—Co. H, 18, Corporal
Reece, Isaac—Co. B, 27, Private
Reed, Benjamin C.G.—Co. E, 21, Captain
Reed, Dexter—Co. I, Private
Reed, John—Co. F, 18, Private
Reed, Nathan—Co. G, 30, Private
Reed, Nathan A.—Co. H, 30, Private
Reed, Samuel O.K.—Co. E, 18, Private
Reese, David J.—Co. K, 18, Private
Reese, Isaac—Co. H, 22, Private
Reese, Samuel—Co. H, 19, Private
Reeves, John—Co. B, 26, Private
Reiche, Gust A.—Co. C, 37, Private
Reid, Edwin—Co. I, 18, 2nd Lieut.
Reid, John W.—Co. E, 23, Sergeant
Reiley, William—Co. A, 22, Private
Reiner, John J.—Co. E, 18, Private
Reynolds, Thomas W.—Co. F, 21, 1st Sergt.
Rhinehart, Zedekiah—Co. D, 25, Private
Rhodes, Hiram B.—Co. F, 23, Corporal
Rhoe, Isaac—Co. H, 20, Private
Rice, Esau—Co. A, 24, Private
Rice, Henry—Co. A, 34, Corporal
Rice, Zenis—Co. A, 26, Private
Richards, Benjamin—Co. H, 25, Private
Richards, Frank F.—Co. H, 24, Private
Richey, George—Co. G, 20, Private
Rickets, William R.—Co. A, 19, Private
Rickey, Joseph—Co. C, 39, Private
Riddle, Alonzo S.—Co. D, 20, Private
Riddle, George F.—Co. K, 23, Private
Riley, Benjamin F.—Co. A, 27, Private
Riley, William B.—Co. F, 22, Private
Risley, Marcus J.—Co. C, 24, Private
Ritchie, John—Co. A, 26, 1st Lieut.
Ritchie, John—Co. G, 26, 1st Lieut.
Roberts, Thomas—Co. E, 25, Private
Robertson, John B.A.—Co. F, 25, Private
Robertson, Thomas C.—Co. K, 19, Private
Robinson, William L.—Co. B, 26, Sergeant
Roney, John C.—Co. H, 21, 1st Lieut.
Root, William H.—Co. C, 24, Private
Ropp, Henry—Co. D, 20, Private
Rorick, Marion—Co. E, 21, Private
Rossman, William C.—Co. F, 26, Captain
Rowe, Thomas—Co. F, 19, Private
Runyan, William—Co. D, 20, Private
Rusk, David S.—Co. E, 24, Sergeant
Rusk, William H.H.—Co. E, 22, Corporal
Rutter, Henry C.—Co. F, 18, Private
Ryan, Michael—Co. B, 43, Private
Sage, Wilber H.—Co. B, 24, 2nd Lieut.

Roster: Third Ohio Volunteer Infantry

Sage, Wilbur H.—F & S, 24, Adjutant
Sanderson, Henry W.—Co. C, 22, 1st Sergt.
Say, Frederick G.—Co. A, 26, Private
Say, George F.—Co. G, 25, Private
Sayers, Samuel—Co. B, 21, Private
Schmedley, James P.—Co. E, 18, Private
Schneller, Andrew—Co. G, 20, Private
Schroder, Joseph—Co. G, 20, Private
Schwab, Charles—Co. G, 26, Private
Schwager, August—Co. G, 26, Private
Schwing, Charles—Co. B, 48, Sergeant
Scott, Andrew—Co. C, 18, Private
Scott, Robert—Co. C, 19, Private
Scroggs, Joseph—Co. H, 31, Private
Seigler, Christopher F.—Co. K, 24, Private
Seyes, Henry H.—F & S, 30, Asst. Surgeon
Shackleford, James H.—Co. I, 19, Sergeant
Shafer, Philip—Co. D, 30, Private
Shafer, Samuel—Co. D, 19, Private
Shank, Joseph W.—Co. D, 20, Private
Shankland, Theodore G.—Co. B, 23, Private
Shaw, Daniel—Co. G, 31, Private
Shaw, Felix B.—Co. I, Private
Shay, Timothy—Co. I, 18, Private
Sheirberg, John F.—Co. C, 21, Private
Sheppard, Abraham—Co. B, 36, Private
Sheppard, George W.—Co. C, 20, Private
Sheppard, Israel—Co. B, 22, Private
Shidler, John L.—Co. F, 24, Corporal
Shields, Lawrence—Co. H, 26, 1st Sergt.
Shinn, Isaac J.—Co. C, 23, Corporal
Shipley, Archibald—Co. A, 22, Private
Shires, Joseph—Co. G, 28, Private
Shives, Timothy—Co. K, 18, Private
Shotwell, Hudson B.—Co. I, 18, Musician
Sigler, James H.—Co. H, 19, Private
Silkniter, John—Co. F, 28, Corporal
Simmons, Wilson—Co. H, 22, Private
Singleton, Robert F.—Co. E, 29, Private
Six, Benjamin—Co. C, 19, Private
Smith, Benjamin S.—Co. H, 21, Private
Smith, Eustace—Co. G, 21, Private
Smith, Henry—Co. F, 19, Private
Smith, Jacob—Co. G, 29, Private
Smith, James—Co. G, 20, Private
Smith, John—Co. H, 20, Private
Smith, Martin—Co. G, 24, Private
Smith, Peter—Co. A, 26, Private
Smith, Robert—Co. I, Private
Smith, Rufus H.—Co. D, 19, Private
Smith, Thomas F.—Co. H, 20, Private
Smith, William—Co. H, 18, Private
Snedeker, Thomas—Co. D, 20, Private
Snyder, Gilbert—Co. E, 22, Private
Snyder, Jacob—Co. E, 23, Sergeant
Snyder, Jesse—Co. I, 21, Private
Souder, John—Co. A, 38, Private
Sowers, George—Co. E, 30, Private
Spellman, Reiland—Co. H, 20, Sergeant
Spencer, Daniel—Co. G, 18, Private
Spring, Noah—Co. E, 22, Private
St. John, James—Co. I, 21, 1st Lieut.
Stafford, Charles—Co. B, 27, Private
Stagg, Michael—Co. A, 32, Private
Starkey, Francis G.—Co. E, 20, Private
Starkey, Tyler Z.—Co. E, 23, Private
Starr, Calvin L.—Co. K, 24, 1st Lieut.
Stauferman, Frank—Co. G, 23, Private
Stauferman, John—Co. G, 19, Private
Stauffer, Ferdinand A.—Co. A, 22, Corporal
Steed, Jacob—Co. A, 29, Private
Stegner, Philip—Co. G, 20, Corporal
Steller, Andrew J.—Co. K, 22, Private
Stevens, George H.—Co. K, 19, Sergeant
Stevens, John—Co. K, 20, Sergeant
Stevenson, Samuel—Co. D, 33, Sergeant
Stevenson, Thomas B.—Co. K, 22, 1st Lieut.
Steward, Henry A.—Co. F, 20, Corporal
Steward, William—Co. F, 20, Private
Stewart, Sylvanus—Co. G, 23, Private
Stewart, Thomas—Co. H, 19, Private
Stidd, David—Co. B, 24, Private
Stiles, James A.—Co. D, 21, Sergeant
Stimpson, Albert—Co. G, 21, Private
Stimson, Cicinnatus—Co. G, 19, Private
Stiner, William—Co. I, 21, Sergeant
Stitizer, George W.—Co. A, 21, Private
Stitt, Elias—Co. K, 50, Private
Stockdall, John A.—Co. D, 24, Private
Stone, John F.—Co. A, 29, Private
Stoner, Jacob—Co. H, 22, Private
Stoner, Joseph—Co. H, 19, Private
Stout, John N.—Co. H, 22, Private
Stout, William—Co. G, 19, Wagoner

Straber, Michael—Co. G, 21, Private
Strahl, Benjamin F.—Co. A, 22, Private
Strait, Cornelius Y.—Co. K, 23, Corporal
Straub, John—Co. I, 22, Private
Strobler, George—Co. D, 23, Private
Strong, Erastus A.—F & S, Chaplain
Stuart, Alexander—Co. B, 20, Private
Sulter, Ernest O.—Co. A, 23, Private
Summers, Alexander—Co. B, 23, Private
Summers, David—Co. B, 25, Private
Suttlers, Edward—Co. B, 21, Private
Sutton, Peter—Co. H, 23, Private
Swan, Robert G.—Co. H, 18, Private
Swaney, George W.—Co. B, 23, Private
Swaney, Solomon—Co. F, 20, Private
Swayze, William A.—Co. A, 31, Captain
Swisher, Alonzo—Co. I, 20, Private
Synder, Elais—Co. E, 28, Wagoner
Talley, Nathaniel W.—Co. H, 18, Private
Tanner, Oscar—Co. E, 22, Private
Tarbutten, John E.—Co. D, 22, Private
Taylor, Alfred K.—F & S, 21, R.Q.M.
Taylor, Alfred K.—Co. E, 21, Sergeant
Taylor, Alfred K.—Co. I, 21, Captain
Teagarden, Lorenzo D.—Co. H, 49, Private
Teetors, Thomas B.—Co. G, Corporal
Thackeray, Thomas—Co. G, 33, Corporal
Thackery, Thomas—Co. K, 33, Corporal
Thomas, Dewar—Co. H, 18, Corporal
Thomas, Henry—Co. E, 29, Private
Thomas, James—Co. E, 24, Private
Thomas, Reese—Co. C, 23, Private
Thomas, Richard—Co. C, 18, Private
Thompson, George W.—Co. E, 23, Private
Thompson, Joel E.—Co. D, 47, 1st Lieut.
Thompson, John B.—Co. H, 31, Private
Thompson, John F.—Co. H, 23, Private
Thompson, John S.—Co. K, 21, Sergeant
Thrall, Robert F.—Co. A, 25, Private
Thurston, William H.—Co. A, 20, Private
Tierney, Owen—Co. H, 33, Private
Tignor, John W.—Co. E, 23, Private
Tillman, Leander D.—Co. A, 24, Corporal
Tippanhancer, Coppie—Co. G, 20, Private
Todd, Thomas—Co. K, 21, Private
Toms, Sylvester—Co. F, 20, Private
Tonar, Finley M.—Co. C, 22, Private
Torbert, James F.—Co. F, 20, Private
Tracy, John H.—Co. B, 34, Private
Tragg, Joel C.—Co. B, 27, Private
Trownsell, Charles T.—Co. F, 23, 2nd Lieut.
Trownsell, Charles T.—Co. G, 23, 2nd Lieut.
Tucker, Aaron T.—Co. C, 30, Private
Tucker, Adam—Co. C, 25, Private
Tucker, Ruell—Co. C, 23, Private
Tydings, Thomas—Co. G, 22, Private
Ulem, John W.—Co. C, 25, 2nd Lieut.
Ulem, John W.—Co. H, 25, 2nd Lieut.
Uncles, Benjamin—Co. B, 21, Private
Underhill, John—Co. I, Private
Underhill, Joseph T.—Co. I, 21, Private
Unine, Francis—Co. A, 27, Private
Van Brimmer, Henry—Co. I, 19, Private
Van Buskirk, Rufus—Co. H, 30, Private
Van Sickle, Thomas—Co. I, 18, Private
Vananda, James—F & S, 38, Major
Vananda, James C.—Co. D, 35, Captain
Vananda, William H.—Co. D, 24, Private
Vance, George—Co. H, 37, Private
Vandine, Walter—Co. A, 22, Private
Vanlein, Joseph—Co. G, 33, Private
Vincent, Michael—Co. I, 21, Private
Violet, Byron W.—Co. H, 18, Corporal
Voight, Frederick—Co. E, 24, Private
Wagoner, John L.—Co. A, 23, Private
Walback, Abraham K.—Co. C, 19, 1st Lieut.
Walker, Christopher—Co. K, 18, Private
Walker, David—Co. C, 18, Sergeant
Walker, John G.—Co. C, 20, Private
Wallom, Charles W.—Co. K, 20, Private
Warden, Albert G.—Co. B, 21, Private
Warff, Amos M.—Co. C, 21, Private
Warfield, Reuben A.—Co. A, 25, Private
Warren, Joseph W.—Co. C, 22, Private
Watson, James—Co. I, 27, Private
Webber, Conrad—Co. G, 20, Private
Weber, Jean—Co. C, 35, Private
Weber, Joseph—Co. G, 24, Private
Wehbring, Charles H.—Co. F, 20, Corporal
Weimer, Andrew—Co. B, 22, Private

Roster: Third Ohio Volunteer Infantry

Weinett, Thomas—F & S, 18, Dr'm Maj.
Welch, Milo—Co. I, 22, Corporal
Welch, Silas—Co. A, 24, Private
Welch, Simon—Co. I, 21, Private
Wellman, Herman D.—Co. G, 20, Private
Wellman, John—Co. G, 21, Private
Wells, George L.—Co. H, 27, 2nd Lieut.
Wells, Kimball C.—F & S, 22, Adjutant
Wells, Kimball C.—Co. K, 22, Private
Wells, William P.—Co. K, 19, Private
Welsh, John T.—Co. G, 20, Private
Wessell, Edward—Co. G, 18, Private
Whip, William—Co. A, 23, Private
White, Emerson—Co. B, 21, Private
White, John B.—Co. I, 24, Private
White, Norman C.—Co. I, 19, Private
White, William D.—Co. E, 22, Private
Whiting, John DeWitt—Co. D, Captain
Whiting, John DeWitt—Co. H, 1st Lieut.
Whitmore, Louis—Co. G, 20, Private
Whittaker, Albert W.—Co. F, 19, Private
Whittaker, James M.—Co. F, 22, Private
Whittier, William M.—Co. H, 23, Private
Wilkins, George—Co. H, 39, Private
Willets, Wendell P.—Co. I, Private
Williams, Charles—Co. H, 18, Private
Williams, Gillman—Co. H, 22, Private
Williams, William—Co. I, Sergeant
Williamson, Jacob L.—Co. I, Private
Williamson, William—Co. H, 19, Private
Willis, Charles—Co. B, 25, Private
Willis, Oliver—Co. B, 23, Private
Wills, George—Co. D, 20, Private
Wilson, James S.—F & S, 26, Adjutant
Wilson, James S.—Co. F, 26, 1st Lieut.
Wilson, Shannon—Co. B, 32, Private
Wilson, William—Co. I, 19, Private
Wilson, William A.—Co. C, 31, Private
Wilson, William W.—Co. C, 19, Sergeant
Winegand, Charles A.—Co. D, 19, Private
Wing, James H.—F & S, 27, Lieutenant Colonel
Wing, James H.—Co. B, 27, Captain
Wingfield, Samuel—Co. D, 23, Private
Wingfield, William—Co. D, 24, Private
Winneman, Christopher—Co. B, 25, Private
Wintermute, Albert—Co. E, 27, Private
Wirick, Martin V.—Co. D, 21, Private
Wirtz, Isaac—Co. A, 21, Private
Wirtz, William—Co. A, 24, Private
Wise, Jacob—Co. D, 27, Corporal
Wolback, Abraham C.—Co. E, 19, 1st Lieut.
Wolf, John—Co. A, 25, Private
Wolf, Michael—Co. B, 31, Private
Wood, Charles W.—Co. I, 18, Private
Wood, Nathans S.—Co. F, 22, Private
Wood, William H.—Co. I, Private
Woodgard, William F.—Co. C, 23, Private
Woodruff, Henry—Co. H, 24, Corporal
Woods, Humphrey—Co. E, 33, Private
Woodward, Joshua—Co. C, 18, Private
Worthington, Artis—Co. A, 27, Sergeant
Wright, George C.—Co. I, Private
Wright, James—Co. I, Private
Yarnall, Thomas H.—Co. D, 18, Private
Young, Henry—Co. B, 20, Private
Young, Jacob—Co. E, 22, Private

Appendix C

Ohio Generals During the Civil War

Brevet promotions after the war, back-dated by Lincoln, are so noted in parentheses.

Allen, Robert
Ammen, Jacob
Anderson, Nicholas L. (3/13/65)
Bailey, Joseph
Banning, Henry B. (3/13/65)
Bates, Joshua Hall
Beatty, John
Beatty, Samuel
Brice, Benjamin W.
Brooks, William T.
Campbell, John Allen (3/13/65)
Carrington, Henry B.
Buckingham, Catharinus
Buckland, Ralph P.
Buell, Don Carlos
Burns, William W.
Bussey, Cyrus
Carroll, Samuel S.
Cist, Henry M. (3/13/65)
Cox, Jacob D.
Crook, George
Custer, George A.
Doolittle, Charles
Ewing, Charles
Ewing, Hugh
Ewing, Thomas, Jr.
Forsyth, James (4/9/65)
Fuller, John
Garfield, James
Garrand, Kenner
Gilbert, Charles
Gilmore, Quincy

Granger, Robert
Grant, Ulysses
Grose, William
Griffin, Charles
Harker, Charles
Harrison, Benjamin (1/23/65)
Hayes, Philip (3/13/65)
Hayes, Rutherford B.
Hazen, William
Hickenlooper, Andrew (3/13/65)
Hobson, Edward
Hooker, Joseph
Kautz, Augustus
Keifer, Joseph
Kennedy, Robert P. (3/13/65)
Kirk, Edward
Leggett, Mortimer
Long, Eli
Lytle, William
Maltby, Jasper
Manson, Mahlon
Mason, John
McClellan, George B.
McCook, Alexander
McCook, Anson (3/13/65)
McCook, Daniel, Jr.
McCook, Edward
McCook, Edwin (3/13/65)
McCook, George (3/13/65)
McCook, Robert
McDowell, Irvin
McLean, Nathaniel

McMillen, William
McPherson, James
Mitchell, Ormsby M.
Mitchell, John G.
Mitchell, Robert B.
Morgan, George W.
Opdyke, Emerson
Osborn, Thomas O.
Patrick, Marsena R.
Paine, Eleazer A.
Paine, Halbert E.
Piatt, Abram S.
Poe, Orlando
Potter, Joseph H.
Pope, John
Potts, Benjamin
Powell, William H.
Reilly, James W.
Robinson, James S.
Rosecrans, William
Rusk, Jeremiah M. (3/13/65)
Sackett, Delos B. (3/13/65)
Scammon, Eliakim B.
Schenck, Robert C.
Scott, Robert K.
Sheridan, Philip H.
Sherman, William T.
Sherwood, Isaac R.
Sill, Joshua W.
Slough, John P.
Smith, Thomas K.
Smith, William S.
Sprague, John W.
Stanley, David S.
Steedman, James B.
Swayne, Wager
Tidball, John C.
Townsend, Edward D. (Adjutant General)
Tuttle, James M.
Tyler, Erastus B.
Van Derveer, Ferdinand
Wade, Melancthon S.
Wagner, George D.
Walcutt, Charles C.
Wallace, William H.L.
Warner, Willard
Weitzel, Godfrey
Welsh, Thomas
Willich, August
Wood, Thomas J.
Woods, Charles R.
Woods, William B.

Appendix D

Third Ohio Volunteer Infantry Regiment: Commands, 1861–1864

June–September 1861. 1st Brigade, Army of the Cumberland
December 1863–June 1864. Second Brigade, Second Division, 14th Army Corps, Army of the Cumberland
Kanawaha Division, Department of the Ohio, Brigadier General Jacob Cox (No divisions at this time)
September–November 1861. 17th Brigade (William Lytle), Brigadier General Joseph Reynolds (No divisions at this time)
November–December 1861. 17th Brigade (Ebenezer Dumont), Third Division, Army of the Ohio
December 1861–September 1862. 17th Brigade (Colonel William Lytle), Third Division (Mitchell), Army of the Ohio
September–November 1862. 17th Brigade (Colonel John Beatty), Third Division (Rousseau), First Corps (A. McCook), Army of the Ohio
December 1862–January 1863. Second Brigade (Beatty), First Division (Rousseau), Center 14th Army Corps (Major General George Thomas), Army of the Cumberland
February–April 1863. Second Brigade, First Division, 14th Army Corps (General William Rosecrans)
May 1863. Streight's Provisional Brigade, 14th Army Corps
June 1863–June, 23, 1864. Unattached

Appendix E

Major General Alexander McCook's Corps: Perryville

First Corps (Perryville)
Second Division: Brigadier General Joshua Sill
Third Division: Brigadier General Lovell Rousseau
   17th Brigade: Colonel John Beatty
               Colonel Curran Pope

- 42nd Indiana
- 88th Indiana
- 15th Kentucky
- Third Ohio
- 10th Ohio
- First Michigan Battery (Loomis)

Appendix F

14th Army Corps (Army of the Cumberland)

Major General William Rosecrans
Stones River
14th Corps (Stones River)
Center Wing: Major General George Thomas
First Division: Major General Lovell Rousseau
Second Brigade: Colonel John Beatty

- 42nd Indiana
- 88th Indiana
- 15th Kentucky
- Third Ohio

Chapter Notes

Explanation of Citations

War of the Rebellion: A Compilation of the Official Records of the Union and Confederate Armies will be cited as OR. The OR comprises 70 volumes (Washington, D.C., 1880–1901).

The minutes of the Third Ohio Infantry Regiment reunion meetings are cited:
Collection Title: United States. Army. Infantry Regiment, Third (1861–1864) records

- Collection Number: MSS2842
- Volumes: 674, 675, 676, 677
- Ohio History Connection, Columbus, Ohio

Preface

1. Issac Morrow is sometimes cited as Marrow in different sources. However, his grave marker states his last name as Morrow.

2. Lawson and Vananda were the only two of the original Third Ohio officers to continue with the regiment from Middle Fork Bridge to Cedar Bluff.

3. Before West Virginia broke from Virginia and joined the Union as a state, it was referred to as western Virginia.

4. After his defeat at the Second Battle of Corinth, Price went to see Jefferson Davis. Davis referred to Price as "the vainest man I ever met."

5. Ebenezer Dumont exaggerated his role at Philippi. The report he filed of the "heroic" actions of his brigade differ greatly from those of some of the men in his own and other brigades at the scene. Dumont gave himself more credit than was warranted.

6. Streight's Raid, however, was charged with disrupting Confederate communication and rail lines. Streight attempted to do what Morgan et al. were doing all over Tennessee, Kentucky and Alabama.

7. Lincoln's Inaugural Address, March 4, 1861, Washington, D.C.

8. Davis, Varina. *Jefferson Davis: A Memoir.* New York: Belford, 1890, p. 19.

Introduction

1. The tension and anger found at the Wheeling Convention on May 14, 1861, is found on many pages of the *Wheeling Intelligencer*. On the 14th, front page, column one states, "The drunken, howling mob, summoned to Richmond by secret messages from leading secessionists." This language on the 14th and subsequent days and weeks is indicative of the tone and disposition of the general population as well as those delegates at the convention.

2. John George Nicolay was Lincoln's only official private secretary. There were several others over the years who were "borrowed" from other departments. They worked as secretaries but did not have that title. Nicolay served throughout most of Lincoln's presidency. Early in the second term, Nicolay became U.S. minister to France.

3. John Milton Hay served as an unofficial secretary to Lincoln throughout his presidency. His notes, diaries and other writings have helped historians research the Lincoln presidency. His library in Providence, Rhode Island, is a good source of primary source data.

4. Nicolay, J.; Hay, J. *Abraham Lincoln: A History.* New York: Century, 1890, p. 28.

5. *Ibid.*

6. Columbiads were big-caliber, smooth-bore guns that were used for seacoast defense. The big 10-inch Columbiad fired a shell weighing 120 lb almost one mile.

7. Second Wheeling Convention: June 11–August 21, 1861. The convention was called to arrange for a referendum to determine whether to form a new state separate from Virginia. Ultimately, western Virginia became West Virginia in 1863.

8. The Library of Congress image of Carlisle taken at this time shows a clean-shaven, "youthful" man.

9. John S. Carlisle was a U.S. senator from Virginia. He was a slave owner and against secession. However, he did not favor the formation of a new state. Arthur I. Boreman was elected president of the Second Wheeling Convention and was important in the process of establishing West Virginia as a separate state.

10. Proceedings of the Second Wheeling Convention, June 12, 1861, afternoon session.

11. *Ibid.*

12. Nicolay, J.; Hay, J. *Abraham Lincoln: A Life*. New York: Century, 1914, p. 193.

13. Senator Stephen Douglas died on June 3, 1861, from typhoid fever complications. He fought against secession right to the end of his life.

14. Napoleon III was desperate to obtain Southern cotton. Unlike Great Britain, France had no cotton reserves. However, Napoleon's minister to the United States, Henri Mercier, agreed that France would not act to break the blockade unless Britain helped. At this stage, Great Britain had already decided to stay out of the war.

15. Lord Richard Lyons was Britain's minister to the United States. Initially antagonistic to U.S. Secretary of State William Seward, the two ultimately became friends. Lyons was critical in maintaining relations between the Lincoln administration and the British government. He worked hard and never panicked when U.S.-British relations sometimes looked like war.

16. Perry, David. *Bluff, Bluster, Lies and Spies: The Lincoln Foreign Policy 1861–1865*. Philadelphia: Casemate, 2016, p. 134.

17. Barnes, James. *The American Civil War through British Eyes*. Kent: Kent State University Press, 2003. Dispatch #183, Russell to Palmerston.

18. Shoddy was a term that came into use during the Civil War. It related to the poor quality of uniforms and equipment being hastily manufactured for the Union army infantry. Boots fell apart after a few miles of walking, and uniforms melted in the rain. The scandal was big news in the newspapers and helped bring about reform.

19. James Gordon Bennett, Sr., founded the *New York Herald*. He was outspoken in his dislike of Lincoln but was in favor of the Union.

20. OR, Vol. 2, p. 48.

21. OR, Vol. 2, p. 51.

22. OR, Vol. 2, p. 52.

23. Hinton Helper was from North Carolina but an abolitionist. He believed that the South was unduly influenced and controlled by a small planter aristocracy.

24. The Confederate states were compromised by the different gauges of their railroads. This was caused, in part, by the fact that each state considered itself as independent of any central authority. This often resulted in a railroad system that was not coordinated throughout the South. This impacted the movement and supply of troops.

25. Nevins, Allan. *The War for the Union: The Organized War 1863–1864*. New York: Scribner's, 1971, p. 23.

26. *Cincinnati Enquirer*, June 22, 1861.

27. Carrington, Henry. "Ohio Militia and the West Virginia Campaign, 1861." Address of General Carrington to Army of West Virginia, at Marietta, Ohio, September 10, 1870. Boston: Blodgett (printers), 1904, p. 12.

28. Catharinus Buckingham was Ohio adjutant general in charge of commissary matters.

29. Diary and Letters of Rutherford B. Hayes, vol. 2.

30. Lamers, William. *The Edge of Glory: A Biography of William S. Rosecrans*. New York: Harcourt Brace, 1961, p. 23.

31. OR, Vol. 2, p. 51.

32. Ironclads, both oceangoing and monitor-class, were significant in dissuading Great Britain from intervening in the Civil War. The Confederacy wanted England to break the blockade to resume

cotton exports. However, Lords Palmerston and Russell realized that the sudden ironclad growth of the U.S. Navy was too great a risk for a wooden British navy. As a result, the American Civil War marked the high point of British power around the world. After the war, Great Britain slowly lost power and influence to the United States.

33. OR, Vol. 2, p. 788.
34. Summers, Festus. *The Baltimore and Ohio in the Civil War*. Gettysburg: Clark Military, 1993, p. 49.
35. Turner, Charles. "Virginia Central Railroad at War 1861-1865." *Journal of Southern History* 12, no. 4 (November 1946): 510-533.
36. Andrews, J. "The Southern Telegraph Company, 1861-1865." *Journal of Southern History* 30, no. 3 (August 1964): 319-344.
37. McClellan to Scott, OR, Vol. 2, p. 44.
38. Plum, William. *The Military Telegraph during the Civil War*. Chicago: Jansen, 1882, p. 104.
39. OR, Vol. 2, p. 49.
40. Johnson, Larry. "Breakdown from Within: Virginia Railroads during the Civil War Era." Master's thesis, University of Louisville, 2004, p. 129.
41. Lincoln secured control of the railroads on January 31, 1862. This was important because of the many private interests controlling the rails, including Secretary of War Simon Cameron.
42. Brigadier General Thomas A. Morris was appointed to command of the Indiana State Militia at the start of the war. His men chased and finally killed Confederate general William Garnett after the Battle of Rich Mountain.
43. Benjamin Franklin Kelley worked for the B&O Railroad and was in command of the First Virginia Infantry (Union) at Philippi. He was badly wounded there but regained his health and returned to command. He became a modest folk hero for his fight at Philippi. His recovery was recorded regularly by all of the local newspapers.
44. *Wheeling Intelligencer*, June 1, 1861.
45. Dayton, Ruth. "The Beginning—Philippi, 1861." *West Virginia Archives and History* 13, no. 4 (July 1952): 254-266.
46. OR, Vol. 2, p. 64.

47. Hall, Granville. *Lee's Invasion of Northwest Virginia, 1861*. Chicago: Mayer and Miller, 1911, p. 61.
48. Kelley recovered and became a local celebrity. The local newspapers carried the progress of his improving health on a regular basis.
49. OR, Vol. 2, p. 69.
50. OR, Vol. 2, p. 72.
51. Reid, Whitelaw. *Ohio in the War: Her Statesmen, Generals and Soldiers*. Cincinnati: Clarke, 1895, p. 47.

Chapter 1

1. OR, Vol. 2, p. 195.
2. Some of the guerrilla bands were commissioned Confederate army officers. John Hunt Morgan and Joseph Wheeler were in this group. Garnett was a West Point graduate who resigned during secession and was commissioned in the Confederate army. Some of the "bushwhackers" were nothing more than criminals taking advantage of a confused military situation.
3. OR, Vol. 2, p. 861.
4. OR, Vol. 2, p. 51.
5. Ibid.
6. Beatty diary, June 28, 1861.
7. *Richmond Dispatch*, June 26, 1861.
8. Camp Garnett was named after Confederate general William Garnett. It was located near the entrance to the road that led to the top of Rich Mountain.
9. Confederate brigadier general John Pegram served as both a cavalry commander and later as a brigade infantry commander. He was wounded at the Wilderness in 1864 and died at Hatcher's Run, Virginia, on February 6, 1865. Pegram was not well liked by his men at Rich Mountain. However, as a cavalry commander, he was responsible for some of the raids on Union supply lines that made war in Kentucky and Tennessee difficult.
10. Beatty diary, June 29, 1861.
11. OR, Vol. 2, p. 195.
12. OR, Vol. 2, p. 198.
13. Beatty diary, July 2, 1861.
14. Beatty diary, July 4, 1861.
15. Colonel John Pegram escaped from Rich Mountain with 400 men. While attempting to connect with the forces of Robert Garnett, Pegram was caught and surrendered to George McClellan on July

12, 1861. Some of his officers were against surrender, but Pegram overruled them.

16. Gilot, Jon-Erik. "A Tremendous Little Man: Newton Schleich in the Civil War." https://emergingcivilwar.com/2017/08/30/a-tremendous-little-man-newton-schleich-in-the-civil-war.

17. OR, Vol. 2, p. 199.

18. Captain Orris Lawson was ultimately promoted to full colonel in 1862. He was one of the original Third Ohio officers who continued with the regiment under Abel Streight in the 1863 raid in northern Alabama.

19. Beatty diary, July 7, 1861.

20. Moore, Frank. *The Rebellion Record*. New York: Putnam, 1862–1866, p. 252.

21. Beatty diary, July 7, 1861.

22. Lamers, William. *The Edge of Glory: A Biography of William S. Rosecrans*. New York: Harcourt Brace, 1961, p. 21.

23. Laidig, Scott. "Brigadier General John Pegram: Lee's Paradoxical Cavalier." February 1998. https://ehistory.osu.edu/articles/brigadier-general-john-pegram-lee%E2%80%99s-paradoxical-cavalier.

24. John Lechter, Virginia governor, 1860–1864. He originally opposed secession but appointed Robert E. Lee as commander of Virginia's army and naval forces.

25. OR, Vol. 2, p. 69.

26. "Confederate Veteran," 1930, p. 149.

27. OR, Vol. 2, p. 50.

28. "Confederate Veteran," 1930, p. 149.

29. Beatty diary, July 8, 1861

30. *Ibid.*

31. Beatty diary, July 10, 1861.

32. *Ibid.*

33. Keifer, Warren J. *The Battle of Rich Mountain and Some Incidents*. Cincinnati: The Commandery, 1911.

34. *Ibid.*

35. *Ibid.*

Chapter 2

1. Roaring Creek was the McClellan campsite that was situated just west of the entrance to the pathway up Rich Mountain.

2. Beatty diary, June 8, 1861.

3. OR, Vol. 2, p. 199.

4. Antoine Jomini was a Swiss military theorist who believed in massing all forces at strategic points to win with few casualties. Dennis Hart Mahan was a professor at West Point. He advocated the combined use of artillery, infantry and cavalry, not as independent actions. William Hardee was a lieutenant colonel in the U.S. and later the Confederate army. His book on *Light Infantry Tactics* was basically a manual of infantry drill. Men like Henry Halleck, Lincoln's general-in-chief, relied on all three authors for direction. Ultimately, Halleck wrote his own tactics manual, which was basically a summary of pieces of all three theorists.

5. Union general Thomas A. Morris was born in Kentucky and served as brigadier general during the engagement at Philippi. He commanded the multi-state regiments that forced Confederate forces under George Porterfield out of that part of western Virginia. Failure at Philippi would have hindered progress in that theater of war, and this might have had an adverse impact on Perryville and Stones River later.

6. OR, Vol. 2, p. 202.

7. Edward Alfred Pollard was the influential editor of the *Richmond Examiner*. He hated Jefferson Davis and Vice President Alexander Stevens even worse. To him, Stevens was "this demon, this malicious, pitiless, pauseless enemy ... this misanthrope, this viperous, heartless, adulterous beast, this living sepulcher of all hideous things, this lonely, friendless, and unfriendly man."

8. Julius DeLagnel was born in New Jersey but resigned from the U.S. Army to fight for the Confederacy. He was chief of artillery in Garnett's Army of the Northwest. After his capture at Rich Mountain, he was exchanged and promoted to brigadier general but declined the promotion in favor of major of artillery. The reason for declining the promotion is unknown.

9. Spherical case (shrapnel) was a metal projectile with a thin casing. It was filled with iron balls and was basically long-range canister shot. The balls were mixed with a sulfur mixture. The projectile had a timed fuse.

10. Lamers, William. *The Edge of Glory: A Biography of William S. Rosecrans*. New York: Harcourt Brace, 1961, p. 30.

11. OR, Vol. 2, p. 206.

12. Beatty diary, July 11, 1861.

Notes—Chapter 3

13. Keifer, J. Warren. *Slavery and Four Years of War*. New York: Putnam, 1900.
14. Beatty diary, July 12, 1861.
15. OR, Vol. 2, p. 207.
16. OR, Vol. 2, p. 257.
17. *Ibid.*
18. OR, Vol. 2, p. 217.
19. *Wheeling Intelligencer*, July 16, 1861, p. 2.
20. OR, Vol. 2, p. 49.
21. Beatty diary, July 18, 1861.
22. Beatty diary, July 14, 1862.
23. When McClellan was called to Washington to take over Union forces after the small engagement at Rich Mountain, Lincoln and the Union were looking for a "hero" to save the day. In a letter to his wife, McClellan complained that this hero worship was not good. He believed that too much was expected of him. Ultimately, McClellan was right.
24. OR, Vol. 2, p. 123.
25. Keifer, J. Warren. *Slavery and Four Years of War*. New York: Putnam, 1900.
26. OR, Vol. 5, p. 192.
27. OR, Vol. 5, p. 185.
28. Keifer, J. Warren. *Slavery and Four Years of War*. New York: Putnam, 1900.
29. Beatty diary, September 29, 1861.
30. Keifer, J. Warren. *Slavery and Four Years of War*. New York: Putnam, 1900.

Chapter 3

1. Ramage, James. *Rebel Raider: The Life of General John Hunt Morgan*. Lexington: University Press of Kentucky, 1986. p. 49.
2. VanDeusen, Glyndon. *William Henry Seward*. New York: Oxford University Press, 1967, p. 294.
3. Beatty diary, September 27, 1861.
4. Beatty diary, October 8, 1861.
5. Ormsby Mitchel was an astronomer, West Point graduate in the same class as Robert E. Lee, mathematics professor and the major general who called the Third Ohio "Obstinate Devils." Mitchel raised the money to build an observatory near Cincinnati, Ohio. He died from yellow fever in South Carolina in September 1862.
6. Beatty diary, January 5, 1862.
7. Beatty diary, February 10, 1862.
8. Beatty diary, February 14, 1862.
9. Beatty diary, March 1, 1862.
10. Beatty diary, March 8, 1862.
11. Beatty diary, April 7, 1862.
12. Ramage, James. *Rebel Raider: The Life of General John Hunt Morgan*. Lexington: University Press of Kentucky, 1986. p. 49.
13. The Fugitive Slave Act was passed in 1850 as part of the Compromise of 1850. It penalized anyone who sheltered runaway slaves with a fine of $1,000. As more and more slaves began to flee the plantations after the start of the Civil War, the act became a problem. Lincoln didn't want to return them to their slave masters, but he also did not want to upset the border slave states. He wanted to retain the allegiance of those four states. Ultimately, the issue grew to a point where Union generals stopped turning away runaway slaves. They were declared "contraband" of war and thus not subject to seizure under the law.
14. Joseph Warren Keifer was part of the original three-month Third Ohio and later remained with the three-year regiment. He served with the Third at Rich Mountain. He was promoted to colonel with the 110th Ohio and breveted to brigadier general in 1864. He saw action at Petersburg and Appomattox. After the war, he was elected to Congress from 1877 to 1883. He served as Speaker of the House, 1881–1883. His books and published recollections of the Civil War remain important sources for the work of the Third Ohio.
15. Keifer, J. Warren. *Slavery and Four Years of War*. Project Gutenberg ebook, chapter 5.
16. William Haines Lytle was a celebrated poet before the war. He was colonel of the 10th Ohio Infantry, and his brigade contained the Third Ohio. He was wounded first in western Virginia in 1861 and later at Perryville in October 1862. At Perryville, he was taken prisoner but was soon exchanged. He was promoted to brigadier general in 1862 but died at Chickamauga, Georgia, in September 1863.
17. The Army of the Cumberland evolved from the Army of the Ohio under Don Carlos Buell. The army was reorganized under William Rosecrans and renamed the Army of the Cumberland on October 24, 1862. The first combat engagement of the Army of the Cumberland was

at Stones River/Murfreesboro, December–January, 1862–1863.

18. Donn Piatt was a lawyer, newspaper writer, and served in the U.S. Legation to Paris, 1854–1855. He served as a major in the Union army but resigned in 1864. He tried to recruit a slave brigade at a time when Lincoln was still careful with the border slave states. Piatt's writings after the war remain a good source of information on many aspects of the war. He also served with John Beatty of the Third Ohio on the Board of Inquiry looking into Buell's failure to catch Bragg at Perryville.

19. Bobrick, Benson. *Master of War: The Life of General George H. Thomas*. New York: Simon and Schuster, 2009, p. 4.

20. Nat Turner was self-educated and deeply religious. He led a four-day rebellion in Virginia that resulted in the death of approximately 60 whites. He and his conspirators were executed, and Virginia passed laws against the education of slaves.

21. Lee, Dan. *Kentuckian in Blue: A Biography of Major General Lovell Harrison Rousseau*. Jefferson: McFarland, 2010, p. 2.

22. Reid, Whitelaw. *Ohio in the War, Volume II*. Cincinnati: More, Wilstach & Baldwin, 1868, p. 600.

23. Beatty diary, April 5, 1862.

24. The Battle of Shiloh/Pittsburg Landing in April 1862 was of interest to the Third Ohio in part because the Army of the Ohio was commanded by Don Carlos Buell. Buell considered himself the hero of Shiloh and would be in command later at Perryville, Kentucky. The Third long remembered that Buell allowed Bragg to get away after Perryville.

25. Beatty diary, April 13, 1862.

26. Henry Shelton Sanford was Lincoln's unofficial secret service official in Europe. Sanford was U.S. minister to Belgium at this time and was in control of the bank accounts for the Union in Europe that allowed him to purchase arms for the Union army. He hired detectives to follow Confederate arms dealers trying to buy weapons in Europe. This allowed him to outbid the rebels. Although his work was not known at the time, Secretary of State William Seward oversaw Sanford's work and congratulated him for his efforts.

27. Beatty diary, April 14, 1862.

28. Beatty diary, April 27, 1862.

29. Confederate brigadier general Danville Leadbetter graduated from West Point and served primarily as an engineer during the war. As an engineer, Leadbetter was frequently involved in the construction of defensive fortifications and artillery positions.

30. OR, Vol. 10, Reports, p. 657.

31. Beatty diary, April 29, 1862.

32. Beatty diary, May 5, 1862.

33. Beatty diary, May 2, 1862.

34. Ohio History Connection. U.S. Army, Infantry Regiment Third (1861–1865) records, vol. 676.

35. Beatty diary, May 2, 1862.

36. John Beatty's diary makes it clear that he favored a scorched earth policy because it deprived the enemy of the local provisions that they also needed to fight.

37. *Louisville Courier Journal*, October 15, 1862.

Chapter 4

1. There are many references in the reports of William Rosecrans and Don Carlos Buell about the lack of water at this time. The newspapers also report a very dry season. John Beatty mentions this in his diary on February 18, 1862: "The country is cavernous, and the only water is that of the ponds. In all of these we discovered dead and decaying horses, mules, and dogs."

2. The Plug Uglies were a criminal street gang originating in Baltimore, Maryland, during the 1850s. They were associated with the Know-Nothings. Both were "nativist" groups who opposed many of those from Europe emigrating to America at this time. They took part in the New York draft riots in 1863 and generally looted and caused harm wherever they went.

3. Benjamin Butler was a lawyer from Massachusetts who helped organize several regiments to march to Washington and relieve the capital. In 1861, Stonewall Jackson temporarily seized control of the B&O Railroad. That rail line was an important communications link for the capital in Washington. Securing an appointment as brigadier general, Butler helped to open communications through Annapolis, Maryland, until the railroad

line could be reopened. He became one of Lincoln's very controversial political generals.

4. Abraham Lincoln, September 22, 1861, in a letter to Orville Browning

5. Prokopowicz, Gerald. *All for the Regiment: The Army of the Ohio 1861–1862*. Chapel Hill: University of North Carolina Press, 2001, p. 160.

6. OR, Vol. 16, p. 1024.

7. Keifer, Warren. *The Battle of Rich Mountain and Some Incidents*. Cincinnati: The Commendary, 1911, p. 20.

8. Brooks, Noah. "Lincoln, Chase and Grant." *Century Illustrated Magazine*, November 1894, p. 23.

9. The work of Jay Cook and Tony Drexel was essential in financing the war for the Union. The federal treasury was always short of money. The states had already spent all that they could afford to outfit their own state regiments. More money was needed quickly. The Confederacy was trying to secure loans in Europe. Finally, Jay Cooke and Tony Drexel had success in selling the government bonds necessary to finance the war. Soon, the new "greenback" came into circulation. This was a gamble that worked.

10. Brooks, Noah. "Lincoln, Chase and Grant." *Century Illustrated Magazine*, November 1894, p. 23.

11. Anaconda Plan was a term invented by the news media. It referred to the plan by Winfield Scott and operationalized by Navy Secretary Gideon Welles to blockade the major deep-water ports of the south. This would block the export of cotton and the importation of war materiel from Europe. Ultimately, the blockade starved the Confederacy to the point where they had trouble feeding their troops as well as the horses that pulled the artillery.

12. Fraser Trenholm and Company had offices in Charleston, South Carolina, and Liverpool, England. Senior partner George Trenholm became Confederate treasury secretary and helped to finance Confederate purchases of guns and saltpeter in Europe.

13. Beatty diary, April 28, 1862.

14. The Army of Tennessee was commanded by Braxton Bragg. It was a Confederate army formed in 1862 and continued to 1865. Some of its commanders included Joseph Johnston and John Bell Hood. The Army of the Tennessee was a Union army commanded by men like Ulysses Grant, William Tecumseh Sherman and Joseph Hooker.

15. Beatty diary, July 18, 1862.

16. McClellan's Peninsula Campaign was designed to capture Richmond and end the war. However, McClellan and Lincoln disagreed on the best plan to achieve this. Lincoln wanted to go overland by rail and foot direct to Manassas and then to Richmond. McClellan wanted to land on the Yorktown peninsula and thus flank Confederate forces guarding the route to Richmond. McClellan won the argument with Lincoln but lost the battle to capture Richmond.

17. Beatty diary, July 7, 1862.

18. Robert McCook was one of the "Fighting McCooks" from Ohio. He was promoted to brigadier general and wounded in a bayonet charge. In March 1862, he was allegedly shot while lying in an ambulance recovering from the bayonet wound. This version was disputed by Southern historians.

19. Beatty diary, August 7, 1862.

20. Ohio brothers Daniel and John McCook had 13 sons between them. They all fought for the Union. Robert, Alexander, Daniel and Edward all became Union generals.

21. Jefferson Davis often acted as his own secretary of war. Acting as secretary of war under Buchannan, he believed that he knew better than some of his generals. As a result, some bypassed the chain of command and communicated directly with Davis. Lincoln did the same at the start of his presidency but soon found that this was not wise. When he put Grant in command, he let Grant have his own way.

22. Beatty diary, August 12, 1862.

23. The Battle of Shiloh/Pittsburg Landing was significant for many reasons. The casualties were great on both sides. However, the North was able to replenish troops to a greater degree than the South. The Union army was soon to be increased by the slaves who had run away from the plantations. Control of this part of Tennessee gave the Union better access to the Mississippi. New Orleans would soon fall as a result.

24. OR, Vol. 18, p. 513.

25. Maurice, Eric. "Send Forward Some

Who Would Fight: How John T. Wilder and His "Lightning Brigade" of Mounted Infantry Changed Warfare." Master's thesis, Butler University, 2016.

26. Josef C. McKibbin served as an aide-de-camp to Generals Halleck and Thomas.

27. Lincoln generally honored the "old boys' club" of army officer seniority. Unfortunately, he selected officers for army command who were senior but not necessarily the best candidate. At Stones River, however, he ignored seniority and promoted Rosecrans over George Thomas. Rosecrans' commission was back-dated to effectively make him senior to Thomas. This was a fairly common practice. However, at the start of his presidency, Lincoln was more respectful of seniority over merit.

28. Beatty diary, October 3, 1862.

29. McWhinney, Grady; Jamieson, Perry. *Attack and Die: Civil War Military Tactics and the Southern Heritage.* Tuscaloosa: University of Alabama Press, 1982, p. 32.

30. Foote, Shelby. *The Civil War: A Narrative: Volume 1: Fort Sumter to Perryville.* New York: Vintage, 1986, p. 713.

31. Foote, Shelby. *The Civil War: A Narrative.* New York: Vintage Press, 1986, p. 728.

32. Kentucky governor George Johnson was killed at the Battle of Shiloh in April 1862. Richard Hawes was appointed to take his place. The inauguration was held in Frankfort, Kentucky, on October 4, 1862.

33. OR, Vol. 16, Reports, p. 1020.

34. OR, Vol. 16, p. 1024.

35. Peskin, Alan. *Garfield: A Biography.* Kent: Kent State University Press, 1978, p. 176.

36. Beatty diary, January 7, 1862.

37. Simon Bolivar Buckner was a Confederate major general and 30th governor of Kentucky. In 1862, he surrendered Fort Donelson to Ulysses Grant. He later served as adjutant to Edmund Kirby Smith.

38. Confederate lieutenant general Leonidas Polk was an Episcopal bishop and a cousin of President James K. Polk. Considered a political general with little experience, Polk was killed during the siege of Atlanta in 1864.

39. OR, Vol. 16, Reports, p. 69.

Chapter 5

1. The Parrott gun was invented by West Point graduate Robert Parrott. The Parrott was rifled and banded at the breach to prevent bursting. The guns were cheap to manufacture and had a long range.

2. William Hardee wrote *Hardee's Rifle and Light Infantry Tactics* in 1861. It was similar to the manual of arms published by the U.S. War Department. Infantry tactical manuals of the time demonstrated how to march, load and fire from a kneeling position and prone position, the responsibilities of skirmishers and so forth. Hardee's was the most respected and utilized manual of its kind at the start of the Civil War.

3. The most common manual of arms used North and South at the start of the war was Confederate general William Hardee's *Hardee's Rifle and Light Infantry Tactics.* The manual addressed many issues including advancing in battle, retreating in battle, firing and loading while kneeling versus lying down and so forth.

4. Beatty diary, October 8, 1862.

5. Richard Hawes was sworn in as provisional governor of Kentucky on November 4, 1862, after Governor George W. Johnson was killed at the Battle of Shiloh.

6. Foote, Shelby. *The Civil War: A Narrative.* New York: Vintage, 1986.

7. Beatty diary, October 8, 1862.

8. William Haines Lytle was already known North and South for his poetry. He died at Chickamauga in September 1863. His death was also mourned North and South.

9. OR, Vol. 16, p. 69.

10. OR, Vol. 16, p. 1044.

11. Private Joseph W. Laybourne, Company D, Third Ohio.

12. OR, Vol. 16, p. 1045.

13. OR, Vol. 16, p. 1040.

14. OR, Vol. 16, p. 71.

15. Minutes of the 2nd Third Ohio reunion, September 2, 1877, Zanesville, Ohio.

16. *Louisville Courier,* October 10, 1862.

17. Beatty diary, October 8, 1862.

18. Kirkpatrick, George Morgan. "Experiences of a Private Soldier in the Civil War." https://freepages.rootsweb.com/~indiana42nd/history/Kirkpatrick_book_part1.htm.

19. OR, Vol. 16, p. 1047.
20. Ohio History Connection. U.S. Army, Infantry Regiment Third (1861–1865) records, vol. 676.
21. Beatty diary, October 8, 1862.
22. Beatty diary, July 6, 1862.
23. Beatty diary, October 13, 1862.
24. *Ibid.*
25. OR, Vol. 16, p. 1042.
26. OR, Vol. 16, p. 1087.
27. Harrison, Lowell. *The Civil War in Kentucky.* Lexington: University of Kentucky Press, 1975, p. 5.
28. OR, Vol. 16, p. 1023.
29. OR, Vol. 16, Reports, p. 6.
30. Beatty diary, July 6, 1862.
31. OR, Vol. 16, Reports, p. 12.
32. Beatty diary, July 18, 1862.
33. Ohio History Connection. U.S. Army, Infantry Regiment Third (1861–1865) records, vol. 677.
34. *Ibid.*

Chapter 6

1. *Nashville Journal Courier,* November 15, 1862.
2. Lamers, William. *The Edge of Glory: A Biography of William S. Rosecrans.* New York: Harcourt Brace, 1961, p. 190.
3. Daniel Silence is listed in the *Nashville Journal Courier* as killed on November 3, 1862. However, his name does not appear on the roster of the Third Ohio Volunteer Infantry Regiment.
4. Initially, Lincoln honored seniority for army promotion. However, war demanded quick changes. Gradually, he allowed the War Department to back-date the desired commission date to promote whoever might be more promising.
5. Lamers, William. *The Edge of Glory: A Biography of William S. Rosecrans.* New York: Harcourt Brace, 1961, p. 182
6. *Ibid.,* p. 183.
7. OR, Vol. 20, Correspondence, p. 6.
8. OR, Vol. 20, Correspondence, p. 31.
9. OR, Vol. 20, Correspondence, p. 60.
10. Sutlers were the traveling storekeepers that supplied luxury goods to soldiers that the government could not supply. Sutlers had to have regimental command approval. Some were appointed by state governors. They sold such items as cheese, cigars, eggs and writing paper.

11. George McClellan initiated the policy of not interfering with the local populations. This went against men like John Beatty of the Third Ohio. Beatty believed that by depriving the local population of sustenance, they could not provide aid or comfort to the enemy.
12. OR, Vol. 20, Correspondence, p. 118.
13. *Ibid.*
14. OR, Vol. 20, Correspondence, p. 123.
15. OR, Vol. 20, Correspondence, p. 39.
16. George W. Brent to John Hunt Morgan, OR, Vol. 20, Reports, p. 64.
17. Beatty diary, December 9, 1862.
18. OR. Vol. 20, Reports, p. 42.
19. OR, Vol. 20, Reports, p. 43.
20. OR, Vol. 20, Reports, p. 40.
21. OR, Vol. 20, Reports, p. 43.
22. OR, Vol. 20, Correspondence, p. 28.
23. Beatty diary, November 11, 1862.
24. A Mary Chesnut diary entry for July 29, 1862, tells a story of Morgan going to court to testify on behalf of secessionists. When he stood to speak, the judge asked who he was, and he introduced himself as John Hunt Morgan. True or not, there were many such stories at the time.
25. OR, Vol. 20, Reports, p. 158.
26. Great Britain decided to spend its money on defensive fortifications rather than oceangoing warships. During the Civil War, most of its fleet was wooden and now vulnerable to ironclad monitors. It decided that there was too much risk getting involved in breaking the Union blockade. Queen Victoria was very active in the decision-making process here.
27. The Confiscation Act allowed Lincoln to seize Confederate property and free slaves in areas under Union control.
28. *Washington Evening Star,* December 11, 1862.
29. *Washington Evening Star,* December 12, 1862.
30. *Richmond Daily Dispatch,* December 13, 1862.
31. Schurz, Carl. *The Reminiscences of Carl Schurz.* Garden City: Doubleday, 1913, p. 399.

Chapter 7

1. OR, Vol. 20, Reports, p. 183.
2. *Chattanooga Daily Rebel,* January 1, 1863, p. 2.

3. Joseph Wheeler was a Confederate cavalry general during the Civil War and U.S. Army major general during the Spanish American War. In 1898, he commanded the cavalry division which included Teddy Roosevelt and the Rough Riders.

4. The Battle of Stones River is also called the Battle of Murfreesboro. The accounts of the time refer to it as the Battle of Stone River, the Battle of Stones River, or the Battle of Murfreesboro.

5. Beatty diary, December 29, 1862.

6. Vance, Wilson. *Stones River: The Turning Point of the Civil War.* New York: Neale, 1914, p. 10.

7. McWhinney, Grady; Jamieson, Perry. *Braxton Bragg and the Confederate Defeat.* Tuscaloosa: University of Alabama Press, 1991, p. 347.

8. Vedettes were different from outposts in that a vedette generally consisted of one or two mounted infantry who were positioned so as to warn the main body of an army. An outpost was often a permanent structure or a larger number of mounted sentinels.

9. Beatty diary, December 26, 1862.

10. Beatty diary, December 31, 1862.

11. McDonough, James. *Stones River: Bloody Winter in Tennessee.* Knoxville: University of Tennessee Press, 1983, p. 85.

12. Beatty diary, December 31, 1862.

13. General Joshua Sill was a West Point graduate who experienced rapid promotion at the start of the Civil War. He died on the first day of the Battle of Stones River by a shot to the face by an Alabama cavalry soldier. General James Negley was a major general, Eighth Division, Army of the Ohio. Poor command decisions at Chickamauga ultimately led to his resignation in 1865.

14. Beatty diary, December 31, 1862.

15. Lamers, William. *The Edge of Glory: A Biography of William S. Rosecrans.* New York: Harcourt Brace, 1961, p. 225.

16. Watkins, Sam. "*Co. Aytch.*" Chattanooga: Times Publishing, 1900, p. 65.

17. The Hotchkiss shell was designed for rifled guns. A lead band at the base facilitated the rifled spin necessary to give the shell great range.

18. Letter of Frank Bond, January 2, 1885, to Louis Garesché (son of adjutant to William Rosecrans).

19. *Ibid.*

20. OR, Vol. 20, p. 373.

21. Beatty diary, January 1, 1863.

22. *Ibid.*

23. Hansen, Harry. *The Civil War: A History.* New York: Duell, Sloan, and Pearce, 1961.

24. OR, Vol. 20, p. 374.

25. Beatty diary, January 1, 1863.

26. Beatty diary, January 3, 1863.

27. OR, Series 1, Vol. 20, Reports, p. 374.

28. Rousseau's report refers to the battle as Murfreesboro. Others sometimes refer to it as Stones River.

29. OR, Vol. 20, p. 96.

30. Beatty diary, January 5, 1863.

31. *Collected Works of Abraham Lincoln*, vol. 6.

32. Ohio History Connection. U.S. Army, Infantry Regiment Third (1861–1864) reports, vol. 676.

Chapter 8

1. Lytle, Andrew. *Bedford Forrest and His Crittter Company.* New York: Minton, 1931, p. 173.

2. Earl Van Dorn was related to President Andrew Jackson and graduated from West Point. He was later promoted to major general in the Confederate army. He is best known as a cavalry officer who damaged bridges, railroads lines and communications in the western theater of war. Unfortunately, in 1863, Van Dorn was shot by the jealous husband of a married woman with whom Van Dorn was having an affair.

3. Miers, Earl. *The American Civil War: A Popular History of the Years 1861–1865 as Seen by the Artist-Correspondents Who Were There.* New York: Ridge Press, 1961, p. 4.

4. Willett, Robert. *The Lightning Mule Brigade: Abel Streight's 1863 Raid into Alabama.* Rockledge: Self-published, 1999, p. 18.

5. *Ibid.*, p. 11.

6. Ferris, Norman B. "Lincoln and Seward in Civil War Diplomacy." *Journal of the Abraham Lincoln Association* 12, no. 1 (1991): 21–42.

7. Kate Chase was the daughter of Salmon Chase, treasury secretary. She

married a wealthy Rhode Island textile magnate primarily to secure the money to finance her father's political ambitions. Kate Chase was the one who hosted the small parties of influential people opposed to Lincoln. Chase was unfaithful to Sprague and they divorced. Kate ultimately died in poverty.

8. Lincoln was more of an auditory than a visual learner. This enabled him to listen better. Auditory learners have a history of good leadership skills among those so skilled. Unfortunately, listening brought Lincoln to Ford's Theater. He understood better when he heard than when he read. For more, see Perry, David. "Abraham Lincoln and John George Nicolay: The Impact of Auditory and Visual Learning Styles on the Civil War." *The Lincoln Herald* 112, no. 2 (Summer 2010): 79–95.

9. Beatty diary, April 7, 1863.

10. https://en.wikisource.org/wiki/Report_of_Col._Abel_D._Streight,_August_22,_1864.

11. Moore, Frank. *The Rebellion Record* (Supplement, 1862), p. 337.

12. Breidenthal diary, April 11, 1863.

13. *Ibid.*

14. It has been suggested by historian Ed Bearss that Streight deliberately chose mules and not horses for the raid. He believed that mules would be best in the northern Alabama territory through which they would be traveling. Apparently, none of the Third Ohio were aware of this.

15. Breidenthal diary, April 16, 1863.

16. Foote, Shelby. *The Civil War: A Narrative.* New York: Vintage Books, 1958, p. 187.

17. OR, Vol. 7, p. 121.

18. Tower muskets were the 1853-model Enfield, muzzle-loading musket assembled in the Tower of London.

19. Admiral Andrew Foote was in charge of the Mississippi River Squadron and was under the command of Ulysses Grant. Foote helped Grant to seize both Forts Henry and Donelson. He later assisted John Pope with the seizure of Island No. 10. This was significant in gaining control of the Mississippi River. Foote died suddenly and unexpectedly in 1863 of complications from kidney disease.

20. Ironclad and timber-clad ships were used together in the Civil War. The timber-clad vessel was a gunboat that was of deeper draft than the monitor-class ironclads. The timber-clads had a large number of big smooth-bore guns. The monitor-class ships were used for river and harbor work. They were shallow draft and lightly armed with fewer guns than the timber-clad boats.

21. Breidenthal diary, April 23, 1863.

22. Grenville Dodge was a Union brigadier general who was wounded at Pea Ridge, Arkansas, in 1862. Much of his work was done in intelligence. This enabled him to successfully obstruct the raids of men like Forrest and Van Dorn. He was promoted to major general in 1864 and helped Sherman with the campaign against Atlanta.

23. Abel Streight filed his report of the raid on August 22, 1864. In the report, he stated that he received Special Order #94 from William Rosecrans to conduct the raid.

24. Breidenthal diary, April 27, 1862, p. 340.

25. Breidenthal diary, April 29, 1862, p. 341.

26. OR, Vol. 23, Reports, p. 287.

27. William Forrest was the brother of Nathan Bedford Forrest. William was the only one of whom Nathan Bedford Forrest was afraid. Captain William Forrest had his own small group within his brother's cavalry brigade. It was called the "Forty Thieves." Brother Nathan often used William to charge ahead in chasing Streight's brigade. He received a serious wound to the thigh at Day's Gap and was out of service.

28. OR, Vol. 23, Reports, p. 11.

29. OR, Vol. 23, Reports, p. 288.

30. Willett, Robert. *The Lightning Mule Brigade: Abel Streight's 1863 Raid into Alabama.* Rockledge: Self-published, 1999, p. 109.

31. *Ibid.*

32. Report of Colonel Abel D. Streight, August 22, 1864.

33. Willett, Robert. *The Lightning Brigade: Abel Streight's 1863 Raid into Alabama.* Rockledge: Self-published, 1999, p. 110.

34. *Ibid.*, p. 110.

35. Breidenthal diary, May 30, 1862.

36. *Ibid.*

37. Alabama Confederate heroine: Emma Sansom, https://civilwartalk.com/threads/alabama-confederate-heroine-emmasansom.77457/.
38. "Alabama Historical Quarterly," vol. 26.
39. Willett, Robert. *The Lightning Brigade: Abel Streight's 1863 Raid into Alabama*. Rockledge: Self-published, 1999, p. 152.
40. Buck and ball was a combination of buckshot and a musket ball loaded into the same charge.
41. Breidenthal diary, May 3, 1863.
42. OR, Vol. 23, Reports, p. 292.
43. *Ibid*.
44. Lytle, Andrew. *Bedford Forrest and His Critter Company*. New York: Minton, 1931, p. 175.

Epilogue

1. Ohio History Connection. U.S. Army, Infantry Regiment Third (1861–1865) records, vol. 676.
2. *Ibid*.
3. Willett, Robert. *The Lightning Mule Brigade: Abel Streight's 1863 Raid into Alabama*. Rockledge: Self-published, 1999, p. 168.
4. *Ibid*., p. 169.
5. *Ibid*., p. 170.
6. *Ibid*.
7. *Ibid*.
8. Reid, Whitelaw. *Ohio in the War, Volume II*. Cincinnati: Moore, Wilstach & Baldwin, 1868, p. 33.
9. Ohio History Connection. U.S. Army, Infantry Regiment Third (1861–1864) reports, vol. 677.

Bibliography

Primary Sources

Alexander, Edward Porter. *Memoirs of a Confederate, a Critical Narrative*. New York: Scribner's, 1907.
The American Encyclopedia and Register of Important Events of the Year 1861. New York: Appleton, 1870.
Appleton's Annual Encyclopedia and Register of Important Events of the Year: 1861–1875. New York: Appleton, 1862.
Basler, Roy, ed. *Collected Works of Abraham Lincoln* (vols. 4–7). New Brunswick: Rutgers University Press, 1953.
Beatty, John. *John Beatty, the Citizen Soldier; or Memoirs of a Volunteer*. Edited by Gregory R. Crane. Perseus Digital Library. http://www.perseus.tufts.edu/hopper/text?doc=Perseus:text:2001.05.0005.
Blaine, James G. *Twenty Years of Congress*. Norwich: Henry Bill, 1886.
Brown, Emma. *The Life and Public Services of James A. Garfield*. Boston: Guernsey, 1881.
Butler, Benjamin F. *Private and Official Correspondence of General Benjamin F. Butler during the Period of the Civil War*. Norwood: Plimpton Press, 1917.
Campbell, John A. *Recollections of the Evacuation of Richmond, April 2nd 1865*. Baltimore: John Murphy, 1880.
Campbell, John A. "A View of the Confederacy from the Inside." *Century Magazine*, October 1889, 950–954.
Carrington, Henry. *Ohio Militia and the West Virginia Campaign, 1861*. Address of General Carrington to Army of West Virginia, at Marietta, Ohio, September 10, 1870. Boston: Blodgett (printers), 1904.
Chase, Salmon P. *Diary and Correspondence*. Annual Report of the American Historical Association. Washington, D.C.: Government Printing Office, 1903.
Cox, Jacob. *Military Reminiscences of the Civil War*. New York: Scribner's, 1900.
Dana, Charles. *Recollections of the Civil War*. New York: Appleton, 1898.
Davis, Jefferson. *The Rise and Fall of the Confederate Government*. New York: Appleton, 1881.
Davis, Varina. *Jefferson Davis: A Memoir*. New York: Belford, 1890.
Dennett, Tyler, ed. *Lincoln and the Civil War in the Diaries and Letters of John Hay*. Westport: Negro Universities Press, 1972.
Dollard, John. *Fear in Battle*. New Haven: Institute of Human Relations, Yale University, 1943.
Executive Documents, Senate of the United States. Washington, D.C.: Government Printing Office, 1871.
Fredericksburg Staff Ride Briefing Book. Washington, D.C.: U.S. Army Center of Military History, 2002.
Fry, James B. *Operations of the Army under Buell from June 10th to October 30th, 1862 and the "Buell Commission."* New York: Van Nostrand, 1884.

Bibliography

Garfield, James. *The Wild Life of the Army: The Civil War Letters*. East Lansing: Michigan State University Press, 1964.
General Orders and Index to General Orders, 1861–1865. Washington, D.C.: Government Printing Office, 1862.
General Orders No. 100: The Lieber Code: Instructions for the Government of Armies of the United States in the Field. Washington, D.C.: Government Printing Office, April, 24, 1863.
General Orders of the War Department. 1861, 1862, 1863.
Gilmore, James R. *Personal Recollections of Abraham Lincoln and the Civil War*. Boston: LC Page, 1898.
Goss, Warren. *Recollections of a Private: A Story of the Army of the Potomac*. New York: Crowell, 1890.
Grant, Ulysses. *Personal Memoirs of U.S. Grant*. Project Gutenberg, June 1, 2004.
Halleck, Henry W. *The Elements of Military Art and Science*. New York: Appleton, 1846.
Hay, Clara. *The Life and Letters of John Hay*. New York: Harper, 1915.
Heitman, Francis B. *Historical Register and Dictionary of the United States Army, from Its Organization, September 29, 1879 to March 2, 1903*. Washington, D.C.: Government Printing Office, 1903.
Helper, Hinton. *The Impending Crisis of the South: How to Meet It*. New York: Burdick, 1860.
Howe, Julia Ward. *Reminiscences, 1819–1899*. Boston: Houghton Mifflin, 1899.
Jomini, Antoine. *Summary of the Art of War*. New York: Putnam, 1838.
Keifer, J. Warren. "Official Reports of J. Warren Keifer, Brevet Major General of Volunteers." *Daily Republic* [Springfield], 1866.
Keifer, J. Warren. *Rich Mountain and Some Incidents*. Cincinnati: The Commendary, 1911.
Keifer, J. Warren. *Slavery and Four Years of War*. New York: Putnam, 1900.
Lee, Robert E. *Memoirs*. Reprint. Secaucus: The Blue and Grey Press, 1983.
Lee, Robert E., Jr., ed. *The Recollections and Letters of General Robert E. Lee*. New York: Doubleday, 1904.
Livermore, Thomas. *Numbers and Losses in the Civil War in America*. New York: Houghton Mifflin, 1901.
Long, A.L. *Memoirs of Robert E. Lee: His Military and Personal History*. New York: J.M. Stoddart, 1886.
Lytle, Andrew. *Bedford Forrest and His Critter Company*. New York: Minton, 1931.
Lytle, William. *The Poems of William Haines Lytle*. Cincinnati: Robert Clark, 1894.
Mahan, D.H. *An Elementary Treatise on Advanced-Guard, Outpost and Detachment of Troops*: New York: Wiley, 1862.
Mahan, D.H. *Treatise on Field Fortifications Containing Instructions on the Laying Out, Constructing, Defending and Attacking Intrenchments*. Richmond: West and Johnson, 1862.
McClellan, George B. *The Armies of Europe*. Philadelphia: Lippincott, 1861.
McClellan, George B. *The Civil War Papers of George B. McClellan: Selected Correspondence 1860–1865*. Edited by Stephen Sears. New York: Ticknor and Fields, 1989.
McClellan, George B. *Manual of Bayonet Exercise*. Washington, D.C.: U.S. War Department, 1862.
McClellan George B. *The Mexican War Diary of George B. McClellan*. Edited by William Meyers. Princeton: Princeton University Press, 1917.
McClellan, George B. *My Own Story*. New York: Webster, 1887.
Official Records of the Union and Confederate Navies, series 1, vols. 4 and 5. Washington, D.C.: Government Printing Office, 1897.
Official Roster of the Soldiers of the State of Ohio in the War of the Rebellion, 1861–1866. Akron: Ohio Roster Commission, 1886.
Pike, James. *The Scout and Ranger, Being the Personal Adventures of Corporal Pike, 4th Ohio Cavalry*. Cincinnati: Hawley, 1865.
Report of the Joint Committee on the Conduct of the War. Washington, D.C.: Government Printing Office, 1863 and 1865.

Schurz, Carl. *The Reminiscences of Carl Schurz*. Garden City: Doubleday, 1913.
Scott, Winfield. *Infantry Tactics*. New York: Harper, 1861.
Scott, Winfield. *Memoirs of Lieut General Winfield Scott, LL.D.* New York: Sheldon, 1864.
Sears, Stephen, ed. *The Civil War Papers of George B. McClellan*. New York: Ticknor, 1989.
Sherman, William T. *Memoirs of General William T. Sherman*. New York: Appleton, 1889.
Statistical Abstract of the United States. Washington, D.C.: Government Printing Office, 1939.
Streight, Abel. *The Crisis of Eighteen Hundred and Sixty One in the United States*. https://www.gutenberg.org/cache/epub/38554/pg38554.txt.
Thomas, George H. *History of the Army of the Cumberland*. Cincinnati: Clarke, 1875.
Townsend, E.D. *Anecdotes of the Civil War in the United States*. New York: Appleton, 1884.
The Union Army: A History of Military Affairs in the Loyal States 1861–1865. Madison: Federal Publishing, 1908.
United States Senate Select Committee to Study Governmental Operations with respect to Intelligence Activities (Church Committee). Washington, D.C.: Government Printing Office, 1975.
Usher, John P. *President Lincoln's Cabinet*. Omaha: Nelson Loomis, 1925.
Villard, Henry. *Memoirs*. Boston: Houghton Mifflin, 1904.
The War of the Rebellion, Official Records of the Union and Confederate Armies. Washington, D.C.: Government Printing Office, 1900.
Wilson, Rufus, ed. *Intimate Memories of Lincoln*. Elmira: Primavera Press, 1945.

Primary Sources (Archival)

The Ohio History Connection, Columbus, Ohio
  Collection: United States. Army. Ohio Infantry Regiment, 3rd (1861–1864) records
  Collection Number: MSS 2842
    Volumes:
    674   Roster
    675   Roll Book
    676   Scrap Book/Minutes
    677   Scrapbook/Minutes
Moore, Frank. *The Rebellion Record: A Diary of American Events, with Documents, Narratives, Illustrative Events, Poetry, etc.* New York: Putnam, 1861–1865.
Henry Shelton Sanford Library and Museum, Sanford, Florida
  Henry Shelton Sanford Papers

- Sanford Letter Books 1861–1877
- Personal Correspondence 1849–1891
- William Henry Seward Correspondence (200 letters)
- Baring Brothers Bank Correspondence, 1850–1869 (35 documents)
- Gideon Welles Correspondence
- John Bigelow Correspondence 1861–1866 (86 letters)
- Frederick Seward Correspondence (22 letters)
- Thurlow Weed Correspondence (70 letters)

Diaries

Before the Storm: The Tuttle Diary during the Stones River Campaign https://www.westerntheatercivilwar.com/post/missing-out-on-stones-river
Captain Robert D. Taylor (Perryville)
The Diary of John Beatty, January–June, 1884. *Ohio History Journal*, vol. LVIII.

Edward Bates
Gideon Welles
Henry A. Breidenthal
Henry Villard
John Milton Hay
The Letters and Diary of Major James A. Connolly: Three Years in the Army of the Cumberland
Mary Boykin Chesnut
Rutherford B. Hayes (Diary and Letters)
Samuel Watkins ("Co Aytch," Kennesaw Mountain)
William T. Sherman

Private Paper Collections

Abraham Lincoln Papers, Library of Congress, Series 2, General Correspondence, 1858–1865.
The Collected Works of Abraham Lincoln (Basler) Vols. 3–8.
Letter from Col. A.B. Moore. 104th Illinois. *Chicago Tribune*, February 14, 1863. "The Disaster at Hartsville."
The Obidiah Jennings Wise Letters, William and Mary Digital Archive, https://digitalarchive.wm.edu/handle/10288/2234.
The Papers of George Brinton McClellan: Box A-18, reel 8; 19 reel 9; 20 reel 9; 17 reel 8; 16 reel 7. Box B-7 reel 46; 8 reel 47 (Library of Congress, microfilm edition).
The Papers of Henry Shelton Sanford, Sanford Museum, Sanford, Florida. Box 15, general correspondence 1849–1891; Box 16, business firms A–Z; Box 36, special projects; Box 41 memoranda; Box 65, clippings; Box 94, general correspondence; Box 95, correspondence 1862–1896; Box 99, 100, 101, 102, letter books.
The Papers of John George Nicolay, Manuscripts Division, Madison Building, Washington. Box 1, notebooks and scrapbooks 1856–1870; Box 2, 1811–1867; Box 3, 1863–1867; Box 7, Letters to Therena Bates; Boxes 8–17. (Sketches in Box 17 and 18 were particularly interesting.)
The Papers of John Milton Hay, The Hay Library, Brown University, Providence, Rhode Island. Microfilm reel 5701:8 and 5701:9.
Sketches of War History: 1861–1865. Paper Read before the Ohio Commandery of the Military Order of the Loyal Legion of the United States. Cincinnati: Clark, 1888.
United States Army. Ohio Infantry Regiment, 3rd (1861–1864) Records. The Ohio History Museum.

- Vol. 0674: Roster, 1889–1922
- Vol. 0675: Roll Book, 1895–1906
- Vol. 0676: Scrapbook, minutes, 1877–1899
- Vol. 0677: Scrapbook, minutes, 1877–1899

Secondary Sources

Alabama Confederate Heroine: Emma Sansom. https://civilwartalk.com/threads/alabama-confederate-heroine-emma-sansom.77457/.
Andrews, J. Cutler. "The Southern Telegraph Company, 1861–1865: A Chapter in the History of Wartime Communication." *Journal of Southern History* 30, no. 3 (August 1964): 319–344.
Axe, David. "Union Spies Saved Washington, D.C. from Becoming a Confederate City. December 2014. https://warisboring.com/union-spies-saved-washington-d-c-from-becoming-a-confederate-city-3aeb5964ceba#.cyat7lt9r.

Bibliography

Ayres, Philip. "Lincoln as a Neighbor." Lincoln Financial Collection, 1918.
Bach, Jennifer. "Acts of Remembrance: Mary Todd Lincoln and Her Husband's Memory." *Journal of the Abraham Lincoln Association* 25, no. 2 (Summer 2004): 25–49.
Ballard, Colin R. *The Military Genius of Abraham Lincoln*. New York: World Publishing, 1952.
Barnes, James. *The American Civil War through British Eyes*. Kent: Kent State University Press, 2003.
Bateman, Robert. "Why Logistics Win Wars." *Esquire Magazine*, October 31, 2013.
Baxter, Nancy. *Gallant Fourteenth: The Story of an Indiana Regiment*. Traverse City: Pioneer Press, 1980.
Beatie, Russel. *The Army of the Potomac*. Cambridge, MA: Da Capo, 2002.
Beatty, John. *The Solid South: Its Political Spirit, Methods and Purposes*. Cincinnati: Self-published, 1880.
Beck, Brandon: *Streight's Foiled Raid on the Western and Atlantic Railroad*. Charleston, SC: History Press, 2016.
Bell, William G. *Secretaries of War and Secretaries of the Army*. Washington, D.C.: Center of Military History, United States Army, 2003.
Bernstein, Iver. *The New York City Draft Riots*. New York: Oxford University Press, 1990.
Beymer, William G. *On Hazardous Service: Scouts and Spies of the North and South*. New York: Harper, 1912.
Blackman, John L. "The Seizure of the Reading Railroad in 1864." *Pennsylvania Magazine of History and Biography* 111, no. 1 (January 1, 1987): 49–60.
Blair, James M. "12th West Virginia Infantry, Company B." http://www.lindapages.com/wvcw/12wvi/12-jmblair.htm.
Bobrick, Benson. *Master of War: The Life of General George H. Thomas*. New York: Simon & Schuster, 2009.
Boritt, Gabor. *The Historian's Lincoln*. Urbana: University of Illinois Press, 1988.
Boritt, Gabor, ed. *Jefferson Davis's Generals*. New York: Oxford University Press, 1999.
Briant, C.C. *History of the 6th Regiment Indiana Volunteer Infantry*. Indianapolis: Burford, 1891.
Bridges, Peter. "Donn Piatt: Diplomat and Gadfly." http://www.unc.edu/depts/diplomat/item/2007/0103/life/bridges_piatt.html.
Brooks, Noah. "Lincoln, Chase and Grant." *Century Illustrated Magazine*, November 1894.
Brown, Genevieve Gist. "A History of the Sixth Regiment West Virginia Infantry Volunteers." *West Virginia History*, July 1948, p. 315
Browning, Robert. *Forrest: The Confederacy's Relentless Warrior*. Washington, D.C.: Brassey's, 2004.
Byrd, Cecil. "Some Notes on Thomas D. Jones, Sculptor of Lincoln." *Indiana University Bookman*, 1957.
Campbell, James Havelock. *McClellan: A Vindication of the Military Career*. New York: Neale, 1916.
Carmony, Donald F. *A Brief History of Indiana*. Indianapolis: Indiana Historical Bureau, 1961.
Cist, Henry. *The Army of the Cumberland*. New York: Scribner's, 1882.
Coggins, Jack. *Arms and Equipment of the Civil War*. Mineola: Dover, 1962.
"Colonel Arthur C. Ducat: One of the Men behind the Man." https://chickamaugablog.wordpress.com/2015/04/19/colonel-arthur-c-ducat-one-of-the-men-behind-the-man/.
Connelly, Thomas. *Army of the Heartland: The Army of Tennessee, 1861–62*. Baton Rouge: Louisiana State University Press, 1967.
Connelly, Thomas. *Civil War Tennessee: Battles and Leaders*. Knoxville: University of Tennessee Press, 1979.
Conrad, Thomas. *The Rebel Scout: A Thrilling History of Scouting Life in the Southern Army*. Washington, D.C.: National Publishing, 1904.
Cope, Alexis. *The 15th Ohio Volunteers and its Campaigns, War of 1861–1865*. Published by the author, 1916.
Cortissoz, Royal. *The Life of Whitelaw Reid*. New York: Scribner's, 1921.

Cox, Jacob. "McClellan in West Virginia." https://www.historycentral.com/CivilWar/WV/Meclellan2.html.
Crook, William H. "Lincoln as I Knew Him." *Harper's*, June 1907, 41–48.
Daniel, Larry. *Shiloh: The Battle that Changed the Civil War.* New York: Simon & Schuster, 1997.
Davis, James A. *The 51st Regiment, Virginia Volunteers, 1861–1865.* Lynchburg: H.E. Howard, 1984.
Davis, Rodney. "Lincoln's 'Particular Friend' and Lincoln Biography." *Journal of the Abraham Lincoln Association* 19, no. 1 (Winter 1998): 21–37.
Davis, William J., ed. *The Partisan Rangers of the Confederate States Army.* Louisville: Fetter Publishing, 1904.
Davison, Eddy. *Nathan Bedford Forrest: In Search of the Enigma.* Gretna: Pelican, 2007.
Dayton, Ruth. "The Beginning—Philippi, 1861." *West Virginia Archives and History* 13, no. 4 (July 1952): 254–266.
Deeben, John P. "To Protect and to Serve: The Records of the D.C. Metropolitan Police, 1861–1930." *Prologue* 40, no. 1 (Spring 2008). https://www.archives.gov/publications/prologue/2008/spring/metro-police.html.
Dirck, Brian R. "Lincoln and Davis as Commanders in Chief." http://www.essentialcivilwarcurriculum.com/lincoln-and-davis-as-commanders-in-chief.html.
Dodge, Grenville. *The Battle of Atlanta and Other Campaigns, Addresses.* Council Bluffs: Monarch, 1910.
Dodge, Grenville. *Personal Recollections of President Abraham Lincoln, General Ulysses S. Grant, and General William T. Sherman.* Council Bluffs: Monarch, 1914.
Eaton, Clement. "Henry A. Wise: Liberal of the Old South." *Journal of Southern History* 7, no. 4 (November 1941): 482–494.
Eckley, Robert S. "Lincoln's Intimate Friend: Leonard Swett." *Journal of the Illinois State Historical Society* 92, no. 3 (Autumn 1999): 274–288.
Farquhar, Michael. "Rebel Rose: A Spy of Grand Dame Proportions." *Washington Post*, September 18, 2000.
Fehrenbacher, Don E. "Lincoln's Wartime Leadership: The First Hundred Days." *Journal of the Abraham Lincoln Association* 9, no. 1 (1987): 2–18.
Ferris, Norman B. "Lincoln and Seward in Civil War Diplomacy." *Journal of the Abraham Lincoln Association* 12, no. 1 (1991): 21–42.
Fish, Carl R. "Lincoln and the Patronage." *American Historical Review* 8, no. 1 (October 1902): 53–69.
Fishel, Edwin. "Military Intelligence, 1861–1863." *CIA Historical Review*, September 18, 1995.
Flower, Frank. *Edwin McMasters Stanton: Autocrat of Rebellion, Emancipation and Reconstruction.* New York: Saalfield, 1905.
Foote, Shelby. *The Civil War: A Narrative: Volume 1: Fort Sumter to Perryville.* New York: Vintage, 1986.
Forsyth, Michael J. "The Military Provides Lincoln a Mandate." *Council on America's Military Past*, 2002. https://history.army.mil/html/bookshelves/resmat/civil_war/articles/article_from_AH53w.pdf.
Frame, Kathryn Hart. "David Hart and the Hart Family in the American Civil War." http://www.richmountain.org/history/davhart.html.
Freiheit, Laurence. "Military Intelligence during the Maryland Campaign." 2008. https://antietam.aotw.org/exhibit.php?exhibit_id=431.
Gabel, Christopher. *Railroad Generalship: Foundations of Civil War Strategy.* Fort Leavenworth: U.S. Army Command and General Staff College, 1997.
Gareschè, Louis. *Biography of Lieut. Colonel Julius P. Gareschè.* Philadelphia: Lippincott, 1887.
Gienapp, William E. "Abraham Lincoln and the Border States." *Journal of the Abraham Lincoln Association* 13, no. 1 (1992): 13–46.
Gilot, Jon-Erik. "A Tremendous Little Man. Newton Schleich in the Civil War." August 30, 2017. https://emergingcivilwar.com/2017/08/30/a-tremendous-little-man-newton-schleich-in-the-civil-war.

Bibliography   193

Golder, Frank. "The American Civil War through the Eyes of a Russian Diplomat." *American Historical Review* 26, no. 3 (April 1921): 454–463.
Goodheart, Adam. "The South Rises Again—and Again and Again." *The Opinionator*, January 27, 2011. https://archive.nytimes.com/opinionator.blogs.nytimes.com/2011/01/27/the-south-rises-again-and-again-and-again/.
Grady, John. "The Confederate Torpedo." *The Opinionator*, August 15, 2014. http://opinionator.blogs.nytimes.com/2014/08/15/the-confederate-torpedo/?_r=1.
Grant, Meredith. "Internal Dissent: East Tennessee's Civil War, 1849–1865." Master's thesis, East Tennessee State University, 2008.
Greene, Francis V. "Lincoln as Commander in Chief." *Scribner's* 46 (July 1909).
Griffith, Paddy. *Battle Tactics of the Civil War*. New Haven: Yale University Press, 1987.
Hagerman, Edward. *The American Civil War and the Origins of Modern Warfare*. Bloomington: Indiana University Press, 1988.
Hall, Granville. *Lee's Invasion of Northwest Virginia 1861*. Chicago: Mayer and Miller, 1911.
Hannaford, E. *The Story of a Regiment: A History of the Campaigns and Association in the Field of the Sixth Regiment of Ohio Volunteer Infantry*. Cincinnati: Self-published, 1868.
Hansen, Harry. *The Civil War: A History*. New York: Duell, Sloan, and Pearce, 1961.
Harrison, Lowell. *The Civil War in Kentucky*. Lexington: University of Kentucky Press, 1975.
Hattaway, Herman. *General Stephen D. Lee*. Jackson: University of Mississippi Press, 1976.
Hattaway, Herman. "Lincoln as Military Strategist." *Civil War History* 26, no. 4 (December 1980): 293–303.
Hattaway, Herman. "Lincoln's Presidential Example in Dealing with the Military." *Journal of the Abraham Lincoln Association* 7, no. 1 (1985): 18–29.
Headley, P.C. *Old Stars, the Life and Military Career of Major General Ormsby M. Mitchel*. New York: C.T. Dillingham, 1883. (Digital reprint, University of Michigan).
Headley, P.C. *The Patriot Boy: The Life and Career of Major-General Ormsby Mitchel*. New York: Appleton, 1865.
Hendrick, Burton. *Lincoln's War Cabinet*. Boston: Little, Brown, 1946.
Henry, Robert. *"First with the Most": Forrest*. New York: Konecky, 1992.
Herndon, William. "Lincoln as a Personality." *Christian Advocate* 84 (February 4, 1909): 164–165.
Hess, Earl. *Civil War Infantry Tactics*. Baton Rouge: Louisiana State University Press, 2015.
Hesseltine, William. "Lincoln's War Governors." *Abraham Lincoln Quarterly* 4, no. 4 (December 1946): 153–200.
History Eighty-Eighth Indiana Volunteers Infantry. Engagements, Chronology, Roster. Mustered into Service August 29th, 1862. Mustered Out, June 7; Disbanded, June 20th, 1865.
Holzer, Harold. "Lincoln Takes the Heat." *Civil War Times* 39, no. 7 (February 2001).
Horn, Stanley. *The Battle of Stones River*. Gettysburg: Historical Times, 1972.
Hurst, Jack: *Nathan Bedford Forrest: A Biography*. New York: Knopf, 1993.
Huston, James. *The Sinews of War: Army Logistics 1775–1953*. Washington, D.C.: Center of Military History, 1997.
Hutchinson, Dennis J. "Lincoln the Dictator." *South Dakota Law Review* 55, no. 2 (2010). https://chicagounbound.uchicago.edu/cgi/viewcontent.cgi?article=2531&context=journal_articles.
Hyman, Harold M. "Lincoln and War Powers: Commentary on Papers by Professor E. Berwanger and Dr. M. Neely." *Journal of the Abraham Lincoln Association* 5, no. 1 (1983): 39–47.
Indiana Infantry, 88th Regiment, 1862–1865. *History Eighty-Eighth Indiana Volunteers Infantry*. Edited by Cyrus Briant. Fort Wayne: W.D. Page, 1895.
Johnson, Adam. *The Partisan Rangers of the Confederate States Army*. Louisville: Fetter, 1904.
Johnson, Albert E.H. "Reminiscences of the Hon. Edwin M. Stanton, Secretary of War." *Records of the Columbia Historical Society* 13 (1910): 69–97.
Johnson, Larry. "Breakdown from Within: Virginia Railroads during the Civil War Era." Master's thesis, University of Louisville, 2004.

Johnson, Robert. *Battles and Leaders of the Civil War*. New York: Century, 1887.
Keifer, Warren. *The Battle of Rich Mountain and Some Incidents*. Cincinnati: The Commandery, 1911.
Killblane, Richard E. *White House Landing: Sustaining the Army of the Potomac during the Peninsula Campaign*. U.S. Army Transportation Corps Publication. E-book, Progressive Management, 2018.
Kurtz, Joel. "Confederate Railroads: Changing Priorities during the War Years." Senior Research Project, Southern Adventist University, 2010. https://knowledge.e.southern.edu/senior_research.
Lackey, Rodney C. "Notes on Civil War Logistics: Facts and Stories." http://www.transportation.army.mil/History/PDF/Peninsula%20Campaign/Rodney%20Lackey%20Article_1.pdf.
Laidig, Scott. "Brigadier General John Pegram: Lee's Paradoxical Cavalier." February 1998. https://ehistory.osu.edu/articles/brigadier-general-john-pegram-lee%E2%80%99s-paradoxical-cavalier.
Lamers, William. *The Edge of Glory: A Biography of William S. Rosecrans*. New York: Harcourt Brace, 1961.
Lee, Dan. *Kentuckian in Blue: A Biography of Major General Lovell Harrison Rousseau*. Jefferson: McFarland, 2010.
Levstik, Frank R. *The 42nd Virginia Regiment, Virginia Volunteers, 1861–1865*. Blacksburg: Virginia Polytechnic Institute, 1968.
Linderman, Gerald E. *Embattled Courage: The Experience of Combat in the American Civil War*. New York: Free Press, 1987.
Lonn, Ella. *Desertion during the Civil War*. New York: Century, 1928.
Marszalek, John F. *Commander of All Lincoln's Armies: A Life of General Henry W. Halleck*. Cambridge, MA: Harvard University Press, 2004.
Marvel, William. *Lincoln's Darkest Year: The War in 1862*. Boston: Houghton, 2008.
Marvel, William. *Mr. Lincoln Goes to War*. New York: Houghton Mifflin, 2006.
Mathes, James. *General Forrest*. New York: Appleton, 1902.
Maurice, Eric. "Send Forward Some Who Would Fight: How John T. Wilder and His 'Lightning Brigade' of Mounted Infantry Changed Warfare." Master's thesis, Butler University, 2016.
McCague, James. *The Second Rebellion: The Story of the New York City Draft Riots of 1863*. New York: Dial Press, 1968.
McClellan, George. "From the Peninsula to Antietam." *Century Magazine*, no. 1 (May 1886).
McDonough, James. *Stones River: Bloody Winter in Tennessee*. Knoxville: University of Tennessee Press, 1983.
McKelvy, David. "The David McKelvy Diary, 1864." *Pennsylvania Magazine of History and Biography* 115, no. 3 (July 1991): 371–413.
McPherson, James. *Embattled Rebel*. New York: Penguin, 2014.
McPherson, James. *Tried by War*. New York: Penguin, 2008.
McWhinney, Grady, and Perry Jamieson. *Attack and Die: Civil War Military Tactics and the Southern Heritage*. Tuscaloosa: University of Alabama Press, 1982.
McWhinney, Grady, and Perry Jamieson. *Braxton Bragg and the Confederate Defeat*. Tuscaloosa: University of Alabama Press, 1991.
Meigs, Montgomery. "General M.C. Meigs on the Conduct of the Civil War." *American Historical Review* 26, no. 2 (January 1921): 285–303.
Miers, Earl. *The American Civil War: A Popular History of the Years 1861–1865 as Seen by the Artist-Correspondents Who Were There*. New York: Ridge Press, 1961.
Merrill, Louis Taylor. "General Benjamin F. Butler in the Campaign of 1864." *Mississippi Historical Valley Review* 33, no.4 (March 1947): 537–570.
Mitchel, F.A. *Ormsby McKnight Mitchel: Astronomer and General*. Boston: Houghton Mifflin, 1887.
Moore, Charles. "Abraham Lincoln. Zachariah Chandler in Lincoln's Second Campaign." *The Century* 50, no. 3 (July 1895): 476–477.

Bibliography

Morton, John. *The Artillery of Nathan Bedford Forest's Cavalry, "The Wizard of the Saddle."* Nashville: M.E. Church, 1909.
Neely, Mark E. "The Lincoln Administration and Arbitrary Arrests: A Reconsideration." *Journal of the Abraham Lincoln Association* 5, no. 1 (1983): 6–24.
Nevins, Alan. *Ordeal of the Union: The Improvised War Vol. 3.* New York: Macmillan, 1959.
Nevins, Alan. *The War for the Union: The Organized War, 1863–1864.* New York: Scribner's, 1971.
Newell, Clayton. *Lee vs McClellan, The First Campaign.* Washington, D.C.: Regency, 1996.
Newman, Leonard. "Opposition to Lincoln in the Elections of 1864." *Science and Society* 8, no. 4 (1944): 305–327.
Nicolay, Helen. "Characteristic Anecdotes of Lincoln." *Century Magazine* (September 1912).
Nicolay, Helen. *Lincoln's Secretary.* Westport: Greenwood, 1949.
Nicolay, John, and John Hay. *Abraham Lincoln: A History.* New York: Century, 1890.
Niven, John. "Lincoln and Chase: A Reappraisal." *Journal of the Abraham Lincoln Association* 12, no. 1 (1991): 1–15.
O'Harrow, Robert. *The Quartermaster: Montgomery C. Meigs, Lincoln's General, Master Builder of the Union Army.* New York: Simon & Schuster, 2016.
Perry, David. "Abraham Lincoln and John George Nicolay: The Impact of Auditory and Visual Learning Styles on the Civil War." *The Lincoln Herald* 112, no. 2 (Summer 2010): 79–95.
Perry, David. *Bluff, Bluster, Lies and Spies: The Lincoln Foreign Policy, 1861–1865.* Philadelphia: Casemate, 2016.
Peskin, Alan. *Garfield: A Biography.* Kent: Kent State University Press, 1978.
Pfeiffer, David A. "Records relating to the U.S. Military Railroads." *Prologue* 43, no. 2 (Summer 2011).
Phillips, Christopher. "Shadow War: Federal Military Authority and Loyalty Oaths in Civil War Missouri." Retrieved June 25, 2024. https://civilwaronthewesternborder.org/essay/shadow-war-federal-military-authority-and-loyalty-oaths-civil-war-missouri.
Piatt, Donn. *General George H. Thomas: A Critical Biography.* Cincinnati: Clarke, 1893.
Pierson, William. "The Committee on the Conduct of the War." *American Historical Review* 23, no. 3 (1918): 550–576. https://www.jstor.org/stable/pdf/1835274.pdf.
Plant, Trevor. "The Shady Side of the Family Tree: Civil War Union Court Martial Case Files." *Prologue* 30, no. 4 (Winter 1998).
Plum, William R. *The Military Telegraph during the Civil War in the United States.* Chicago: Jansen, 1882.
Porter, George. *Ohio Politics during the Civil War Period.* New York: Longmans, Green. 1911.
Pratt, Harry E. "The Repudiation of Lincoln's War Policy in 1862: Stuart/Swett Congressional Campaign." *Journal of the Illinois State Historical Society* 24, no. 1 (1931): 129–140.
Prokopowicz, Gerald. *All for the Regiment: The Army of the Ohio 1861–1862.* Chapel Hill: University of North Carolina Press, 2001.
Putnam, Bayard. "Open Letters: The Tool-House at Home, Zachariah Chandler." *Century* 50, no. 3 (July 1895).
Ramage, James. *Rebel Raider: The Life of General John Hunt Morgan.* Lexington: University Press of Kentucky, 1986.
Reid, Whitelaw. "Lincoln as I Knew Him." *Leslie's Illustrated Weekly*, February 9, 1911.
Reid, Whitlaw. *Lincoln.* London: Harrison, 1910.
Reid, Whitelaw. *Ohio in the War: Her Statesmen, Generals and Soldiers.* Cincinnati: Clarke, 1895.
Reid, Whitlaw. *Ohio in the War, Volume II.* Cincinnati: Moore, Wilstach & Baldwin, 1868.
Rhodes, Albert. "A Reminiscence of Abraham Lincoln." *St. Nicholas Magazine*, November 1876, 8–10.
Rice, Judith. "Ida Tarbell: A Progressive Look at Lincoln." *Journal of the Abraham Lincoln Association* 19 (Winter 1998): 57–72.
Richards, Kent D. "The Young Napoleons: Isaac I. Stevens, George B. McClellan and the

Cascade Mountains Route." *Columbia: The Magazine of Northwest History* 3, no. 4 (Winter 1989–1990).

Rietveld, Ronald. "The White House Community." *Journal of the Abraham Lincoln Association*. 20, no. 2 (Summer 1999): 17–48.

Rogers, Earl. "McClellan's Candidacy with the Army." *Century Magazine* (October 1890): 959–960.

Russell, Francis. "Butler the Beast?" *American Heritage* 19, no. 3 (April 1968). https://www.americanheritage.com/butler-beast.

Schafer, Joseph. "Who Elected Lincoln?" *American Historical Review* 47, no. 1 (October 1941): 51–63.

Schaffer, Dallas. "Rich Mountain Revisited." *West Virginia* History 28, no. 1 (October 1966): 16–34.

Schuckers, J.W. *The Life and Public Services of Salmon Portland Chase*. New York: Appleton, 1874.

Sears, Stephen. *Controversies and Commanders: Dispatches from the Army of the Potomac*. Boston: Houghton Mifflin, 1999.

Sears, Stephen. *George B. McClellan: The Young Napoleon*. New York: Ticknor, 1988.

Segal, Charles, ed. "Conversations with Lincoln." *American Historical Review*, January 1921, 299.

Seventy-Third Regimental History Association. *History of the Seventy-Third Indiana Volunteers*. Washington, D.C.: Carnahan Press, 1909.

Shannon, Fred A. *The Organization and Administration of the United States Army 1861–1865*. Cleveland: Clark, 1928.

Shaw, James. *History of the Tenth Regiment Indiana Volunteer Infantry*. Lafayette: Self-published (Regimental Association), 1912.

Shrader, Charles R. *United States Army Logistics, 1775–1992*. Washington, D.C.: Center of Military History, 1997.

Simpson, Brooks D. "Lincoln and his Political Generals." *Journal of the Abraham Lincoln Association* 21, no. 1 (Winter 2000): 63–77.

Smith, Adam. "Jewel of Liberty: Abraham Lincoln's Re-election and the End of Slavery." *Journal of the Abraham Lincoln Association* 20, no. 1 (1999): 67–83.

Smith, Gene. "The Destruction of Fighting Joe Hooker." *American Heritage Magazine*, October 1993. https://www.americanheritage.com/destruction-fighting-joe-hooker-0.

Solensky, Richard. "The Confederacy's Special Agent." March 2008. http://www.damninteresting.com/the-confederacys-special-agent.

Spillard, F. Horral. *History of the Forty-Second Indiana Volunteer Infantry*. Chicago: Donohue and Henneberry, 1892.

Stahr, Walter. *Seward: Lincoln's Indispensable Man*. New York: Simon & Schuster, 2012.

Stahr, Walter. *Stanton, Lincoln's War Secretary*. New York: Simon & Schuster, 2017.

Starr, John W. *Lincoln and the Railroads*. New York: Dodd Mead, 1927.

Stone, Charles P. "Washington on the Eve of the War." *Century Illustrated Monthly Magazine* (1883), 458–466.

Summers, Festus. *The Baltimore and Ohio in the Civil War*. Gettysburg: Clark Military, 1993.

Swick, Gerald D. "The First Battle of the Civil War: Philippi." March 14, 2011. https://www.historynet.com/the-first-battle-of-the-civil-war.

Tap, Bruce. "Amateurs at War: Abraham Lincoln and the Committee on the Conduct of the War." *Journal of the Abraham Lincoln Association* 23, no. 2 (Summer 2002): 1–18.

Temple, Oliver. *East Tennessee and the Civil War*. Cincinnati: Clarke, 1899.

"Third Regiment Ohio Volunteer Infantry (Three Months Service)." https://www.ohiocivilwarcentral.com/3rd-regiment-ohio-volunteer-infantry-three-months-service.

Trueman, C.N. "The Cost of the American Civil War." March 25, 2015. http://www.historylearningsite.co.uk/the-american-civil-war/the-cost-of-the-american-civil-war/.

Turner, Charles W. "The Virginia Central Railroad at War: 1861–1865." *Journal of Southern History* 12, no. 4 (November 1946): 510–533.

Turner, George. *Victory Rode the Rails*. Lincoln: University of Nebraska Press, 1981.

Vance, Wilson. *Stones River: The Turning Point of the Civil War.* New York: Neale, 1914.
VanDeusen, Glyndon. *William Henry Seward.* New York: Oxford University Press, 1967.
Voigt, David Q. "Too Pitchy to Touch: President Lincoln and Editor Bennett." *Abraham Lincoln Quarterly* 6, no. 3 (September 1950).
Walther, Eric. "The Fire-Eaters and Seward Lincoln." *Journal of the Abraham Lincoln Association* 32, no. 1 (Winter 2011): 18–32.
Warner, Ezra. *Generals in Gray: Lives of the Confederate Commanders.* Baton Rouge: Louisiana State University Press, 1959.
Watkins, Sam. *"Co. Aytch."* Chattanooga: Times Publishing, 1900.
Waugh, John. *The Class of 1846.* New York: Warner, 1994.
Weber, Jennifer. "Lincoln's Critics: The Copperheads." *Journal of the Abraham Lincoln Association* 32, no. 1 (Winter 2011): 33–47.
Wert, Jeffrey D. *The Sword of Lincoln.* New York: Simon & Schuster, 2005.
Whyte, James H. "Divided Loyalties in Washington during the Civil War." *Columbia Historical Society* 60 (1960): 103–122.
Willett, Robert S. *The Lightning Mule Brigade: Abel Streight's 1863 Raid into Alabama.* Rockledge: Self-published, 1999.
Williams, T. Harry. *Lincoln and His Generals.* New York: Knopf, 1952.
Wills, Brian. *A Battle from the Start: The Life of Nathan Bedford Forrest.* New York: Harper, 1993.
Wise, Barton. *The Life of Henry A. Wise of Virginia 1806–1876.* New York: Macmillan, 1899.
Woodworth, Steven. *Jefferson Davis and His Generals.* Lawrence: University Press of Kansas, 1990.
Work, David. *Lincoln's Political Generals.* Urbana: University of Illinois Press, 2009.
Wrone, David. "Lincoln: Democracy's Touchstone." *Journal of the Abraham Lincoln Association*, Vol. 1 (1979): 71–83.
Wyeth, John. *That Devil Forrest: The Life of General Nathan Bedford Forrest.* Baton Rouge: Louisiana State University Press, 1989.
Young, Bennett. *Confederate Wizards of the Saddler: Being Reminiscences of One Who Rode with Morgan.* Boston: Chapple, 1914.
Young, James Harvey. "Anna Elizabeth Dickinson and the Civil War: For and Against Lincoln." 1944. https://www.oah.org/site/assets/files/8710/07_mvhr_1944_young.pdf.

Newspapers, Journals, and Magazines

Alabama Historical Quarterly, vol. 26.
Century Illustrated
Century Magazine
Chattanooga Daily Rebel
Cincinnati Daily Enquirer
Civil War History, vol. 6, no. 1
Civil War Quarterly
Columbia: The Magazine of Northwest History
Confederate Veteran. Nashville, United Daughters of the Confederacy, vol. 38, 1893.
Daily Huntsville Confederate
Daily Rebel Banner
The Guerilla (Charleston, West Virginia)
Journal of Southern History, vol. 30, no. 3
Knoxville Whig
Louisville Courier Journal
Magazine of American History
Magazine of History with Notes and Queries
Maryland Historical Magazine: The Maryland Historical Society (vol. 88)
Mississippi Valley Historical Review, vol. 9, no. 2.

Nashville Daily Union
Nashville Union and American
New York Tribune
Ohio Historical Journal, vol. LVIII
Pennsylvania Magazine of History and Biography
Register of the Kentucky Historical Society.
Richmond Dispatch
Richmond Enquirer
South Carolina Historical and Genealogical Magazine
Washington Star
West Virginia Archives and History
West Virginia History: A Journal of Regional Studies
Wheeling Intelligencer

Index

Numbers in **_bold italics_** indicate pages with illustrations

Anaconda Plan 74, 125
Anderson, Capt. Charles D. 140

Beatty, Lt. Col. John **_28_**, 33–34, 37; battle of Bridgeport 69–70; battle of Middle Fork Bridge 40, 42–46; battle of Paint Rock 75–76, 85, 87–91; battle of Perryville 108, 115–123; battle of Rich Mountain 52, 54, 55, 57, 59, 66, 69; battle of Stones River (Murfreesboro) 129; promotion to brigadier general 129–130
Beatty, Gen. Samuel 120
Beauregard, Gen. Pierre T. 132
Bennett, James Gordon 12
Black Warrior River 136, 137
Blount's Plantation 138
Blountsville 125, 134, 137
Bond, Maj. Frank S. 118
Bond, Maj. Lewis H. 144
border states 73–74
Boreman, Arthur **_9_**
Bottom, Henry P. 89
Bragg, Gen. Braxton 75; Munfordville 77, 79–97; Perryville **_81_**; Stones River 111–114, 120
Breckenridge, Maj. Gen. John 115, 120–121
Breidenthal, Serg. Henry 130–133, 136–137, 139–140, 142, 143
Brent, Gen. George W. 94, 104
Bridgeport 69
Buckingham, Adj. Gen. Carinthius 15
Buckner, Gen. Simon Bolivar 83, 91
Buell, Gen. Don Carlos 48, 73, 77, **_78_**, 79–95; court of inquiry 95, 100; Perryville 96–97
Bull Run 32; *see also* Manassas
Burnside, Gen. Ambrose 108–109
Butler, Gen. Benjamin **_46_**, 63, 72

Cameron, Simon 18
Camp Garnett 29, 30, 41–42
Carlisle, John 9
Carrick's Ford 44
Cedar Bluff 139
Chalmers, Gen. James 79
Chase, Kate 127, 184n7
Chase, Salmon 127–128
Cheat Mountain 32, 44, 49, 51
Coffey, George 141
Columbiad **_8_**
Conscription 107
Cook, Jay 74, 181n9
Cox, Gen. Jacob 36
Crittenden, Gen. Thomas 19, 105, 115, 121

Davis, Jefferson 35
Day's Gap 133–134, 135
DeLangel, Capt. Julius 41, 49
Dennison, Gov. William 10, 16, 22
Dodge, Gen. Grenville 132–133
Doughty, John B. 131
Ducat, Lt. Col. Arthur C. 103, 105
Dumont, Gen. Ebeneezer 19, 21, 55, 59, 104–105, 175n5
Duncan, Pvt. Thomas D. 137

Elk Water 51

Farragut, Adm. David 75
Foote, Adm. Andrew 131–132
Forrest, Gen. Nathan Bedford 3, 104, 126, **_127_**, 133, 137; with Emma Sansom 138
Forrest, Capt. William 134–135
Fraser (Trenholm & Co.) 56, 74
Fredericksburg 108–109

Gadsden 137
Garfield, Adj. James 83, 127
Garnett, Gen. Robert 12, 22, 25, 29, 35 44

199

Index

Garrett, John W. 16
Geresché, Lt. Col. Julius 107, 118
Grant, Gen. Ulysses 67, 131–132

Halleck, Gen. Henry 80, 97, 100–102, 104
Hardee, Gen. William 40, 85–*86*, 115–117, 178*ch*1*n*15, 182*ch*5*n*2
Harman, Maj. Michael 35
Harris, Col. Leonard A. 88, 93
Hart, David 41
Hart, Joseph *38*
Hartsville 4, 104, 105–106
Hathaway, Col. Gilbert 139
Haughey, Thomas 145
Hawes, Gov. Richard 82
Hayes, Col. Rutherford B. 16
Heck, Lt. Col. Jonathan 29, 44
Helper, Hinton 13
Hog Mountain 137

Imbrie, Capt. James 98
Ironclad 177*Prefn*17, 183*ch*5*n*26, 185*ch*8*n*20
Irvine, Col. James 19

Jackass Cavalry 131, 136–137, 139
Jackson, Brig. Gen. Henry 51
Jackson, Brig. Gen. James S. 88
Jackson, Gen. Thomas (Stonewall) 25–28, *27*
Johnston, Gen. Albert Sydney 132
Jomini, Antoine 40, 178*n*4

Keifer, Col. Joseph on Beatty 37–39, *43*, 49, 51–52, 63, 73, 178*n*33, 179*n*13, 179*n*14, 179*n*5, 180*n*7; on Morrow 37
Kelley, Col. Benjamin 17, 19, 21–22
Kirkpatrick, Pvt. George 92

Laurel Hill 23, 29, 31–32, 44–45
Lawson, Col. Orris 33, 34, 122–123, 130, 135
Leadbetter, Brig. Gen. Danville 69
Lee, Gen. Robert E. 14, 48, 49, 50, 115
Lincoln, Abraham 18, 48, 62–63, 72–73, 80, 99, 100, 104, 107, 124–125, 128
Loomis, Capt. Cyrus 82, 87–88, 89, 91, 94, 110, 123
Loring, Gern. Alonzo 16, 49
Lyons, Richard (Lord) 11
Lytle, Col. William *64*, 84, 87–89, 92

Mahan, Denis 40
Manassas 33; *see also* Bull Run
Mason, James 57
McClellan, Gen. George 12, 17–18, 20, 22, 25–*26*, 30–31, 40, 46

McCook, Gen. Alexander 83, 88, 94, 107, 115–116
McCook, Gen. Robert 33, 77
Middle Fork Bridge 29, 32–35, 37, 39
Milroy, Brig. Gen. Robert 19
Mitchell, Gen. Ormsby 47, 57–*58*, 66
Moore, Col. Absalom 106
Morgan, Gen. John Hunt 3, 54, 59–60, *62*, 103–104, 106, 126, 128, 144
Morris, Gen. Thomas 19, 20, 35
Morrow, Col. Issac 35, 37, 54, 59
Munfordville 79, 149
Murfreesboro 111, *113*, 115–123, *119*

Napoleon gun *110*
Negley, Gen. James 116
Nicolay, John George 104, 108, 176*Intro.* *n*12, 185*n*8

Obstinate Devils 66

Paint Rock 69–70
Palmerston, (Lord, Henry Temple) 54
Parrott Gun 53
Pegram, Col. John 3, 29, *31*–32, 37, 104, 128, 177*ch*1*n*9, 178*ch*1*n*15, 178*ch*1*n*23
Peninsula Campaign 76
Perryville 79, 85–93, 141
Philippi 13, *14* 16, 20–21
Piatt, Donn 64, 180*n*18
Pittsburg Landing 67, 132; *see also* Shiloh
Pointer, Capt. Henry 140
Polk, Gen. Leonidas 84, 115
Pollard, Edward 41, 178*n*7
Pope, Gen. John 76
Porterfield, Col. George 12, 13, 16, 19–20, 21
Price, Gen. Sterling 3

Reid, Whitelaw 144
Reynolds, Gen. Joseph 48, 50, 51
Rich Mountain 32, 40–45
Roaring Creek 35, 40
Roddey, Gen. Philip 133
Rosecrans, Gen. William 33, 35–*36*, 41–42, 99–104, 111, 116, 120, 123–124
Rousseau, Gen. Lovell 65–*66*, 76, 88, 91–92; men of iron 93, 116, 118, 121
Russell, John (Lord) 11

Sand Mountain 134, 136
Sanford, Henry Shelton 68, 75, 180*n*26
Sansom, Emma 138
Schleich, Gen. Newton 15, 33
Schurz, Gen. Carl 109

Index

Scorched Earth 73
Scott, Gen. Winfield 49, 74, 125
Seward, William Henry 54–*55*
Shackleford, Brig. Gen. James M. 144
Sheridan, Gen. Philip 116, 118
Shiloh 67; *see also* Pittsburg Landing
Shoddy 12, 176n18
Sill, Gen. Joshua 82, 116, 184n13
Simonson, Capt. Peter 9, 110
Smith, Gen. Kirby 75, 82, 95
Stafford, Pvt. Charles 139
Stanton, Edwin 17, 96
Stones River 3, 112, *113*
  115–123, *119*, 123, 141; *see also* Murfreesboro
Streight, Brig. Gen. Abel 126, *128*, 130, 133, 135–136, 138
Streight's Raid 128, *129*, 134, 139–140, 142
Stuart, Maj. Gen. J.E.B. |115
Sutlers 101

Tafel, Col. Gustav 106
Terrill, Brig. Gen. William 88
Thomas, Gen. George 64–*65*, 80, 100, 105, 115, 118, 121–122

Tilghman, Brig. Gen. Lloyd 131–132
Timberclad 185*ch*8n20
Tomkins, Christopher 27
Townsend, Adj. Edward 25, 31
Trent 56
Turchin, Gen. Ivan 47
Turner, Nat 64

Vananda, Maj. James 134, 136
Van Dorn, Gen. Earl 126, 184n2
Vicksburg 75–76

Walker, Pvt. J. Gilbert 97
Watkins, Pvt. Sam 118
Welles, Gideon 125
Wheeler, Gen. Joseph (Fighting Joe) 3, 104, 111–*112*
121, 123, 128
Wheeling Convention 7, 9
Wilder, Col. John 79
Wilkes, Capt. Charles 56
Winegard, Pvt. Charles A. 123
Wisdom, John 139
Wise, Gen. Henry 36
Wise, O. Jennings 37

www.ingramcontent.com/pod-product-compliance
Lightning Source LLC
Chambersburg PA
CBHW032044300426
44117CB00009B/1184